TEST BANK

Human Resource Management

Ninth Edition

Robert L. Mathis
University of Nebraska at Omaha

John H. Jackson
University of Wyoming

Prepared by
Roger A. Dean
Washington and Lee University

South-Western College Publishing
Thomson Learning

Australia • Canada • Denmark • Japan • Mexico • New Zealand • Philippines
Puerto Rico • Singapore • South Africa • Spain • United Kingdom • United States

Publisher: Dave Shaut
Acquisitions Editor: Charles E. McCormick, Jr.
Developmental Editor: Judith O'Neill
Marketing Manager: Joseph A. Sabatino
Production Editor: Deanna R. Quinn
Manufacturing Coordinator: Dana Began Schwartz
Printer: Globus Printing

COPYRIGHT ©2000 by South-Western College Publishing, a division of Thomson Learning.
The Thomson Learning logo is a registered trademark used herein under license.

The text of this publication, or any part thereof, may be reproduced for use in classes for which *Human Resource Management, 9th edition,* by Mathis and Jackson, is the adopted textbook. It may not be reproduced in any manner whatsoever for any other purpose without written permission from the publisher.

Printed in the United States of America
1 2 3 4 5 02 01 00 99

For more information contact South-Western College Publishing, 5101 Madison Road, Cincinnati, Ohio, 45227 or find us on the Internet at http://www.swcollege.com

For permission to use material from this text or product, contact us by
- telephone: 1-800-730-2214
- fax: 1-800-730-2215
- web: http://www.thomsonrights.com

ISBN 0-538-89008-8

This book is printed on acid-free paper.

TABLE OF CONTENTS

Chapter 1
Changing Nature of Human Resource Management — 1

Chapter 2
Strategic Human Resource Planning — 15

Chapter 3
Individuals, Jobs, and Effective HR Management — 29

Chapter 4
Global Human Resource Management — 43

Chapter 5
Diversity and Equal Employment Opportunity — 59

Chapter 6
Implementing Equal Employment — 73

Chapter 7
Analyzing and Identifying Jobs — 87

Chapter 8
Recruiting in Labor Markets — 101

Chapter 9
Selecting and Placing Human Resources — 115

Chapter 10
Training Human Resources — 129

Chapter 11
Human Resource Development and Careers — 143

Chapter 12
Performance Management and Appraisal — 157

Chapter 13
Compensation Strategies and Practices — 173

Chapter 14
Variable Pay and Executive Compensation — 189

Chapter 15
Managing Employee Benefits — 203

Chapter 16
Health, Safety, and Security — 217

Chapter 17
Employee Rights and Discipline — 231

Chapter 18
Labor/Management Relations — 245

INTRODUCTION

The questions in this Test Bank were specifically written to accompany *Human Resource Management*, Ninth Edition, by Mathis and Jackson. A wide variety of test questions have been written and are provided in several formats: multiple choice, true/false, and essay. Over 1,500 questions are provided in all.

Question Arrangement

Within each chapter, questions are grouped together by format (multiple choice, true/false, or essay). Within each format group, questions are ordered according to textbook presentation.

Multiple Choice Questions

Each question notes the correct answer (A, B, C, or D) and gives the textbook page number where the answer can be found. In this example from Chapter 10, the correct answer is "C" and the answer can be found in the textbook on p. 317.

4. _____ is a process whereby people acquire capabilities to aid in the achievement of organizational goals.
   A. Reinforced learning
   B. Orientation
   C. Training
   D. Employee development

   ANSWER: C, 317

True/False Questions

Each question notes the correct answer (True or False) and gives the textbook page number where the answer can be found. In this example from Chapter 5, the correct answer is "False" and the answer can be found in the textbook on p. 158. For each true/false question where the correct response is "False," an explanation is provided to underscore why the statement is false.

73. The EEOC is part of the Department of Labor, and is responsible for requiring that federal contractors take affirmative action to overcome the effects of prior discrimination practices.

    ANSWER: False, 158
    It is the task of the OFCCP to require federal contractors and subcontractors take affirmative action. The EEOC is an independent agency responsible for enforcing employment-related provisions of the 1964 Civil Rights Act.

Essay Questions

Essay questions cover larger spans of material than do multiple choice or multiple choice questions. Full solutions are provided along with page numbers keyed to the student text where answers can be found.

Testing Software

With Thomson Learning Testing Tools™, instructors are able to select questions, modify them, add questions, and print multiple versions of the same exam. Free to adopters of *Human Resource Management*, this Windows-compatible software is a fully integrated suite of test creation, delivery, and classroom management tools. ISBN 0-538-89012-6

Chapter 1

Changing Nature of Human Resource Management

Multiple Choice

1. In an organization, the management of human resources means that people must be
    A. supervised and controlled.
    B. recruited, compensated, trained, and developed.
    C. strategically managed.
    D. monitored and disciplined as necessary.

    ANSWER: B, 4

2. The text defines _____ as "the design of formal systems in an organization to ensure the effective and efficient use of human talent to accomplish the organizational goals."
    A. personnel administration
    B. strategic management
    C. human capital
    D. human resource management

    ANSWER: D, 4

3. Which of the following has resulted from the explosive growth of information technology?
    A. Organizations of all types have had to change.
    B. Manufacturing facilities have been built off-shore.
    C. Government regulations have changed the way HR is practiced.
    D. Most businesses have been unable to adapt rapidly enough.

    ANSWER: A, 4

4. Percentagewise, the fastest growing occupations are related to
    A. education and skills training.
    B. the financial industry.
    C. information technology or health care.
    D. legal or regulatory compliance.

    ANSWER: C, 4

1

Chapter 1

5. _____ of all U.S. jobs are in service industries.
   A. Approximately 60 %
   B. Over 80%
   C. Over 90%
   D. Less than 50%

   ANSWER: B, 5

6. Temporary workers, independent contractors, and leased employees are collectively referred to as
   A. part-time workers.
   B. virtual employees.
   C. non-organizational employees.
   D. contingent workers.

   ANSWER: D, 6

7. Why are companies increasing their use of contingent workers?
   A. To reduce legal liability for employers.
   B. To avoid minimum wage payments.
   C. To replace employees taking voluntary early retirement.
   D. To meet affirmative action goals.

   ANSWER: A, 7

8. It is anticipated that the white labor force will _____ of the workforce by 2006.
   A. increase to over 80%
   B. be less than 50%
   C. decline to about 73%
   D. total approximately 60%

   ANSWER: C, 7

9. Immigration of individuals into the United States is heavily weighted towards
   A. males.
   B. non-whites.
   C. Western Europeans.
   D. Mexicans and Central Americans.

   ANSWER: B, 8

10. Many employees are less willing than in the past to accept relocations and transfers if it means
    A. living in a more diverse city.
    B. additional responsibility.
    C. the additional cost of buying a new house.
    D. sacrificing family or leisure time.

    ANSWER: D, 9

11. Under the Family and Medical Leave Act of 1993, employees are required to provide up to _____ weeks of unpaid parental/family leave.
    A. 12
    B. 18
    C. 26
    D. 36

    ANSWER: A, 10

12. Which of the following activities are NOT usually involved as an organization "rightsizes"?
    A. Outplacing workers
    B. Closing facilities
    C. Increasing layers of managers
    D. Merging with other organizations

    ANSWER C, 10

13. A common transformation during organizational restructuring has been to
    A. increase managerial control of the workforce.
    B. make organizations flatter by removing several layers of management.
    C. refocus the organization's attention on one overriding goal.
    D. change from a bureaucratic structure to one that is less formal.

    ANSWER: B, 10

14. The central focus for human resource management must be on
    A. cost efficiency and the design of staffing strategies.
    B. personnel policies.
    C. ensuring employee satisfaction and personal wellbeing.
    D. contributing to organizational success.

    ANSWER: D, 10

15. _____ can be measured as the amount of output per employee.
    A. Productivity
    B. Effectiveness
    C. Profitability
    D. Efficiency

    ANSWER: A, 10

16. Through _____, managers attempt to anticipate forces that will influence the future supply of and demand for employees.
    A. staffing
    B. HR development
    C. HR planning
    D. HR analysis

    ANSWER: C, 12

Chapter 1

17. One activity that affects all other HR activities is
    A. staffing.
    B. compliance with equal employment opportunity laws and regulations.
    C. HR planning and analysis.
    D. human resources development.

    ANSWER: B, 12

18. The aim of _____ is to provide an adequate supply of appropriately qualified individuals to fill jobs in the organization.
    A. HR planning and analysis
    B. human resource development
    C. diversity assessment and training
    D. staffing

    ANSWER: D, 12

19. HR development includes which of the following activities?
    A. performance management
    B. wage and salary administration
    C. environmental scanning
    D. diversity assessment and analysis

    ANSWER: A, 13

20. A major issue of concern in compensation and benefits is the
    A. equalization of pay between men and women.
    B. use of stock options at all levels of the organization.
    C. increase in the cost of benefits.
    D. design of early retirement packages.

    ANSWER: C, 13

21. Workplace _____ has (have) grown in importance in response to the increasing number of acts or workplace violence.
    A. safety
    B. security
    C. monitoring
    D. employee assistance programs

    ANSWER: B, 13

22. An activity of HR management that is important to facilitating good employee relations is
    A. a voluntary workplace suggestion system.
    B. the distribution of a company newsletter.
    C. an employee assistance program.
    D. the development and communication of HR policies and rules.

    ANSWER: D, 13

23. What are the three HR management roles?
    A. administrative, operational, strategic
    B. personnel, human relations, planning
    C. staffing, appraisal, compensation
    D. short term, intermediate term, longer term

    ANSWER: A, 15

24. The administrative role of HR management is heavily oriented to
    A. recruitment and selection.
    B. tactical activities.
    C   processing and record keeping.
    D. workforce development

    ANSWER: C, 14

25. Recruiting and selecting for current openings are typical _____ activities.
    A. personnel
    B. operational
    C. strategic
    D. HR planning

    ANSWER: B, 15

26. The _____ role of HR management emphasizes that the people in an organization are valuable resources representing a significant organizational investments.
    A. human capital
    B. administrative
    C. operational
    D. strategic

    ANSWER: D, 16

27. The strategic focus of HR must be on the _____ implications of HR issues.
    A. longer term
    B. maintenance oriented
    C. interpersonal
    D. organizational

    ANSWER: A, 16

28. The human resources in an organization are the ones who
    A. justify their pay and benefits.
    B. are hard to quantify in terms of costs and benefits.
    C. design, produce, and deliver products and services to customers.
    D. usually regarded as expenses by financial managers.

    ANSWER: C, 16

6   Chapter 1

29. It is recommended that HR _____ when organizational strategic planning is being done.
    A. concentrate on personnel issues
    B. have a "seat at the table"
    C. leave strategic decisions to financial planners
    D. stress intermediate implications of strategic alternatives

    ANSWER: B, 16

30. To be strategic contributors, HR professionals must
    A. count how many activities and tasks were performed.
    B. improve the quality of the human resources available to operational managers.
    C. limit the organization's exposure to legal liability.
    D. measure what their activities produce as organizational results.

    ANSWER: D, 17

31. Human capital is the _____ of human resources to the organization.
    A. total value
    B. marginal value
    C. market cost
    D. replacement cost

    ANSWER: A, 18

32. _____ is composed of the people in the organization and what capabilities they have and can utilize in their jobs.
    A. Human Resources
    B. Organizational personnel
    C. Human capital
    D. Human asset management

    ANSWER: C, 18

33. Which of the following statements is TRUE?
    A. HR managers have found the "key" to motivating most employees.
    B. Human capital experts have predicted a skills shortage for U.S. organizations that could hurt their competitive edge.
    C. Human resources include only the on-the-job activities of the individuals associated with the organization.
    D. HR management is concerned primarily with implementing personnel policies.

    ANSWER: B, 18

34. The human capital in organizations is valuable because of
    A. the amount of time and money invested in their development.
    B. low unemployment, making it difficult to replace employees.
    C. the total compensation and benefits packages.
    D. the capabilities that the people have.

    ANSWER: D, 20

35. HR development includes which of the following activities?
    A. assessing the capabilities of each employee
    B. wage and salary administration
    C. job analysis
    D. scanning the external labor market

    ANSWER: A, 20

36. What action has been recommended once the gap between capabilities needed in the organization and those existing in employees is identified?
    A. Job analysis should be conducted to determine needed knowledge and skills.
    B. Compensation packages must be reviewed to insure competitiveness.
    C. Training and development activities must be designed.
    D. An affirmative action plan should be developed.

    ANSWER: C, 20

37. Which of the following should be the focus throughout the development of human resource capabilities?
    A. Ensuring competitive pay and benefit plans
    B. Providing guidance to employees and creating awareness of career growth possibilities within the organization
    C. Training and development activities
    D. Communicating promotional opportunities to employees to encourage them to remain loyal members of the organization, thus reducing turnover

    ANSWER: B, 20

38. The formal reward system in organizations must be aligned with
    A. wage and salary surveys.
    B. the external labor market.
    C. achieving affirmative action goals.
    D. the strategic goals for the organization.

    ANSWER: D, 20

39. As compared to traditional compensation programs, HR is having to
    A. develop and implement performance-oriented reward programs.
    B. provide cost-of-living adjustments (or COLAs).
    C. offer across-the-board pay increases.
    D. emphasize benefit packages rather than salary.

    ANSWER: A, 20

40. Study results show that the greatest amount of time and costs of HR management are concentrated at the _____ level, while HR management adds the greatest value at the _____ level.
    A. operational, administrative
    B. administrative, operational
    C. administrative, strategic
    D. strategic, operational

    ANSWER: C, 21

8   Chapter 1

41. In order to ensure legal compliance, the role of HR is to
    A. centralize compliance activities within the HR unit.
    B. ensure that the organization and its managers know of the HR laws and regulations.
    C. use independent contractors and contingency workers as much as possible to minimize exposure.
    D. request regular compliance reviews by government regulators.

    ANSWER: B, 21

42. What is the most commonly required retention time for records kept by employers who are subject to the Fair Labor Standards Act?
    A. one year
    B. six months
    C. five years
    D. three years

    ANSWER: D, 22

43. _____ is contracting with another organization to provide functions that were previously handled internally.
    A. Outsourcing
    B. Reengineering
    C. Downsizing
    D. Business process reengineering

    ANSWER: A, 22

44. Which of the following HR activities are most often outsourced?
    A. pre-employment testing
    B. employee surveys
    C. pension administration
    D. training and development

    ANSWER: C, 23

45. HR management is the responsibility of
    A. only the organization's HR unit
    B. all managers and supervisors in the organization.
    C. the union representatives.
    D. all employees of the organization.

    ANSWER: B, 22

46. The areas of contact between the HR unit and managers within the organization are called
    A. management prerogatives.
    B. accountability points.
    C. subsystem contacts.
    D. interfaces.

    ANSWER: D, 22

47. Before 1900, most hiring, firing, training, and pay-adjustment decisions were made by
    A. individual supervisors.
    B. HR generalists.
    C. employment managers.
    D. senior management and owners.

    ANSWER: A, 24

48. What was the impact of the scientific management studies conducted by Frederick W. Taylor?
    A. illustrated the need for a specialized personnel function
    B. revealed the impact of work groups on individual workers
    C. helped management increase worker productivity
    D. resulted in the passage of the National Labor Relations Act

    ANSWER: C, 24

49. What was the effect the Hawthorne Studies conducted by Elton Mayo?
    A. illustrated the need for a specialized personnel function
    B. revealed the impact of work groups on individual workers
    C. helped management increase worker productivity
    D. resulted in the passage of the National Labor Relations Act

    ANSWER: B, 24

50. The National Labor Relations Act of 1935,
    A. established the minimum wage.
    B. mandated labor/management cooperation.
    C. encouraged employers to establish HR departments.
    D. led to the growth of unions.

    ANSWER: D, 24

51. HR management as an organizational function traditionally was viewed as
    A. a staff function.
    B. a cost center.
    C. a line function.
    D. a profit center.

    ANSWER: A, 27

52. A person with responsibility for performing a variety of HR activities is an
    A. HR unit manager.
    B. HR specialist.
    C. HR generalist.
    D. HR professional.

    ANSWER: C, 27

10   Chapter 1

53. Individuals who have in-depth knowledge and expertise in a limited area of HR are
    A. HR unit managers.
    B. HR specialists.
    C. HR generalists.
    D. HR professionals.

    ANSWER: B, 27

54. Two trends in HR management are evident in a growing number of organizations today. These include
    A. centralization of HR activities.
    B. cost containment through wage concessions.
    C. hostility towards the growing influence of labor unions.
    D. outsourcing of HR activities.

    ANSWER: D, 27

55. The benefits resulting from outsourcing some HR activities include
    A. the outside contractor is likely to maintain more current systems and processes.
    B. responsibility for legal compliance is shifted to the outside contractor.
    C. it is usually less expensive for the organization.
    D. the HR units gains more control for HR decisions.

    ANSWER: A, 29

56. Ethics deals with
    A. what is required by law.
    B. religious values.
    C. what ought to be done.
    D. what is acceptable to the general society.

    ANSWER: C, 30

57. Deciding how much flexibility to offer an employee with family problems, while denying other employees similar flexibility, may require considering
    A. mixed outcomes
    B. multiple alternatives.
    C. extended consequences.
    D. uncertain consequences.

    ANSWER: B, 30

58. To respond in situations with ethical dimensions, the HR manager should
    A. ignore civil law because ethical decisions are at a higher level.
    B. investigate how the "typical" manager would respond in a similar situation.
    C. review the Uniform Guidelines developed by the EEOC.
    D. comply with all organizational standards of ethical behavior.

    ANSWER: D, 30

59. If HR professionals are to contribute strategically to their organizations, they must
    A. have an understanding of the financial, technological, and other facets of the organization.
    B. be professionally certified in human resources.
    C. be knowledgeable of all relevant laws and regulations.
    D. have an advanced degree in human resource management.

    ANSWER: A, 32

60. For generalists, the largest professional HR organization is
    A. the International Personnel Management Association (IPMA).
    B. the American Society for Training and Development (ASTD).
    C. the Society for Human Resource Management (SHRM).
    D. the Human Resource Certification Institute (HRCI).

    ANSWER: C, 33

True and False

61. Although change is sweeping work organizations throughout the United States, the way human resource managers do their work remains constant.

    ANSWER: False, 4
    Workforce 2000 has highlighted some important workforce challenges and their impact on the HR function.

62. Health care jobs are declining as Americans have become more health and fitness conscious and less susceptible to addictive behaviors.

    ANSWER: False, 4
    Health care jobs are actually growing as a result of the aging of the U.S. population and workforce.

63. It is estimated that manufacturing jobs will represent only 12% to 15% of all U.S. jobs by the year 2006.

    ANSWER: True, 5

64. One consequence of the shift to a service economy is that the number of jobs requiring semi-skilled and less educated workers are expected to grow at a more rapid rate than the number of other jobs.

    ANSWER: False, 6
    Workforce changes mean that people without high school diplomas or college degrees are at a disadvantage, as many occupational groups and industries require more educated workers.

Chapter 1

65. One reason for the growth in contingent workers is the reduced legal liability faced by employers.

    ANSWER: True, 7

66. Projections by the U.S. Bureau of Labor Statistics are that the racial/ethic mix of the U.S. workforce will continue to shift, such that by 2006 the white labor force will be less than 50%

    ANSWER: False, 7
    The white labor force is expected to decline from 80% in 1986 to about 73% by 2006.

67. During the 1990 the number of working women and dual-career couples actually declined.

    ANSWER: False, 9
    Both groups have increased, such that 70% of all women with children under age six are in the workforce, and dual-career couples comprise about 60% of all married couples.

68. As a result of the decline of the traditional family, many employees are less willing than in the past to accept relocations and transfers.

    ANSWER: True, 9

69. The Family and Medical Leave Act requires employers with at least 50 workers to provide up to 12 weeks of paid parental/family leave.

    ANSWER: False, 10
    The Family and Medical Leave Act requires up to 12 weeks of <u>unpaid</u> leave.

70. Through HR development, managers attempt to anticipate forces that will influence the future supply of and demand for employees.

    ANSWER: False, 12
    It is through HR planning that managers attempt to anticipate forces that will influence the future supply of and demand for employees.

71. The operational role of HR management requires HR professionals to identify and implement the HR portion of organizational strategic plans developed by top management.

    ANSWER: True, 15

72. In terms of strategic planning, human resources is primarily a staff function providing advice and support to the financial, technological, and production functions of the organization.

    ANSWER: False, 16
    To be a strategic partner, HR must have a "seat at the table", being viewed in the same context as the financial, technological, and other resources that are managed in organization

73. In organizations where they are viewed as strategic contributors, HR professionals participate in the discussions prior to top management making final decisions regarding mergers, acquisitions, and downsizing.

    ANSWER: True, 17

74. Organizations can downsize the importance of the HR function by increasing its use of independent contract workers, consultants, and temporary workers.

    ANSWER: False, 19
    HR professionals are needed to develop policies, negotiate contracts, evaluate staffing suppliers, and monitor work performance of these non-employees.

75. HR professionals must cost justify their existence and administratively deliver HR activities efficiently and responsively.

    ANSWER: True, 22

76. As can be expected, the medium HR cost per employee increases as an organization grows.

    ANSWER: False, 27
    The cost per employee of having an HR department is greater in organizations with fewer than 250 employees. In most organizations, the same activities must be provided irrespective of the number of employees.

77. In terms of HR activities, the greatest amounts of outsourcing were in the areas of payroll, benefits, recruiting, and training.

    ANSWER: True, 29

78. A survey of HR professionals indicated that the most common unethical incidents by employees were lying to supervisors, employee drug or alcohol use, and falsification of records.

    ANSWER: True, 31

79. "Liking to work with people" is a major qualification necessary for success in HR.

    ANSWER: False, 32-33
    This is one of the greatest myths about HR careers. HR professionals must have the technological and education needed for success in this field.

80. Professional certification has grown in importance for HR professionals.

    ANSWER: True, 33

Essay

81. Describe changes that are facing organizations with respect to workforce availability and quality. How can HR management help organizations adjust to these changes?

    ANSWER: 5-7
    Low unemployment, coupled with the need for workers with specialized skills, has caused significant workforce shortages. HR management has become active partners with public schools in addition to developing training programs for employees at all levels. Organizations have also increased their use of contingent workers to meet shortfalls in skilled workers and to provide flexibility.

82. Discuss the challenges of changing demographics facing HR management.

    ANSWER: 7-10
    The three major demographic challenges are the increased racial diversity of the workforce, more women are in the labor force than ever before, and the workforce is older than ever before. HR managers must ensure that the diverse workforce is treated fairly. This impacts all staffing activities and may require diversity-oriented training. Problems have emerged in balancing work and family. Older workers often need greater medical care which affects benefit programs and creates a growth in medically related jobs.

83. Define and clarify the three roles of HR management.

    ANSWER: 14-16
    Administrative - processing and record keeping. Operational - coordinating the management of HR activities with the actions of managers and supervisors throughout the organization. Strategic - emphasizes that people are valuable resources representing significant organizational investments.

84. What is meant by the "interface" concept?

    ANSWER: 22
    Interfaces refers to the areas of contact between the HR unit and managers within the organization. It recognizes that HR management is a joint activities of HR professionals and managers. Many HR decisions are made jointly.

85. Discuss why ethical issues permeate HR management. Give examples of typical ethical decisions faced by an HR manager.

    ANSWER: 30-32
    Ethical decisions relate to questions of fairness, justice, truthfulness, and social responsibility. The most common unethical incidents by employees were lying to supervisors, drug and alcohol use, and falsification of records. HR managers may be pressured to compromise their ethical standards in order to meet financial, scheduling, or other operational goals.

Chapter 2

Strategic Human Resource Planning

Multiple Choice

1. _____ planning is the process of identifying organizational objectives and the actions needed to achieve those objectives.
   A. Manpower
   B. Strategic
   C. Human resource
   D. Operational

   ANSWER: B, 40

2. The strategic planning process begins with
   A. the process of studying the environment of the organization.
   B. an internal assessment of what the organization can and cannot do.
   C. a study of workforce patterns and conditions, social values and lifestyles.
   D. identifying and recognizing the philosophy and mission of the organization.

   ANSWER: D, 40

3. Defining the philosophy and mission of an organization addresses all of the following questions, except:
   A. What government rules and regulations impact this organization's activities?
   B. Why does the organization exist?
   C. What unique contribution does the organization make?
   D. What are the underlying values and motivations of key managers and owners?

   ANSWER: A, 40

4. _____ is the process of examining the external forces to identify opportunities and threats.
   A. HR planning
   B. Strategic planning
   C. Environmental scanning
   D. Competitive analysis

   ANSWER: C, 40-41

5. Internal strengths and weaknesses must be identified in light of
   A. the results of the environmental scanning process.
   B. the philosophy and culture of the organization.
   C. the organizational capabilities.
   D. the findings of the human resource audit.

   ANSWER: B, 41

6. _____ examines the strengths and weaknesses of the organizations internally and the opportunities and threats externally.
   A. HR planning
   B. Competitive analysis
   C. Strategic planning
   D. SWOT analysis

   ANSWER: D, 41

7. A unique capability in an organization that creates high value and that differentiates that organization from its competitors is referred to as
   A. a core competency.
   B. the organizations culture.
   C. a strategic advantage.
   D. a differentiated function.

   ANSWER: A, 41

8. Ways that human resources can become a core competency include:
   A. recruiting and hiring a diverse workforce that is representative of society at large.
   B. making extensive use of contingent workers to ensure a constant inflow of new employees with contemporary ideas.
   C. attracting and retaining employees with unique professional and technical capabilities.
   D. encouraging all HR employees to be professionally certified.

   ANSWER: C, 41

9. Using a VRIO framework as the foundation for HR management means that people are truly seen as _____, not as _____.
   A. resources; employees
   B. assets; expenses
   C. expenses; resources
   D. employees; assets

   ANSWER: B, 42

10. "A pattern of shared values and beliefs giving members of an organization meaning and providing them with rules for behavior" is a definition of
    A. organizational norms.
    B. organizational commitment.
    C. organizational ethics.
    D. organizational culture.

    ANSWER: D, 42

11. An organization's _____ shapes its members' responses and defines what an organization can or is willing to do.
    A. culture
    B. ethics
    C. mission
    D. climate

    ANSWER: A, 42

12. The culture of an organization
    A. develops very early in the organization's life cycle.
    B. is imposed by management to give the organization meaning.
    C. provides the members with norms of expected behavior.
    D. is devoid of rituals and symbols.

    ANSWER: C, 43

13. Which of the following is true about a firm that has been in existence for less than two years?
    A. It will have duplicated the culture of a competitor.
    B. It is unlikely to have developed a stabilized culture.
    C. The culture of the firm will mirror the founder's personality.
    D. No culture will be evident.

    ANSWER: B, 43

14. Which of the following statements is FALSE?
    A. An organization's culture can be a source of competitive advantage.
    B. Culture must be compatible with organizational strategies.
    C. Culture affects the way external forces are viewed.
    D. Organizations often duplicate a competitor's culture to achieve similar results.

    ANSWER: D, 43

15. A high-risk and entrepreneurial spirit pervades the organization in which life cycle stage?
    A. embryonic
    B. growth
    C. maturity
    D. decline

    ANSWER: A, 43

16. Which of the following is a characteristic of an organization's growth stage?
    A. The organization and its culture are stabilized.
    B. There is an increased resistance to change.
    C. The organization needs investments to expand facilities, marketing, and human resources.
    D. HR activities are handled reactively and training seems less important.

    ANSWER: C, 43

18   Chapter 2

17. In the _____ stage, HR development is focused on high-potential, scarce-skilled employees.
    A. embryonic
    B. shakeout
    C. maturity
    D. growth

    ANSWER: B, 45

18. When organizational size and success enable an organization to develop more formalized plans, policies, and procedures, it has entered the
    A. growth stage.
    B. decline stage.
    C. shakeout stage.
    D. maturity stage.

    ANSWER: D, 45

19. In the _____ stage of an industry life cycle, the organization and its culture are stabilized.
    A. maturity
    B. decline
    C. shakeout
    D. growth

    ANSWER: A, 45

20. Downsizing and outplacement are more likely to occur in the _____ stage.
    A. shakeout
    B. growth
    C. decline
    D. maturity

    ANSWER: C, 45

21. A cost-leadership strategy is more appropriate in a _____ environment.
    A. highly competitive
    B. relatively stable
    C. dynamic
    D. decentralized

    ANSWER: B, 46

22. Which of the following strategies would be more appropriate in a rapidly changing environment, characterized by the need to continually find new products and new markets?
    A. aggressiveness
    B. cost-leadership
    C. flexibility
    D. differentiation

    ANSWER: D, 46

23. The _____ strategy requires an organization to adopt a longer HR planning horizon of "building" its own employees to fit its specialized needs.
    A. cost-leadership
    B. flexibility
    C. differentiation
    D. aggressiveness

    ANSWER: A, 46

24. _____ analyzes and identifies the need for and availability of human resources so that the organization can meet its objectives.
    A. Labor market analysis
    B. Strategic planning
    C. Human resource planning
    D. Environmental scanning

    ANSWER: C, 47

25. Which of the following statements best describes the responsibility for HR planning?
    A. HR planning is the responsibility of the top HR executive.
    B. Typical HR planning responsibilities involve the HR unit and other managers in the organization.
    C. The top HR executive and subordinate staff specialists have most of the responsibility
    D. HR planning is the responsibility of the organization's top management.

    ANSWER: B, 47

26. The HR unit's responsibilities during the planning process typically include
    A. integration of HR plans with departmental plans.
    B. monitoring the HR plan to identify changes needed.
    C. review of employee-succession plans in line with HR plans.
    D. implementation of HR plans as approved by top management

    ANSWER: D, 47

27. _____ are the means used to aid the organization in anticipating and managing the supply and demand for human resources.
    A. HR strategies
    B. Economic forecasting
    C. Strategic forecasting
    D. Labor market analyses

    ANSWER: A, 49

28. Scanning the external environment especially affects HR planning because
    A. the corporate culture is the responsibility of the HR unit.
    B. of the demographic patterns of the internal workforce.
    C. the organization must draw from the same labor market that supplies all other employers.
    D. the organization must meet certain affirmative action quotas.

    ANSWER: C, 50

20   Chapter 2

29. The ability of an organization to compete for critical human resources is
    A.   governed by EEO regulations.
    B.   one measure of organizational effectiveness.
    C.   a test of how well management provide competitive wages.
    D.   one input to the environmental scanning process.

    ANSWER: B, 50

30. External environmental factors that affect the labor supply include
    A.   life-style choices of employees.
    B.   corporate philosophy and mission.
    C.   environmental scanning.
    D.   government influence.

    ANSWER: D, 51

31. Under a "closed-import" policy, foreign firms may
    A.   establish more American-based manufacturing operations using American labor.
    B.   not import large numbers of foreign products to sell here by American firms.
    C.   not sell more than the government's quota limit in the U.S.
    D.   seek to become partners with American firms.

    ANSWER: A, 51

32. Tax credits for employee day care and financial aid for education may affect
    A.   EEOC compliance.
    B.   retirement patterns.
    C.   employer practices in recruiting and retraining workers.
    D.   an expanding array of government rules.

    ANSWER: C, 51-52

33. As the unemployment rate declines,
    A.   the need for overtime also declines.
    B.   people available for work may be less educated, less skilled, or unwilling to work.
    C.   it becomes easier to fill jobs.
    D.   early retirement plans become more attractive.

    ANSWER: B, 52

34. One geographic factor affecting the supply of human resources is the
    A.   urban/rural ratio.
    B.   gross population profile.
    C.   total labor workforce audit.
    D.   impact of international competition on the area.

    ANSWER: D, 52

35. Which of the following has been a geographic trend that has forced changes in HR plans?
    A. the reluctance on the part of many workers to accept geographic relocation
    B. the movement of better educated workers to the Southwest
    C. the deterioration of inner cities
    D. the influx of foreign workers into certain regions

    ANSWER: A, 52

36. A business that fails to offer competitive pay scales will often
    A. have a generous benefits package.
    B. attract a committed workforce.
    C. have a much lower-quality workforce.
    D. employ "protected-class" workers.

    ANSWER: C, 52

37. In which of the following scheduling arrangements do employees work a set number of hours per day but vary starting and ending times?
    A. virtual office
    B. flextime
    C. work sharing
    D. compressed workday

    ANSWER: B, 53

38. _____ occurs when a full week's work is accomplished in fewer than five days.
    A. Flextime
    B. Virtual office
    C. Telecommuting
    D. Compressed workweek

    ANSWER: D, 54

39. _____ employees go to work via electronic computing and telecommunications equipment.
    A. Telecommuting
    B. Virtual
    C. Hoteling
    D. Contingent

    ANSWER: A, 54

40. In which of the following work arrangements do workers check in with an office concierge, carry their own nameplates with them, and are assigned to work cubicles or small offices?
    A. telecommuting
    B. virtual office
    C. hoteling
    D. contingent workplace

    ANSWER: C, 54

22   Chapter 2

41. In the _____ arrangement, work is done anywhere, anytime, and people are judged more on results than on "putting in time."
    A. telecommuting
    B. virtual office
    C. hoteling
    D. flexiplace

    ANSWER: B, 54

42. A comprehensive analysis of all current jobs provides a basis for
    A. auditing jobs.
    B. an internal analysis of jobs and people.
    C. human asset accounting.
    D. forecasting what jobs will need to be done in the future.

    ANSWER: D, 54

43. A planner should examine which of the following questions when auditing jobs?
    A. How essential is each job?
    B. What is the demographic profile of the current job holders?
    C. What type of training will be needed to fill each job?
    D. Who is responsible for staffing the organization?

    ANSWER: A, 54-55

44. What is the basic source of data on employees and their skills?
    A. employee evaluations
    B. supervisory files
    C. HR records of the organization
    D. personnel update forms completed by employees

    ANSWER: C, 55

45. A(n) _____ is an integrated system designed to provide information used in HR decision making.
    A. human capital operating system
    B. human resource information system
    C. management tracking and evaluation system
    D. strategic personnel management system

    ANSWER: B, 56

46. Which of the following is the most basic use of an HRIS in an organization?
    A. centralization of all job postings
    B. EEO and affirmative action tracking
    C. maintaining job description and job specification information
    D. automation of payroll and benefits activities

    ANSWER: D, 56

47. "What information is available?" "to what uses will the information be put?" and "who needs the information?" are questions about
    A. the data to be included in the HRIS.
    B. the design, implementation, and training elements of an HRIS.
    C. the capacity and capabilities of the HRIS equipment.
    D. HRIS security and privacy.

    ANSWER: A, 58

48. _____ is an Internet-linked network that allows employees access to information provided by external entities.
    A. An intranet
    B. E-mail
    C. An extranet
    D. A listserve

    ANSWER: C, 58

49. Controls must be built into the HRIS to
    A. enable employees to readily access their personal files.
    B. restrict indiscriminate access to HRIS data on employees.
    C. permit supervisors to access and update the files of their subordinates.
    D. provide access to the system by "computer illiterates."

    ANSWER: B, 59

50. _____ uses information from the past and present to identify expected future conditions.
    A. Modeling
    B. Simulating
    C. Predicting
    D. Forecasting

    ANSWER: D, 59

51. The most common forecasting methods used are
    A. a combination of quantitative method and subjective judgment.
    B. computer simulation models.
    C. various "rules of thumb."
    D. mathematical models.

    ANSWER: A, 59

52. An intermediate planning range usually projects _____ into the future.
    A. beyond five years
    B. three to five years
    C. one to five years
    D. six months to one year

    ANSWER: C, 60

24   Chapter 2

53. Which of the following is a purely judgmental method of forecasting?
    A. simulation models
    B. the Delphi Technique
    C. staffing ratios
    D. a transition matrix

    ANSWER: B, 61

54. When general guidelines are applied to a specific situation within the organization, which forecasting method is being used?
    A. the Delphi technique
    B. simulation models
    C. estimates
    D. rules of thumb

    ANSWER: D, 61

55. Government labor force population estimates and trends in industry are used to
    A. forecast the external supply of human resources.
    B. estimate the internal supply of labor.
    C. implement a human resource information system (HRIS).
    D. predict terminations, retirements, and deaths of employees.

    ANSWER: A, 61

56. The internal supply of human resources is influenced by
    A. actions of competing employers.
    B. government regulations and pressures.
    C. training and development programs.
    D. changing workforce composition and patterns.

    ANSWER: C, 62

57. Succession analysis, one method used to forecast the supply of people for certain positions, relies on
    A. stand-in potential.
    B. replacement charts.
    C. succession tables.
    D. worker profile analysis.

    ANSWER: B, 62

58. Reducing the size of an organizational work force is called
    A. re-engineering.
    B. downshifting.
    C. reorganizing.
    D. downsizing.

    ANSWER: D, 63

59. _____ occur(s) when individuals who quit, die, or retire are not replaced.
    A. Attrition
    B. Buyouts
    C. Hiring freezes
    D. Downsizing

    ANSWER: A, 66

60. _____ is (are) a group of services provided to displaced employees to give them support and assistance.
    A. Job counseling
    B. Career guidance
    C. Outplacement
    D. Buy-outs

    ANSWER: C, 67

True and False

61. Other than an altruistic notion of "social responsibility," there is little practical incentive for employers to hire welfare recipients.

    ANSWER: False, 39
    Low unemployment rates have left many employers little option but to hire welfare recipients. In addition, state governments are providing tax incentives and wage subsidies to encourage the hiring of welfare recipients.

62. The process of strategic planning begins with scanning the environment to identify workforce patterns and conditions, social values and lifestyles, and technological developments.

    ANSWER: False, 40
    Strategic planning begins with identifying and recognizing the philosophy and mission of the organization. The next requirement is to scan the environment.

63. Environmental scanning is especially important when rapid changes are occurring.

    ANSWER: True, 40

64. Human resources can be thought of as a core competency in that they create high value and differentiate the organization from its competitors.

    ANSWER: True, 41

65. A relatively new firm probably has not developed a stabilized organizational culture.

    ANSWER: True, 43

26 Chapter 2

66. The differentiation strategy requires an organization to "build" its own employees to fit its specialized needs.

    ANSWER: False, 46
    This strategy is appropriate for the cost-leadership strategy.

67. In most organizations that do HR planning, the responsibility for this planning is shared by senior organizational executives and HR staff specialists.

    ANSWER: False, 47
    The top HR executives and subordinate staff specialists have most of the responsibilities for HR planning. Other managers provide data for the HR specialists to analyze.

68. HR management and ultimately HR planning are critical in small and entrepreneurial organizations.

    ANSWER: True, 47

69. Family-owned businesses are relieved from most HR planning responsibilities when the business is passed on from one generation to another.

    ANSWER: False, 48
    HR planning is especially critical when there is a mix of family and nonfamily employees.

70. Effective HR planning requires that an organization considers the allocation of people to jobs over long periods of time, not just for the next month of even the next year.

    ANSWER: True, 50

71. Lower HR costs is a good evaluation of the success of HR planning.

    ANSWER: False, 50
    HR costs _may_ be lower, but more important are such measurements as projected levels of demand against actual levels at some point in the future.

72. The most telling evidence of successful HR planning is an organization in which the human resources are consistently aligned with the needs of the business over a period of time.

    ANSWER: True, 50

73. One measure of organizational effectiveness is the ability of an organization to compete for a sufficient supply of human resources with the appropriate capabilities.

    ANSWER: True, 50

74. Employers find it easier to fill jobs as the unemployment rate decreases.

    ANSWER: False, 52
    As the unemployment rate decreases, there are fewer qualified people looking for work.

75. The starting point for evaluating internal strengths and weaknesses is an audit of the jobs currently being done in the organization.

    ANSWER: True, 54

76. Human resource information systems (HRIS) are merely HR record-keeping systems that have been computerized.

    ANSWER: False, 56
    An HRIS is an integrated system designed to provide information used in HR decision making. It is useful for both record keeping and strategic planning.

77. Because of the high degree of uncertainty in the environment, it is virtually impossible to forecast with enough accuracy to benefit an organization's long-range plans.

    ANSWER: False, 59
    Usually experienced people are able to forecast with enough accuracy to benefit organizational long-range planning.

78. Simulation models use input from a group of experts who fill out separate questionnaires anonymously.

    ANSWER: False, 61
    The Delphi Technique, a judgment method, uses input from a group of experts.

79. The Worker Adjustment and Retraining Notification (WARN) Act requires employers to give a 60-day notice before a layoff or facility closing involving more than 50 people.

    ANSWER: True, 63

80. Research has concluded that those who are still around after downsizing are so glad to have a job that they pose no problems to the organization.

    ANSWER: False, 65
    Performance of survivors and the communications throughout the organization may be affected as the survivors experience guilt because they were spared while their friends were not.

ESSAY

81. Why is strategic planning essential for organizational success? Describe some of the ways human resources can become a core competency.

    ANSWER: 40-42
    Strategic planning is the process of identifying organizational objectives and the actions needed to achieve them. It involves analyzing such areas as finance and marketing in addition to human resources to determine the capacities of the organization to meet its objectives. HR can become a core competency through attracting and retaining employees with unique professional and technical capabilities, investing in training and development, and compensating them in ways to keep them competitive with their counterparts in other organizations.

82. What is organizational culture? Why must HR managers consider the culture of the organization?

    ANSWER: 42-43
    Organizational culture is the pattern of shared values and beliefs giving members of an organization meaning and providing them with rules for behavior. Culture affects the attraction and retention of competent managers. The culture of an organization may be incompatible with otherwise excellent strategies.

83. Discuss the impact of the external environment on the supply of labor.

    ANSWER: 50-52
    Government influences include rules and regulations, tax credits, educational policies, and immigration policies. Economic conditions such as inflation, growth, and unemployment affects labor supply. Geographic and competitive concerns impact the supply of labor, in addition to changes in the composition of the workforce and the use of varied work patterns.

84. What are some of the alternatives to the traditional work schedule of a full-time, eight-hour day at the employers place of business?

    ANSWER: 53-54
    Alternatives include flextime, compressed workweek, voluntary part-time, job sharing, telecommuting, hoteling, and virtual office.

85. What is the purpose of a human resource information system (HRIS)?

    ANSWER: 56
    Administrative and efficiency - to improve the efficiency in which data on employees and HR activities is compiled; strategic - having accessible data enables HR planning and managerial decision making to be based to a greater degree on information rather than on managerial perceptions and intuition.

Chapter 3

Individuals, Jobs, and Effective HR Management

Multiple Choice

1. Which of the following is a measure of the quantity and quality of work done, considering the cost of resources it took to do the work.
    A. efficiency
    B. productivity
    C. effectiveness
    D. profitable output

    ANSWER: B, 75

2. _____ can be viewed as the ratio between input and output, or the value added by an organization.
    A. Profitable output
    B. Effectiveness
    C. Economic value
    D. Productivity

    ANSWER: D, 75

3. At the national level, high productivity is of concern because it lead to
    A. higher standards of living.
    B. increases in national wage levels.
    C. higher labor costs.
    D. increased worker satisfaction and motivation.

    ANSWER: A, 75

4. _____ is the total labor cost per unit of output.
    A. Value added (labor)
    B. Production fixed cost
    C. Unit labor cost
    D. Output infracosts

    ANSWER: C, 75

5. The productivity of an individual depends upon
   A. age and experience.
   B. innate ability, effort exerted, and support.
   C. talents and personality factors.
   D. motivation and job design.

   ANSWER: B, 76

6. When recruiting and selecting employees, HR professionals are especially concerned with
   A. employee motivation.
   B. personality factors.
   C. compensation and benefits provided.
   D. the job candidates' innate ability.

   ANSWER: D, 76

7. When a firm outsources, it
   A. contracts with someone else to perform activities previously done by its employees.
   B. replaces workers with equipment that can perform the task more efficiently.
   C. "reengineers" the work methods.
   D. downsizes, eliminating jobs that no longer add value to the firm.

   ANSWER: A, 76

8. W. Edwards Deming argued that _____ is important to quality production.
   A. recruiting and hiring the best qualified workers
   B. using high quality raw material
   C. getting the job done right the first time
   D. employee motivation

   ANSWER: C, 77

9. _____ is (are) a comprehensive management process focusing on the continuous improvement of organizational activities to enhance the quality of the goods and services supplied.
   A. Quality circles
   B. Total Quality Management
   C. Shamrock teams
   D. A production cell

   ANSWER: B, 77

10. Which of the following is recognized as being at the heart of the TQM concept?
    A. quality control
    B. employee motivation
    C. productivity
    D. customer focus

    ANSWER: D, 77

11. Which of the following is not identified as a dimension of customer service?
    A. organizational culture
    B. confidence in employees' knowledge
    C. dependable and accurate performance
    D. physical facilities and equipment

    ANSWER: A, 78

12. What has been a major impact of mergers and acquisitions, contingent work, and outsourcing jobs?
    A. These actions have helped to hinder union-organizing activities.
    B. Feelings of job security have risen since employees believe that their organization now is more competitive.
    C. These actions have caused recognizable damage to loyalty and length of service.
    D. Union membership has increased.

    ANSWER: C, 79

13. What is a psychological contract?
    A. The written employment contract between a job applicant and a prospective employer.
    B. The unwritten expectations that employees and employers have about the nature of their work relationships.
    C. The total sum of a new employee's experiences during the first days on the job.
    D. The trade-off between wages and benefits in the overall compensation package.

    ANSWER: B, 79

14. A(n) _____ is the unwritten expectations that employees and employers have about the nature of their work relationships.

    A. employment contract
    B. applicant assessment
    C. biographical sketch
    D. psychological contract

    ANSWER: D, 79

15. _____ are encompassed by psychological contracts.
    A. Both tangible and intangible items
    B. Only wages, benefits, employee productivity, and attendance
    C. Only intangible items such as loyalty, fair treatment, and job security
    D. All aspects of the working experience

    ANSWER: A, 80

Chapter 3

16. The transformation in the psychological contract mirrors an evolution in which organizations have moved from employing individuals to perform tasks to
    A. outsourcing most routine activities.
    B. contracting with contingent workers to perform the activities.
    C. employing individuals to produce results.
    D. employing groups of people to work as a team.

    ANSWER: C, 80-81

17. Rather than _____, increasingly employers are expecting employees to _____.
    A. expecting teams to produce results; work independently
    B. paying them to put in time; accomplish organizational results
    C. offering long-term employment; accept short-term assignments
    D. giving regular cost-of-living raises; work as independent contractors

    ANSWER: B, 81

18. _____ is the desire within a person causing that person to act.
    A. Attitude
    B. Loyalty
    C. Precept
    D. Motivation

    ANSWER: D, 82

19. Content theories of motivation are concerned with
    A. the needs that people are attempting to satisfy.
    B. the aspirations of a broad range of people.
    C. expectations, desires, and goals.
    D. the needs that people are attempting to satisfy..

    ANSWER: A, 82

20. Which one of the following is the correct order of Maslow's hierarchy of needs?
    A. psychological, security, recognition, love, self-actualization
    B. existence, relatedness, growth
    C. physiological, safety, belonging, esteem, self-actualization
    D. basic, security, self-esteem, social, achievement

    ANSWER: C, 82

21. People using Maslow's hierarchy assume that workers in modern, technologically advanced societies
    A. are concerned primarily with a lack of belonging and love.
    B. have basically satisfied their physiological, safety, and belonging needs.
    C. are primarily motivated by money.
    D. will rarely reach the top of the hierarchy.

    ANSWER: B, 82

22. Based on Herzberg's theory, what happens if all the hygiene or maintenance factors are satisfactory?
    A. productivity increases
    B. workers are motivated
    C. absenteeism and turnover are likely to increases
    D. people may not be motivated to work harder

    ANSWER: D, 82

23. Herzberg's theory suggests that managers should
    A. use motivators as tools to enhance employee performance.
    B. understand that a satisfied worker is more productive than a dissatisfied worker.
    C. ignore hygiene factors since they do not motivate workers.
    D. initially concentrate on higher order needs.

    ANSWER: A, 82

24. Which of the following is a motivator in Herzberg's theory?
    A. salary
    B. supervision
    C. recognition
    D. interpersonal relations

    ANSWER: C, 83

25. Which of the following statements is true about process theories of motivation?
    A. Managers should seek to satisfy their employees' needs.
    B. People are different and are motivated by a variety of factors.
    C. Managers should use a Theory Y approach to enhance employee satisfaction and motivation.
    D. Hygiene factors should be satisfied so that the employees can concentrate on motivators.

    ANSWER: B, 83

26. The Porter and Lawler model indicates that if _____, they will become dissatisfied.
    A. hygiene factors are not inadequate
    B. good performance is not recognized
    C. goals are set too high or too low
    D. expectations are not met

    ANSWER: D, 83

27. The essence of the Porter and Lawler view of motivation is
    A. perception.
    B. equitable rewards.
    C. job satisfaction.
    D. job design.

    ANSWER: A, 84

34 Chapter 3

28. According to Porter and Lawler, _____ leads to _____.
    A. motivation; performance
    B. expectations; satisfaction
    C. performance; satisfaction
    D. satisfaction; performance

    ANSWER: C, 84

29. _____ refers to organizing tasks, duties, and responsibilities into a productive unit of work.
    A. Job analysis
    B. Job design
    C. Job characteristics
    D. Job evaluation

    ANSWER: B, 84

30. Job design involves the content of jobs and
    A. the interrelationships among all jobs in the organization.
    B. the job's requirements.
    C. the qualifications needed for someone to effectively perform the jobs' functions.
    D. the effect of jobs on employees.

    ANSWER: D, 84

31. Job enlargement involves
    A. broadening the scope of a job by expanding the number of different tasks to be performed.
    B. increasing the depth of a job to provide more autonomy.
    C. increasing the amount of impact the job has on other people.
    D. shifting a person from job to job to increase variety.

    ANSWER: A, 85

32. When you increase the depth of a job by adding employee responsibility for planning, organizing, controlling, and evaluating the job, _____ has occurred.
    A. job enlargement
    B. task significance
    C. job enrichment
    D. task character improvement

    ANSWER: C, 85

33. Job _____ refers to the number of similar operations of a job.
    A. enlargement
    B. scope
    C. depth
    D. rotation

    ANSWER: B, 85

34. Job _____ is the process of shifting a person from job to job.
    A. enlargement
    B. scope
    C. responsibility
    D. rotation

    ANSWER: D, 85

35. Which of the following is not an example of actions that enrich a job?
    A. Rotating a person among different jobs to break the monotony.
    B. Increasing a person's accountability for work by reducing external control.
    C. Giving feedback reports directly to employees.
    D. Giving a person an entire job rather than just a piece of the work.

    ANSWER: A, 85

36. Who developed the job-characteristics model?
    A. Maslow
    B. Herzberg
    C. Hackman and Oldham
    D. Porter and Lawler

    ANSWER: C, 86

37. The extent to which the work requires several different activities for successful completion indicates its
    A. enlargement.
    B. skill variety
    C. task identity.
    D. enrichment

    ANSWER: B, 86

38. _____ is the amount of impact the job has on other people.
    A. Experienced responsibility
    B. Autonomy
    C. Task identity
    D. Task significance

    ANSWER: D, 87

39. "Rethinking and redesigning work to improve cost, service, and speed" describes the _____ process.
    A. reengineering
    B. job enrichment
    C. Codetermination
    D. job enlargement

    ANSWER: A, 87

Chapter 3

40. _____ includes such techniques as creating work teams, training employees in multiple skills, pushing decision making down the organizational hierarchy, and reorganizing operations and offices to simplify and speed work.
    A. Job enrichment
    B. Codetermination
    C. Reengineering
    D. Job enlargement

    ANSWER: C, 87

41. Reengineering assumes the ultimate focus of all organizational work should be
    A. the shareholders (or owners) of the organization.
    B. the customer.
    C. the employees.
    D. senior management.

    ANSWER: B, 88

42. A organizational group formed to address specific problems and which may continue to work together to improve work processes or the quality of products and services, is called
    A. a production cell.
    B. self-directed work team.
    C. shamrock team.
    D. a special-purpose team.

    ANSWER: D, 88

43. The _____ is a small group of employees who monitor productivity and quality and suggest solutions to problems.
    A. quality circle
    B. special-purpose team
    C. production cell
    D. TQM

    ANSWER: A, 88

44. _____ are groupings of workers who produce entire products or components of products.
    A. Quality circles
    B. Shamrock teams
    C. Production cells
    D. Self-directed work teams

    ANSWER: C, 88

45. The _____ is composed of individuals who are assigned a cluster of tasks, duties, and responsibilities to be accomplished.
    A. special-purpose team
    B. Self-directed work teams
    C. quality circle
    D. autonomous work group

    ANSWER: B, 88

46. Which of the following has not been identified for the successful use of self-directed work teams?
    A. Teams value and endorse dissent.
    B. Teams use "shamrock" structures and have some variation in membership.
    C. Teams have authority to make decisions.
    D. Teams encourage a high level of organizational commitment.

    ANSWER: D, 89

47. _____ is a positive emotional state resulting from evaluating one's job experiences.
    A. Job satisfaction
    B. Job survival intentions
    C. Employee loyalty
    D. Organizational commitment

    ANSWER: A, 89

48. "The degree to which employees believe in and accept organizational goals and desire to remain with the organization" is a definition of
    A. job satisfaction.
    B. employee involvement.
    C. organizational commitment.
    D. loyalty.

    ANSWER: C, 91

49. If an employee is sick, or has a sick child, and is unable to come to work, the resulting time off is usually referred to as
    A. sick-leave time.
    B. involuntary absenteeism.
    C. explainable absenteeism.
    D. recognized time off.

    ANSWER: B, 91-92

50. Which of the following was suggested as an absenteeism control option?
    A. negative reinforcement
    B. perceptual changes
    C. equity controls
    D. positive reinforcement

    ANSWER: D, 92

51. _____ is a process in when employees leave the organization and have to be replaced.
    A. Turnover
    B. Vacancy
    C. Residual
    D. Changeover

    ANSWER: A, 93

38 Chapter 3

52. _____ occurs when an employee is fired.
    A. At-will-termination
    B. Dehiring
    C. Involuntary turnover
    D. Voluntary withdrawal

    ANSWER: C, 93

53. _____ for organizations is often defined as the extent to which goals have been met.
    A. Assessment
    B. Effectiveness
    C. Appraisal
    D. Efficiency

    ANSWER: B, 94

54. "The degree to which operations are done is an economical manner" is a definition of
    A. assessment.
    B. effectiveness.
    C. appraisal.
    D. efficiency.

    ANSWER: D, 94

55. An employer who chose not to provide an on-site child-care facility for all employees because the cost of operating the facility would exceed any benefits achieved as a result of reduced absenteeism and turnover, would be concerned with
    A. efficiency.
    B. effectiveness.
    C. benefit administration.
    D. liability management.

    ANSWER: A, 94

56. A(n) _____ is a formal research effort that evaluates the current status of HR management in an organization.
    A. HRIS
    B. personnel assessment
    C. HR audit
    D. HR research

    ANSWER: C, 96

57. _____ is the analysis of data from HR records to determine the effectiveness of past and present HR practices.
    A. Strategic assessment
    B. HR research
    C. A performance review
    D. An HR audit

    ANSWER: B, 97

58. Attitude surveys, questionnaires, interviews, and experiments are all examples of _____ research methods.
    A. experimental
    B. interactive
    C. primary
    D. secondary

    ANSWER: D, 97

59. With regard to exit interviews, which of the following statements is <u>false</u>?
    A. Departing employees are usually eager to use the occasion to voice their "gripes."
    B. HR specialists are usually better at gaining useful information than supervisors.
    C. It is often more useful to contact departing employees a month or so after departure when they may be more willing to provide information.
    D. A major reason employees commonly give for leaving their jobs is an offer for more pay elsewhere.

    ANSWER: A, 100

60. One approach to assessing HR effectiveness is _____, which compares specific measures of performance against data on those measures in "best practice" organizations.
    A. HR appraisal
    B. HR imitation
    C. benchmarking
    D. compa-valuation

    ANSWER: C, 100

True and False

61. The actual monetary value of a skilled workforce to an organization can be determined using an HR audit formula.

    ANSWER: False, 74
    Although there is no formula to put a precise dollar amount on the workforce, when a company is sold, a skilled workforce can bring a premium price.

62. Having an effective strategy is essential because it can guarantee an organization's success.

    ANSWER: False, 74
    Simply having an effective strategy does not guarantee success for an organization if the individual employees do not implement that strategy.

63. Lower rates of productivity results in higher labor costs and a less competitive position for a nation's products in the world marketplace.

    ANSWER: True, 75

64. A useful way to measure organizational HR productivity is by unit labor cost, which is computed by dividing the average cost of workers by their average levels of output.

    ANSWER: True, 75

65. Total quality management (TQM) programs have had overwhelming success and impact in most of the organizations that have adopted the approach.

    ANSWER: False, 77
    A nationwide study of over 1,000 executives and managers found that only 45% of the organizations that had implemented TQM thought their programs had been successful.

66. Psychological contracts include both tangible items (such as wages, benefits, employee productivity, and attendance) and intangible items (such as loyalty, fair treatment, and job security).

    ANSWER: True, 80

67. In most organizations today, employees exchange their efforts and capabilities for a secure job that offers rising wages, comprehensive benefits, and career progression within the organization.

    ANSWER: False, 80
    While this may have been true in the past, the new psychological contract rewards employees for contributing to organizational success in the competitive marketplace for goods and services.

68. Performance and reaction to compensation are related to motivation.

    ANSWER: True, 82

69. People using Maslow's theory of motivation assume that workers are motivated by the lower order physiological, safety, and belonging needs.

    ANSWER: False, 82
    It is assumed that these needs have been met in modern, technologically advanced societies. They concentrate on the needs for esteem and self-actualization.

70. Job design involves the content of jobs and the effect of jobs on employees.

    ANSWER: True, 84

71. Job enlargement is achieved by adding employee responsibility.

    ANSWER: False, 85
    Job enlargement broadens the scope of a job while job enrichment increases the depth by adding employee responsibility.

72. In the job-characteristics model, task identity is defined as the extent of individual freedom and discretion in the work and its scheduling.

    ANSWER: False, 86
    This is in fact the definition of "autonomy." Task identity is defined as the extent to which the job includes a whole identifiable unit of work.

73. Production cells are small groups of employees who monitor productivity and quality and suggest solutions to problems.

    ANSWER: False, 88
    Quality circles monitor productivity and quality. Production cells are groupings of workers who produce entire products or components of products.

74. The self-directed work team is composed of individuals who are assigned a cluster of tasks, duties, and responsibilities to be accomplished.

    ANSWER: True, 88

75. Research has consistently found that improving job satisfaction will lead to a more productive workforce.

    ANSWER: False, 90
    There is no consistent relationship between satisfaction and productivity.

76. If employees are committed to an organization, they are likely to be more productive.

    ANSWER: True, 91

77. Absenteeism tends to be highest in governmental agencies, utilities, and manufacturing firms, and lowest in retail/wholesale firms, possibly because retail/wholesale firms use a large percentage of part-time workers.

    ANSWER: True, 92

78. A good way to eliminate voluntary turnover is to improve employee recruitment and selection.

    ANSWER: True, 93-94

79. Effectiveness can be thought of as the cost per unit of output.

    ANSWER: False, 94
    Effectiveness is the extent to which goals have been met. Efficiency is concerned with the cost per unit of output.

80. Attitude surveys allow employees to air their views about their jobs, their supervisors, their coworkers, and organizational policies and practices.

    ANSWER: True, 99

42   Chapter 3

Essay

81. Traditionally, loyalty and long service with one employer were the norm. How has this changed? Why?

    ANSWER: 79
    The idea of reciprocity is very much an issue in the decline of loyalty and length of service by employees. Workers have seen massive lay-offs, mergers and acquisitions, and outsourcing jobs as indications of a loss of job security. They have responded with reductions in loyalty to their employers, and an unwillingness to commit to long-term employment at one organization.

82. If a panel discussion were possible between Maslow, Herzberg, and Porter and Lawler, how would each respond to the statement: "Pay is the most effective tool management has for motivating the performance of its workers?"

    ANSWER: 82-84
    Maslow would argue that pay was important only to the extent that it helped satisfy unmet needs. Since most workers in developed countries had satisfied their lower-order needs, pay was only useful as a form of recognition to satisfy esteem needs. Herzberg viewed pay as a hygiene factor, not a motivator. Porter and Lawler focused on the value an employee placed on pay, and the perceived equity in which it was awarded.

83. How has reengineering affected the design of jobs and work?

    ANSWER: 87-88
    Reengineering is rethinking and redesigning work to improve cost, service, and speed. The process may include such techniques as creating work teams, retraining employees in multiple skills, pushing decision making down the organization, and reorganizing operations and offices to simplify and speed work.

84. What is meant by job satisfaction? What are the advantages of a satisfied workforce?

    ANSWER: 89-91
    Job satisfaction is a positive emotional state resulting from evaluating one's job experiences. Job satisfaction, while not directly linked to productivity, does impact organizational commitment. A satisfied employee is less likely to be absent or to voluntarily leave the organization.

85. Why is HR record keeping important? What could be the possible outcome for an organization that kept incomplete employee records?

    ANSWER: 95
    HR records are needed for compliance with government regulations, serve as important documentation in defending legal challenges, and are useful in evaluating HR effectiveness. An HR unit without accurate and complete records would not be able to defend itself internally or externally when challenged.

Chapter 4

Global Human Resource Management

Multiple Choice

1. For firms such as Colgate and Coca-Cola, foreign sales and profits account for
    A. almost 90 percent of total sales and profits.
    B. over 60 percent of total sales and profits.
    C. about 40 percent of total sales and profits.
    D. less than 20 percent of total sales and profits.

    ANSWER: B, 110

2. The automobile, steel, and electronics industries have _____ facilities because of competition from firms in Japan, Taiwan, Korea, and Germany.
    A. modernized
    B. refurbished
    C. built more modern
    D. closed unproductive

    ANSWER: D, 110

3. One positive aspect of foreign-owned firms investing in the Unites States is
    A. they helped to replace some of the jobs lost at U.S. firms due to downsizing.
    B. foreign investment keeps the prime rate low.
    C. foreign-owned firms promote mutual understanding and tolerance for diversity.
    D. they minimize the need for tariff barriers.

    ANSWER: A, 110

4. What was the purpose of GATT, which was signed at the end of 1994.
    A. to place restrictions on employers to ensure that HR practices meet certain standards
    B. to ensure standard HR practices in competing nations
    C. to provide general guidelines on trade practices among nations
    D. to stabilize currency transactions among competing nations

    ANSWER: C, 110

Chapter 4

5. NAFTA expanded trade opportunities among Canada, the United States, and Mexico, but also
   A. required U.S. companies to pay U.S. wage rates in their Mexican plants.
   B. placed restrictions on employers to ensure that HR practices in Mexico meet certain standards.
   C. banned the import of goods made in Mexican sweat shops.
   D. limited trade with nations that did not sign the agreement.

   ANSWER: B, 110

6. What is the purpose of the Commission of Labor Cooperation (CLC), which was established as part of NAFTA?
   A. to maintain a comparable minimum wage for workers in the United States, Canada, and Mexico
   B. to facilitate free trade among the United States, Canada, and Mexico
   C. to monitor labor union organizing efforts and practices in cooperating nations
   D. to review complaints regarding occupational safety and health, child labor, benefits, and labor-management relations

   ANSWER: D, 110-111

7. One highlight of recent years in Latin America is
   A. the resurgence of the economies of the largest countries.
   B. their relatively low birthrates.
   C. their reluctance to do business with U.S. companies.
   D. the rapidly improving working conditions.

   ANSWER: A, 111

8. Japanese society has been changing because of
   A. a move away from western values to a more traditional lifestyle.
   B. an eagerness to open up the economy to foreign business.
   C. a rapidly aging population.
   D. a relatively high birthrate.

   ANSWER: C, 111

9. Because India and China have huge populations, a growing number of foreign firms are establishing operations there. Difficulties faced by these firms include
   A. the cost of labor is higher than in other less-developed countries.
   B. the difficulty of attracting foreign managers and professionals to these countries.
   C. a strong national opposition against foreign investment.
   D. an unstable government.

   ANSWER: B, 111

10. The opening up of Eastern Europe gives U.S.-based firms expanded opportunities to sell products and services, in addition
    A. there is a shortage of workers available in those countries.
    B. there is security from trade restrictions.
    C. automated manufacturing facilities can be started up to tap the labor pool.
    D. wage rates are relatively low.

    ANSWER: D, 111

11. What has been a consequence of the high costs imposed on employers in Western European countries such as Germany and France?
    A. many European-headquartered firms have shifted production to the U.S.
    B. low unemployment
    C. a resurgence in economic nationalism
    D. Western European firms rarely lay off employees

    ANSWER: A, 111-112

12. In many parts of Africa, excluding South Africa, opportunities for international operations are
    A. limited for non-African firms due to the Africa Economic Agreement.
    B. facilitated by a modern infrastructure.
    C. inhibited by civil strife and corrupt governments.
    D. encouraged by the General Agreement on Tariffs and Trade (GATT).

    ANSWER: C, 112

13. U.S. firms are accustomed to a relatively _____ political system.
    A. turbulent
    B. stable
    C. homogeneous
    D. heterogeneous

    ANSWER: B, 112

14. The Foreign Corrupt Practices Act (FCPA)
    A. controls the practices of foreign firms operating in the U.S.
    B. is a U.N. sponsored pact regulating multinational organizations.
    C. permits U.S. firms to offer bribes if that is an acceptable way of doing business.
    D. prohibits U.S. firms from engaging in bribery in foreign countries.

    ANSWER: D, 113

15. With respect to foreign investment, many lesser developed countries
    A. are receptive in order to create jobs for their growing populations.
    B. are receptive only if the multinational firms employ nationals for senior positions.
    C. impose high barriers to entry to discourage foreign competition.
    D. insist on state ownership of a significant share of the firm.

    ANSWER: A, 113

16. _____ is (are) defined as the societal forces affecting the values, beliefs, and actions of a distinct group of people.
    A. Society
    B. Norms
    C. Culture
    D. Globalization

    ANSWER: C, 116

17. The dimension of _____ refers to the inequality among the people of a nation.
    A. status difference
    B. power distance
    C. gentry
    D. elitism

    ANSWER: B, 116

18. In which of the following countries is there the largest power distance?
    A. the Netherlands
    B. the United States
    C. Germany
    D. Russia

    ANSWER: D, 116

19. More collective action and less individual competition is likely in those countries that de-emphasize
    A. individualism.
    B. collectivism.
    C. free enterprise.
    D. socialism.

    ANSWER: A, 116

20. _____ values identified by Hofstede were assertiveness, performance-orientation, success, and competitiveness.
    A. Individualism
    B. Integrative
    C. Masculine
    D. Feminine

    ANSWER: C, 116

21. Which of the following are feminine values identified by Hofstede?
    A. assertiveness, success
    B. quality of life, close personal relationships
    C. justice, equity
    D. traditional family relationships, conflict avoidance

    ANSWER: B, 116

22. Hofstede's dimension of _____ refers to the preference of people in a country for structured rather than unstructured situations.
    A. structure orientation
    B. formalization
    C. bureaucracy
    D. uncertainty avoidance

    ANSWER: D, 116

23. Nations high on the uncertainty-avoidance dimension tend to be
    A. more resistant to change and more rigid.
    B. more intriguing and challenging.
    C. more acceptable for women.
    D. more flexible and to have more "business energy."

    ANSWER: A, 116

24. We can expect to find greater entrepreneurship and risk taking in cultures that are more
    A. masculine.
    B. feminine.
    C. flexible.
    D. rigid.

    ANSWER: C, 117

25. Long-term values, according to Hofstede, include
    A. a respect for traditions.
    B. thrift and persistence.
    C. resistance to change.
    D. strategic optimism.

    ANSWER: B, 117

26. _____ values include respecting tradition and fulfilling social obligations.
    A. Rigid
    B. Flexible
    C. Long-term
    D. Short-term

    ANSWER: D, 117

27. In which of the following countries did the people score highest on long-term orientation?
    A. Hong Kong
    B. the United States
    C. Russia
    D. France

    ANSWER: A, 117

28. The first phase of international interaction consists of
    A. multinational enterprise.
    B. multinational exploration.
    C. importing and exporting.
    D. global organization.

    ANSWER: C, 118

29. A(n) _____ operates in various countries with each foreign business unit operating separately.
    A. global organization
    B. multinational enterprise
    C. foreign subsidiary
    D. international enterprise

    ANSWER: B, 119

30. A(n) _____ has corporate units in a number of countries that are integrated to operate as one organization worldwide.
    A. international enterprise
    B. multinational enterprise
    C. importing and exporting organization
    D. global organization

    ANSWER: D, 119

31. HR management in _____ moves people, especially key managers and professionals, throughout the world.
    A. global organizations
    B. importing and exporting organizations
    C. multinational enterprises
    D. international enterprises

    ANSWER: A, 119

32. Employees who are not citizens of the country in which they work but are citizens of the country where the organization is headquartered are
    A. resident aliens.
    B. host-country nationals.
    C. expatriates.
    D. third-country nationals.

    ANSWER: C, 121

33. A(n) _____ is an employee working in a unit or plant who is a citizen of the country in which the unit or plant is located, where the unit or plant is operated by an organization headquartered in another country.
    A. resident alien
    B. host-country national
    C. expatriate
    D. third-country national

    ANSWER: B, 122

Global Human Resource Management

34. An employee who is a citizen of one country, working in a second country, and employed by an organization headquartered in a third country is called a(n)
    A. second-country national.
    B. host-country national.
    C. expatriate.
    D. third-country national.

    ANSWER: D, 122

35. Why do many multinational enterprises use expatriates?
    A. to ensure that foreign operations are linked effectively with the parent organization
    B. to ensure that the values and culture of the home country are maintained in the foreign operation
    C. it is less expensive in terms of salary and benefits
    D. to establish clearly that it is making a commitment to the host country

    ANSWER: A, 122

36. _____ expatriates move from one country to another. Often, they prefer to work internationally rather than in the home country.
    A. Volunteer
    B. Career development
    C. Global
    D. Traditional

    ANSWER: C, 123

37. Using host-country nationals is important if the organization wants to
    A. emphasize that a global approach is being taken.
    B. establish clearly that it is making a commitment to the host country.
    C. ensure that foreign operations are linked effectively with the parent organization.
    D. indicate that it is setting up a foreign operation.

    ANSWER: B, 123

38. Organizations often hire _____ because they know the culture, politics, laws, and business customs better than an outsider would.
    A. second-country nationals
    B. expatriates
    C. third-country nationals
    D. host-country nationals

    ANSWER: D, 123

39. Organizations will use third-country nationals as a way to
    A. emphasize that a global approach is being taken.
    B. it is less expensive in terms of salary and benefits.
    C. indicate that it is setting up a foreign operation.
    D. establish clearly that it is making a commitment to the host country.

    ANSWER: A, 123

50   Chapter 4

40. The selection process for international assignments should
    A. test language skills.
    B. examine the employee's willingness to be separated from family and friends.
    C. provide a realistic picture of the life, work, and culture to which the employee may be sent.
    D. be guided by the fact that a good employee in the domestic operation will usually make a good expatriate.

    ANSWER: C, 124

41. Most staffing failures among those selected for foreign assignments occur because of
    A. a lack of fluency in the host-country language.
    B. cultural adjustment problems.
    C. a compensation package that fails to account for differences in living expenses.
    D. separation anxiety.

    ANSWER: B, 124

42. The most common reason(s) for turning down international assignments is(are)
    A. pre-assignment visits by the employee to the host country.
    B. a fear for the personal safety of family members.
    C. a lack of understanding of the business culture and legal environment of the host country.
    D. family considerations and spouses' careers.

    ANSWER: D, 125

43. Why have many U.S. firms been reluctant to consider women for international assignments?
    A. Customs and cultural considerations in some foreign countries pose significant problems for women.
    B. Women generally do not function effectively in foreign countries.
    C. Most husbands were unwilling to accompany their wives on international assignments.
    D. It is generally more expensive to relocate female employees.

    ANSWER: A, 126

44. The Civil Rights Act of 1991 states that, with respect to U.S. citizens working internationally for U.S.-controlled companies,
    A. all EEO laws and regulations apply in all circumstances.
    B. the EEO regulations of Title VII do not apply internationally.
    C. all EEO laws and regulations apply, except when they conflict with the laws of the foreign country.
    D. all EEO laws and regulations apply, except when they conflict with the customs, culture, or laws of the foreign country.

    ANSWER: C, 126

45. Which of the following was not given as a type of training activity for international assignments?
    A. pre-departure orientation for employees and their families
    B. on-the-job training upon arrival in the host country
    C. continuing employee training and development
    D. repatriation training and development

    ANSWER: B, 127

46. A foreign organization, operating in the U.S., which plans to appoint an expatriate manager to a U.S. position must first
    A. prove to the Immigration and Naturalization Service that no American is qualified for the position.
    B. demonstrate that the expatriate is fluent in English.
    C. obtain clearance from the Equal Employment Opportunity Commission.
    D. train the U.S. workers to ensure acceptance of the foreign boss.

    ANSWER: D, 127

47. The process of bringing expatriates home is called
    A. repatriation.
    B. naturalization.
    C. reentry.
    D. re-nationalization.

    ANSWER: A, 128

48. The _____ approach provides international employees with a compensation package that equalizes cost differences between the international assignment and the same assignment in the home country of the individual or the corporation.
    A. equalization
    B. global market
    C. balance-sheet
    D. home-country reference

    ANSWER C, 129

49. One basic premise of the balance-sheet approach is that
    A. international assignments are usually long term.
    B. expatriate employees generally will have international assignments lasting two to three years.
    C. international employees should be compensated for the hardships encountered overseas.
    D. expatriate employees will receive a significant salary increase on their return to the U.S.

    ANSWER: B, 130

Chapter 4

50. The major focus of most international compensation programs is to
    A. provide a compensation package that avoids U.S. tax liability.
    B. compensate international employees for the hardships encountered overseas.
    C. recognize that most overseas assignments provide the employee with invaluable psychological rewards.
    D. keep the expatriates "whole" for a few years until they can be reintegrated into the home country compensation program.

    ANSWER: D, 130

51. The _____ to compensation requires that the international assignment be viewed as continual, not just temporary.
    A. global market approach
    B. balance-sheet approach
    C. equalization plan approach
    D. home country reference approach

    ANSWER: A, 130

52. Under a tax equalization plan,
    A. the IRS reimburses expatriates for taxes paid to foreign governments.
    B. the IRS gives special consideration to U.S. citizens working overseas.
    C. expatriates are protected from negative tax consequences.
    D. expatriates are still expected to pay their fair share of income taxes.

    ANSWER: C, 130

53. Global firms often contract with such organizations as International SOS, Global Assistance Network, or U.S. Assist to
    A. provide bodyguard protection for expatriates.
    B. provide emergency medical services for expatriates.
    C. maintain security devices for employees' families.
    D. ensure labor union free operations in the host country.

    ANSWER: B, 131

54. According to the International Labor Organization, in which of the following countries were men least likely to report attacks on the job?
    A. France
    B. Argentina
    C. Switzerland
    D. United States

    ANSWER: D, 132

55. The share of female workers reporting violence on the job was highest in
    A. Argentina.
    B. England.
    C. Switzerland.
    D. United States.

    ANSWER: A, 132

56. In _____ labor unions either do not exist or are relatively weak.
    A.   Australia
    B.   Scandinavia
    C.   China
    D.   Germany

    ANSWER: C, 132

57. A practice whereby union or worker representatives are given positions on a company's board of directors is called
    A.   collective bargaining.
    B.   co-determination.
    C.   worker councils.
    D.   participative management.

    ANSWER: B, 133

58. Which of the following is predicted about European unions in the next decade?
    A.   Unions will grow in both membership and strength.
    B.   The European Parliament will make union membership a mandatory condition of employment.
    C.   Unions will be banned from political activity.
    D.   Unions will have less power as a result of competition worldwide.

    ANSWER: D, 133

59. In _____, local unions bargain with individual employers to set wages and working conditions.
    A.   the United States
    B.   Scandinavia
    C.   Australia
    D.   Germany

    ANSWER: A, 133

60. In _____, unions argue their cases for wages and working conditions before arbitration tribunals.
    A.   the United States
    B.   Scandinavia
    C.   Australia
    D.   Germany

    ANSWER: C, 133

True and False

61. There are a number of provisions in GATT that are likely to affect HR practices in the United States.

    ANSWER: True, 110

62. While promoting free trade, NAFTA also requires U.S. organizations operating in Mexico to pay U.S. level wages.

    ANSWER: False, 111
    While NAFTA didn't specifically address wage rates, it did place restrictions on employers to ensure that their HR practices in Mexico met certain standards.

63. The Commission on Labor Cooperation (CLC) was established as part of NAFTA to standardize labor negotiation for firms operating in the United States, Canada, and Mexico.

    ANSWER: False, 111
    The CLC was established to review complaints filed in the United States, Canada, or Mexico regarding occupational safety and health, child labor, benefits, and labor-management relations.

64. The high costs imposed on employers in Western European countries such as Germany and France have led many European-headquartered organizations to shift production to new plants in the United States.

    ANSWER: True, 111-112

65. HR professionals need to ensure that global organizations standardize their HR practices to maintain consistency throughout their operations.

    ANSWER: False, 112
    Doing business globally requires management practices, including HRM, be adapted to reflect different organizational/workforce values.

66. Flexible labor laws in Western Europe make it easier to lay off workers and close plants than is possible in the United States.

    ANSWER: False, 113
    Laws on labor unions and employment make it difficult to reduce the number of workers because required payments to ex-employees can be very high.

67. In some countries, because of religious or ethical differences, employment discrimination may be an accepted practice.

    ANSWER: True, 113

68. Cultural differences not only exist between nations, but within countries also.

    ANSWER: True, 116

Global Human Resource Management

69. Many MNEs use host-country nationals to ensure that foreign operations are linked effectively with the parent organization.

    ANSWER: False, 122
    Expatriates are used to ensure that foreign operations are linked effectively with the parent corporations.

70. Host-country nationals are important in indicating a commitment to the host country.

    ANSWER: True, 123

71. The use of third-country nationals is a way to emphasize that a global approach is being taken.

    ANSWER: True, 123

72. Most staffing "failures" for those selected for foreign assignments occur because of difficulties with the jobs or inadequate technical skills.

    ANSWER: False, 124
    Most failures occur because of cultural adjustment problems.

73. The Civil Rights Act of 1991 extended coverage of EEO laws and regulations to U.S. citizens working internationally for U.S.-controlled companies.

    ANSWER: True, 126

74. The Civil Rights Act if 1991 extended coverage of EEO laws and regulations to all employees of U.S.-controlled companies working anywhere in the world.

    ANSWER: False, 126
    Coverage is limited to U.S. citizens working internationally for U.S.-controlled companies.

75. The U.S.-based subsidiary of a Japanese-owned firm would be exempt from EEO laws and regulations if Japanese culture prescribes alternate practices.

    ANSWER: False, 126
    In most cases EEO regulations and laws do apply to foreign-owned firms.

76. One of the greatest deterrents to accepting foreign assignments is employees' anxiety about continued career progression.

    ANSWER: True, 128

77. The balance-sheet approach to international employees attempts to equalize salary differences between expatriates and host-country employees.

    ANSWER: False, 129
    The approach attempts to equalize cost differences between the international assignment and the same assignment in the home country of the individual or the corporation.

78. A basic premise of the balance-sheet approach is that expatriate employees generally will have international assignments lasting two to three years.

    ANSWER: True, 130

79. Under a tax equalization plan, the corporation attempt to ensure that all international employees pay taxes at the same rate.

    ANSWER: False, 130
    The intent of the tax equalization plan is to ensure that expatriates will not pay any more or less in taxes than if they had stayed in the United States.

80. Union militancy is increasing in some lesser-developed countries, such as Brazil, Mexico, Poland, and Romania.

    ANSWER: True, 133

Essay

81. Identify and discuss some of the legal, political, economic, and cultural issues affecting global HR management.

    ANSWER: 112-118
    Legal and political issues - NAFTA, GATT, EEO, Foreign Corrupt Practices Act. Economic issues - different economic systems, economic conditions including cost of living, wages, benefits, levels of unemployment. Cultural factors - differing values, beliefs, actions within and between different countries.

82. A U.S. manufacturing firm is considering the possibility of moving its production facilities to a less-developed country. What are some of the ethical questions management should discuss before making the final decision?

    ANSWER: 112-113
    Foreign Corrupt Practices Act - what is the distinction between legal agent fees and bribery? Conflict between EEO laws and host-country laws and customs, and the role of women in the host country.

83. What are the advantages and disadvantages of using host-country nationals rather than expatriate employees?

    ANSWER: 121-123
    Host-country nationals indicate a commitment to the host country. They know the culture, politics, laws, and business customs better than an outsider would. They can better tap into the power networks. Also less expensive in terms of compensation, benefits, and training.

84. What are some of the actions HR professionals should take to prepare a manager for an international assignment?

ANSWER: 126-127
Careful selection. Pre-departure orientation and Training for the employee and family members - including language, culture, history, and living conditions of the host country.

85. Discuss the unique challenges involved in international compensation. Describe some of the approaches available for international compensation.

ANSWER: 128-130
Consider living costs, tax policies, fluctuations in the value of the U.S. dollar, costs of housing, schooling of children, and yearly transportation home. Alternatives include the balance-sheet approach and the global market approach. The tax equalization plan attempts to minimize negative tax consequences.

Chapter 5

Diversity and Equal Employment Opportunity

Multiple Choice

1. Which of the following statements is true about "diversity?"
    A. Diversity requires organizations to initiate affirmative action programs.
    B. Diversity recognizes the difference among people.
    C. Diversity is a natural consequence of civil rights enforcement.
    D. The best response to diversity is to ignore it.

    ANSWER: B, 142

2. Which of the following occurs as a result of diversity?
    A. Usually diversity initially leads to reduced tensions and conflicts.
    B. Outright hostility and physical resistance have been common occurrences.
    C. Diversity causes reverse discrimination.
    D. Organizations may be able to adapt better to the subtle differences in various customer markets.

    ANSWER: D, 142

3. The U.S. Department of Labor has projected that _____ of the entrants to the workforce between 1990 and 2005 will be white men.
    A. only one third
    B. less than 25 percent
    C. about half
    D. at least 60 percent

    ANSWER: A, 143

4. Which of the following was not given as an implication for HR management activities of more women working?
    A. greater flexibility in work patterns and schedules
    B. job placement assistance for working spouses whose mates are offered relocation transfers
    C. less attention to legal issues such as sex discrimination
    D. more variety in benefits programs and HR policies

    ANSWER: C, 143-144

Chapter 5

5. The fastest-growing segments of the U.S. population are
   A. women heads of households.
   B. racial and ethnic groups.
   C. persons under age 25.
   D. Americans with disabilities.

   ANSWER: B, 144

6. During the 1950s most immigrants were Europeans, whereas in the 1990s, _____ predominated.
   A. Eastern Europeans
   B. Central and South Americans
   C. Africans
   D. Hispanics and Asians

   ANSWER: D, 144

7. Implications of the increase in racial and ethnic cultural diversity include:
   A. the potential for work-related conflicts among various racial and ethnic groups will increase.
   B. employer-sponsored cultural awareness and diversity training will become less necessary.
   C. English-only workplaces will become necessary.
   D. enforced dress codes will become common in the workplace.

   ANSWER: A, 144

8. In the U.S., the medium age of the population will _____ by 2000.
   A. remain constant
   B. exhibit a normal distribution
   C. increase
   D. decrease

   ANSWER: C, 145

9. A recent change in Social Security regulations
   A. permits individuals to retire at age 60 while collecting full Social Security payments.
   B. allows individuals over age 65 to earn more per year without affecting their Social Security payments.
   C. increased the employer's share of Social Security contributions.
   D. removes the automatic cost-of-living adjustments to monthly payments.

   ANSWER: B, 145

10. Which of the following was not listed as an implication of the shifting age of the U.S. workforce?
    A. Service industries will actively recruit senior workers for many jobs.
    B. Retirement benefits, particularly pension and health-care coverage, will increase in importance.
    C. Baby boomers will have more multiple careers as they leave organizations.
    D. More promotion opportunities will exist for midcareer baby boomers.

    ANSWER: D, 145

Diversity and Equal Employment Opportunity 61

11. The Centers for Disease Control estimates that _____ Americans with disabilities are covered by the ADA.
    A. at least 43 million
    B. approximately 25 million
    C. more than 80 million
    D. less than 20 million

    ANSWER: A, 145

12. A consequence of the Americans with Disabilities Act is that employers must
    A. redesign jobs to provide employment for persons with a variety of disabilities.
    B. establish an affirmative action plan for hiring persons with disabilities.
    C. define more precisely what are the essential tasks in jobs.
    D. revise their medical insurance plans to provide coverage for disabled employees.

    ANSWER: C, 146

13. The largest group of individuals with disabilities is the
    A. mentally retarded.
    B. hearing impaired.
    C. HIV infected.
    D. blind.

    ANSWER: B, 146

14. Which of the following is the primary reason why women and African-American professionals and managers leave their jobs?
    A. lack of diversity -training programs
    B. inequitable salaries and benefits
    C. overt discrimination and prejudice related to sex or race
    D. lack of opportunity for career growth

    ANSWER: D, 147

15. Why were companies cited as the best places to work for women and minorities?
    A. They tended to be more successful in recruiting and retaining diverse employees.
    B. They were more successful financially.
    C. They had instituted comprehensive affirmative action programs.
    D. They were smaller and often family owned.

    ANSWER: A, 147

16. What is the purpose of diversity training?
    A. to draw attention to differences
    B. to teach the necessary behaviors for getting along in a diverse workforce
    C. to eliminate infringements on legal rights and to minimize discrimination, harassment, and lawsuits
    D. to implement affirmative action programs

    ANSWER: C, 149

62   Chapter 5

17. _____ is concerned with developing organizational initiatives that value all people equally, regardless of their differences.
    A. Affirmative action
    B. Diversity management
    C. Equal employment opportunity (EEO)
    D. Cultural diversity

    ANSWER: B, 150

18. _____ is a broad concept holding that individuals should have equal treatment in all employment-related actions.
    A. Cultural diversity
    B. Affirmative action
    C. Diversity management
    D. Equal employment opportunity (EEO)

    ANSWER: D, 150

19. Individuals who fall within a group identified for protection under equal employment laws and regulations, are members of a(n)
    A. protected class.
    B. affirmative action category.
    C. EEO classification.
    D. minority group.

    ANSWER: A, 150

20. Which of the following is not a basis for protection under federal laws?
    A. military experience
    B. age
    C. sexual orientation
    D. gender

    ANSWER: C, 150

21. "A process in which employers identify problem areas, set goals, and take positive steps to guarantee equal employment opportunities for people in a protected class" is a definition of
    A. cultural diversity.
    B. affirmative action.
    C. diversity management.
    D. equal employment opportunity (EEO).

    ANSWER: B, 151

22. _____ may exist when a person is denied an opportunity because of preferences given to protected-class individuals who may be less qualified.
    A. Quotas
    B. Unlawful discrimination
    C. Affirmative action
    D. Reverse discrimination

    ANSWER: D, 151

Diversity and Equal Employment Opportunity   63

23. What was the intent of the California's Civil Rights Initiative?
    A. to restrict the use of affirmative action
    B. to grant civil-rights protection for persons of differing sexual orientations
    C. to ensure that protected-class members have equal opportunity in all aspects of employment
    D. to eliminate discrimination in university admissions

    ANSWER: A, 154

24. In the _____ case, a federal court restricted the use of race in university admissions.
    A. California Civil Rights Initiative
    B. Adarand
    C. Hopwood v. State of Texas
    D. Griggs v. Duke Power

    ANSWER: C, 154

25. Under the Equal Pay Act, men and women should receive the same pay when
    A. their jobs are comparable.
    B. they are performing substantially the same work.
    C. their education and experience is equivalent.
    D. they are equal seniority.

    ANSWER: B, 155

26. Executive Order 11246
    A. prohibited mandatory retirement programs.
    B. mandated affirmative action programs to eliminate unlawful discrimination against protected-class individuals.
    C. prohibited federal contractors from discriminating against individuals with disabilities.
    D. required federal contractors and subcontractors to eliminate employment discrimination and prior discrimination through affirmative action.

    ANSWER: D, 155

27. The Age Discrimination in Employment Act protects people in what age range?
    A. over age 40
    B. 40-65 years old
    C. over age 65
    D. under age 25

    ANSWER: A, 155

28. When can an organization use age as a selection criterion?
    A. never
    B. after a job offer is made
    C. when it is a *bona fide* occupational qualification
    D. if the applicant is over age 70

    ANSWER: C, 155

29. Under the Pregnancy Discrimination Act, employers must
    A. provide a leave, but not disability insurance.
    B. treat pregnant women like all other employees for employment-related purposes, including benefits.
    C. not discriminate against women. The act does not require leave.
    D. provide pregnant persons with 12 weeks unpaid leave.

    ANSWER: B, 155

30. Under the Immigration Reform and Control Act, it is the employer's responsibility
    A. to notify the Immigration and Naturalization Service when an illegal alien applies for a job.
    B. to verbally ask applicants about their eligibility to work in the U.S.
    C. to check with the Social Security office to insure the individual has the right to work.
    D. not to hire illegal aliens.

    ANSWER: D, 155

31. Which of the following types of organizations does not fall under Title VII?
    A. federal government departments
    B. educational institutions
    C. private employers of 15 or more persons
    D. large labor unions

    ANSWER: A, 156

32. What was the major purpose for passing the Civil Rights Act of 1991?
    A. prohibit discrimination based on sexual preference
    B. protect individuals with disabilities from employment discrimination
    C. overturn or modify seven U.S. Supreme Court decisions
    D. eliminate reverse discrimination preferences

    ANSWER: C, 156

33. Relying on reasoning in the *Griggs v. Duke Power* decision, the Civil Rights Act of 1991 emphasized the importance of _____ in establishing validity.
    A. test reliability
    B. job relatedness
    C. affirmative action
    D. job descriptions

    ANSWER: B, 156-157

34. The 1991 Civil Rights Act requires that the plaintiff bringing a discrimination charge must
    A. show a pattern of discrimination.
    B. identify the majority-group member(s) who benefited from the illegal actions.
    C. provide evidence of financial harm caused by the employer's actions.
    D. identify the particular employer practice being challenged.

    ANSWER: D, 157

Diversity and Equal Employment Opportunity 65

35. Under the 1991 Civil Rights Act, employers must show that an individual's race, color, religion, sex, or national origin
    A. played no factor in the challenged employment practice.
    B. was not the deciding factor in the employment decision.
    C. did not limit that individual's employment options.
    D. caused no financial hardship to the individual.

    ANSWER: A, 157

36. The _____ allows victims of discrimination on the basis of sex, religion, or disability to receive both compensatory and punitive damages in cases of intentional discrimination.
    A. Civil Rights Act of 1994
    B. *Griggs v. Duke Power* decision
    C. Civil Rights Act of 1991
    D. *Price Waterhouse v. Hopkins* decision

    ANSWER: C, 157

37. _____ is the practice of adjusting employment test scores on the basis of the race or gender of test takers.
    A. Discriminatory intent
    B. Race norming
    C. Affirmative adjustment
    D. Business necessity

    ANSWER: B, 157

38. With respect to U.S. citizens working abroad, the 1991 Civil Rights Act
    A. does not apply internationally.
    B. takes precedence over local laws.
    C. requires corporations to abide by local laws and customs.
    D. extends coverage of U.S. EEO laws, except where local laws conflict.

    ANSWER: D, 157

39. What is the composition of the EEOC?
    A. five members appointed by the President and confirmed by the Senate
    B. the members of the Federal District Appeals Court
    C. the senior career-staff members of the Department of Labor
    D. five members appointed by the Civil Rights Commission

    ANSWER: A, 158

40. The EEOC uses _____ who pose as applicants for jobs to determine whether employers would discriminate in their treatment of the individuals.
    A. lawyers
    B. entrapers
    C. "matched pair" testers
    D. African-American candidates

    ANSWER: C, 159

Chapter 5

41. The purpose of the OFCCP is to
    A. evaluate the comparable worth of federal government jobs.
    B. require that federal contractors and subcontractors take affirmative action to overcome the effects of prior discriminatory practices.
    C. help victims of discrimination file claims and obtain relief.
    D. monitor labor market changes.

    ANSWER: B, 158

42. One factor that affects the enforcement of civil rights and affirmative action legislation is
    A. the amount of lobbying being done by special interest groups.
    B. the number of grievances being reported to government agencies.
    C. the mass media's attention and editorials.
    D. the philosophies of the U.S. presidential administration.

    ANSWER: D, 158

43. In addition to federal laws, many states and municipalities have passed their own laws which often
    A. prohibit discrimination in areas beyond those addressed by federal laws.
    B. weaken the effect of the federal laws.
    C. are in conflict with federal laws, thus making enforcement difficult.
    D. are written to protect the rights of the majority group.

    ANSWER: A, 159

44. The _____ has ultimate responsibility for interpretation of EEO laws and regulations.
    A. President of the United States
    B. Equal Employment Opportunity Commission
    C. U.S. Supreme Court
    D. Congress of the United States

    ANSWER: C, 160

45. Discrimination becomes illegal when
    A. you make a notation of an applicant's protected-class status.
    B. two different standards are used to judge different individuals.
    C. you recruit job applicants with your AAP in mind.
    D. a validated test adversely affects a protected class.

    ANSWER: B, 160

46. _____ occurs when protected-class members are treated differently from others.
    A. Adverse impact
    B. Discrimination
    C. Disparate impact
    D. Disparate treatment

    ANSWER: D, 161

47. _____ occurs when there is a substantial under representation of protected-class members as a result of employment decisions that work to their disadvantage.
    A. Disparate impact
    B. Adverse treatment
    C. Disparate treatment
    D. Discrimination

    ANSWER: A, 161

48. The landmark case that established the importance of disparate impact as a legal foundation of EEO law is
    A. *Adarand Constructors v. Pena*
    B. *Bakke*
    C. *Griggs v. Duke Power*
    D. *University of Texas Law School*

    ANSWER: C, 161

49. A practice necessary for safe and efficient organizational operations is called
    A. a *bona fide* occupational qualification.
    B. a business necessity.
    C. a validity generalization.
    D. 4/5ths rule.

    ANSWER: B, 161

50. A _____ is a characteristic providing a legitimate reason why an employer can exclude persons on otherwise illegal bases of consideration.
    A. validity generalization
    B. business necessity
    C. 4/5ths rule
    D. *bona fide* occupational qualification

    ANSWER: D, 161

51. When does the burden of proof fall on the employer?
    A. when the court rules that a *prima facie* case has been made
    B. when there was no Affirmative Action Plan in place
    C. when it is a class action suit
    D. the burden of proof always remains on the complainant

    ANSWER: A, 162

52. Under the Uniform Guidelines, the 4/5ths rule is used to determine if
    A. the employer is guilty of preferential treatment.
    B. a protected-class member has suffered from disparate treatment.
    C. disparate impact has occurred.
    D. illegal discrimination exists.

    ANSWER: C, 163

Chapter 5

53. Employers can check for _____ by comparing the percentage of employed workers in a protected class in the organization with the percentage of protected-class members in the relevant labor market.
    A. external validity
    B. disparate impact externally
    C. internal disparate impact
    D. labor pool balance

    ANSWER: B, 163

54. _____ is the extent to which a test actually measures what it says it measures.
    A. Job relatedness
    B. Accuracy
    C. Reliability
    D. Validity

    ANSWER: D, 165

55. The consistency with which a test measures an item is its
    A. reliability.
    B. repeatability.
    C. stability.
    D. validity.

    ANSWER: A, 165

56. A test his _____ if it reflects an actual sample of the work done on the job in question.
    A. reliability
    B. criterion validity
    C. content validity
    D. validity generalizability

    ANSWER: C, 166

57. In measuring criterion-related validity, a test is the _____ and the desired KSAs and measures of job performance are the _____.
    A. validator; job stats
    B. predictor; criterion variables
    C. X-variable; Y-variables
    D. measure; scores

    ANSWER: B, 166

58. The validation strategy that tests current employees and correlates the scores with their performance ratings is called
    A. predictive validity.
    B. construct validity.
    C. criterion validity.
    D. concurrent validity.

    ANSWER: D, 167

Diversity and Equal Employment Opportunity

59. _____ validity shows a relationship between an abstract characteristic inferred by research and job performance.
    A. Construct validity
    B. Predictive validity
    C. Concurrent validity
    D. Criterion

    ANSWER: A, 168

60. _____ is the extension of the validity of a test with different groups, similar jobs, or other organizations.
    A. Construct validity
    B. Judgment validity
    C. Validity generalization
    D. Utility

    ANSWER: C, 169

True and False

61. Only one-third of the entrants to the workforce between 1990 and 2005 will be white males.

    ANSWER: True, 143

62. High birthrates in the minority community is responsible for much of the growth of racial and ethnic groups in the workforce.

    ANSWER: False, 144
    Much of the growth in the various racial and ethnic groups is due to immigration from other countries.

63. Employment-related benefits and work schedules must remain unchanged to avoid giving special treatment for individuals with disabilities.

    ANSWER: False, 146
    The Americans with Disabilities Act requires employers to make reasonable accommodations for individuals with disabilities. This may require providing additional benefits and/or flexible work schedules to accommodate the special needs of disabled persons.

64. In the absence of national legislation, only a few cities and states have passed laws outlawing discrimination against individuals with differing sexual orientations.

    ANSWER: True, 146

65. Diversity management is concerned with developing affirmative action initiatives to achieve a workforce that reflects the ethnic, gender, and lifestyle makeup of the surrounding community.

    ANSWER: False, 150
    The purpose of diversity management is to develop organizational initiatives that value all people equally, regardless of their differences.

66. Affirmative action occurs when employers identify problem areas, set goals, and take positive steps to guarantee equal employment opportunities for people in a protected class.

    ANSWER: True, 151

67. The Civil Rights Act of 1991 permits the use of quotas as a way of achieving equal employment opportunity.

    ANSWER: False, 151
    The act specifically prohibits the use of quotas.

68. The purpose of the California Civil Rights Initiative (CCRI) is to guarantee, legislatively, that minorities and women gain equal access to employment and educational opportunities in the State of California.

    ANSWER: False, 154
    The initiative stipulates that the State shall not discriminate against or grant preferential treatment to any individual or group on the basis of race, sex, color, ethnicity, or national origin.

69. If employers violate the principles of EEO accidentally or through ignorance, they still may be required to pay back wages, reinstate individuals to their jobs, reimburse attorney fees, and pay punitive damages.

    ANSWER: True, 155-156

70. Under the 1991 Civil Rights Act, an employer cannot simply require that all job applicants have a minimum level of education, such as a high school diploma. They must be able to defend the requirement as job related for the position.

    ANSWER: True, 157

71. The Civil Rights Act of 1991 permits the adjustment of employment test scores on the basis of the race and gender of test takers to achieve affirmative action goals.

    ANSWER: False, 157
    The practice, called "race norming," is prohibited by the Act.

72. The 1991 Civil Rights Act extended coverage of U.S. EEO laws to U.S. citizens working abroad, except where local laws conflict.

    ANSWER: True, 157

Diversity and Equal Employment Opportunity

73. The EEOC is part of the Department of Labor, and is responsible for requiring that federal contractors take affirmative action to overcome the effects of prior discrimination practices.

    ANSWER: False, 158
    It is the task of the OFCCP to require federal contractors and subcontractors take affirmative action. The EEOC is an independent agency responsible for enforcing employment-related provisions of the 1964 Civil Rights Act.

74. Discrimination is defined as illegally preferring one individual over another based upon such factors as race, sex, religion, or sexual orientation.

    ANSWER: False, 160
    The word "discrimination" simply means that differences among items or people are recognized.

75. The Civil Rights Act of 1964, Title VII, prohibited discrimination in all employment-related situations.

    ANSWER: False, 160
    The Act prohibits discrimination in employment-related situations in which different standards are used to judge different individuals, or the same standard is used but it is not related to the individuals' jobs. Not all discrimination is illegal.

76. The burden of proof shifts to the defendant once the court rules that a *prima facie* case of discrimination has been made.

    ANSWER: True, 162

77. The Uniform Guidelines are used by enforcement agencies to examine recruiting, hiring, promotion, and many other employment-related practices.

    ANSWER: True, 162

78. Content validity is a logical, nonstatistical method used to identify the KSAs and other characteristics necessary to perform a job.

    ANSWER: True, 166

79. Concurrent validity studies use a sample of current applicants for the data collection.

    ANSWER: False, 167
    Concurrent validity tests current employees and correlates the scores with their performance ratings.

80. When the validity of a test extends to different groups, similar jobs, or other organizations it has construct validity.

    ANSWER: False, 169
    Validity generalization is the extension of the validity of a test.

Chapter 5

Essay

81. What is meant by the term "diversity?" Why is diversity management an important concern for HR management?

    ANSWER: 142-165
    Diversity refers to differences among people, including age, race, color, religion, gender, and ethnic and national origin. A diverse population affects an organization's application pool, providing an opportunity to tap a broader set of people, ideas, and experiences. This can help an organization better adapt to customer needs. Diversity brings the possibility of conflict. Laws and court rulings prohibit discrimination based on many diverse characteristics.

82. Discuss the following statement with reference to EEO laws and regulations: *"This is my business ... I founded it ... I can hire and fire whomever I choose without interference from the government."*

    ANSWER: 155
    An assortment of federal, state, and local laws limit the ability of a business to hire and fire at will. Regulations prohibit discrimination based on disability, age, race, color, religion, sex, ethnic and national origin, etc. A business owner acting upon the sentiment expressed could face legal actions and possibly social and business consequences.

83. What is illegal discrimination? How can you determine if illegal discrimination has occurred?

    ANSWER: 160-162
    Discrimination can be illegal in employment where different standards are used to judge different individuals, or the same standard is used but it is not related to the individuals' jobs. You would need to consider such items as the 4/5ths rule, disparate treatment, disparate impact, business necessity, job relatedness, and *bona fide* occupational qualifications.

84. How would you validate a test that has been developed to select bank tellers?

    ANSWER: 165-169
    The concurrent validity approach would test current bank tellers and correlate the scores with their performance ratings. To measure predictive validity, test results of applicants are compared with their subsequent job performance.

85. Discuss the interrelationships among equal employment opportunity, affirmative action, and reverse discrimination.

    ANSWER: 150-154
    Equal employment requires that individuals be treated equally in employment-related actions. Affirmative action focuses on hiring, training, and promotion of protected-class members where they are under represented in an organization. Reverse discrimination may exist when a person is denied an opportunity because of preferences given to protected-class members.

Chapter 6

Implementing Equal Employment

Multiple Choice

1. What was the original purpose of the Civil Rights Act of 1964?
    A. to end all employment discrimination
    B. to address race discrimination
    C. to establish equal pay for equal work
    D. to provide legal remedies for victims of unlawful discrimination

    ANSWER: B, 176

2. The Immigration Reform and Control Act
    A. permits employers to hire only U.S. citizens.
    B. permits employers to require more documentation for some prospective employees than for others to ensure that illegal aliens are not hired.
    C. prevents employers from discriminating against undocumented aliens seeking work.
    D. makes it illegal for an employer to discriminate in hiring based on national origin.

    ANSWER: D, 176

3. Which of the following is a requirement of the Immigration Reform and Control Act, as revised?
    A. Employers who knowingly hire illegal aliens must be penalized.
    B. Civil Rights Act protection must be extended to undocumented workers.
    C. Employers are required to verify the citizenship and/or immigration status of job candidates suspected of being foreign born.
    D. Employers cannot require workers speak only English in the workplace.

    ANSWER: A, 176

4. Under the Immigration Reform and Control Act, employers are required to examine identification documents
    A. before a job offer is extended.
    B. after a job offer is extended but before the new employee begins work.
    C. within 72 hours of hiring the new employee.
    D. never.

    ANSWER: C, 178

Chapter 6

5. Which of the following is true with regard to conviction and arrest records?
    A. Using conviction records has been shown to be discriminatory.
    B. Only job-related convictions can be considered.
    C. All convictions may be considered in employment decisions.
    D. Recent job-related arrests may be considered in employment decisions.

    ANSWER: B, 178

6. "Actions that are sexually directed, are unwanted, and subject the worker to adverse employment conditions or create a hostile work environment," is a definition of
    A. *quid pro quo* discrimination.
    B. gender discrimination.
    C. sexual assault.
    D sexual harassment.

    ANSWER: D, 178

7. With regard to workplace relationships and romances, employment attorneys generally recommend that the HR manager
    A. remind both parties of the company policy on sexual harassment.
    B prohibit all workplace relationships and romances.
    C. document all such relationships to minimize future harassment claims.
    D. do nothing, since such romances are a part of human social interaction.

    ANSWER: A, 179

8. According to EEOC statistics, over 90 percent of the sexual harassment charges filed have involved harassment of
    A. men by men.
    B. women by women.
    C. women by men.
    D. men by women.

    ANSWER: C, 179

9. *Quid pro quo* harassment occurs when
    A. the harassment has the effect of unreasonably interfering with work performance or psychological well-being.
    B. a supervisor links specific employment outcomes to the individual's granting sexual favors.
    C. intimidating or offensive working conditions are created.
    D. an employee demands sexual preference as a condition of employment.

    ANSWER: B, 179

10. _____ occurs when the harassment has the effect of unreasonably interfering with work performance or psychological well-being.
    A. *Quid pro quo* harassment
    B. Sexual misconduct
    C. Victimization
    D. Hostile environment harassment

    ANSWER: D, 179

11. In what landmark case did the Supreme Court rule that in determining if a hostile environment exists, it should be considered whether the conduct was physically threatening or humiliating, rather than just offensive?
    A. *Harris v. Forklift Systems*, Inc.
    B. *Meritor Savings Bank v. Vinson*
    C. *EEOC v. Mitsubishi Motor Manufacturing of America*
    D. *Washington v. Davis*

    ANSWER: A, 180

12. Which of the following is necessary to prove sexual harassment involving the creation of a hostile environment?
    A. the employee is a member of a protected class
    B. sexual extortion existed
    C. the conduct interfered unreasonably with an employee's work performance
    D. the complainant suffered loss of earnings or job loss

    ANSWER: C, 180

13. An employer may avoid liability for sexual harassment in which of the following situations?
    A. the victim and alleged harasser were both heterosexual males
    B. the employer took reasonable care to prohibit sexual harassment
    C. the employee did not suffer any tangible employment action
    D. the employer had no knowledge of the offensive behavior

    ANSWER: B, 180

14. Employers generally are held responsible for sexual harassment
    A. if the victim reported the incident.
    B. unless they had no knowledge of the harassment behaviors.
    C. if they knew of the behavior.
    D. unless they take appropriate action in response to complaints.

    ANSWER: D, 181

15. Which of the following should be included in an employer's sexual harassment policy?
    A. Disciplinary action will be taken against sexual harassers up to and including termination.
    B. Assurances of confidentiality for all parties involved in the complaint.
    C. The complainant will be assigned to another section or supervisor.
    D. Instructions to report complaints through strictly controlled channels.

    ANSWER: A, 182

16. An employer's defense in a sexual harassment complaint is aided when
    A. the victim is immediately transferred to another supervisor.
    B. the alleged harasser is moved to a work site remote from the complainant.
    C. the employer promptly investigates the complaint and punishes the identified harassers.
    D. the employer immediately dismisses the alleged harasser.

    ANSWER: C, 183

76 Chapter 6

17. The major provision of the Pregnancy Discrimination Act was that
    A. employers could not discriminate against employees based on family status.
    B. maternity leave was to be treated the same as other personal or medical leaves.
    C. pregnant employees are entitled to 12 weeks unpaid maternity leave.
    D. pregnant employees are entitled to 12 weeks of paid maternity leave.

    ANSWER: B, 183

18. Which of the following has been a general ruling in cases filed under the Pregnancy Discrimination Act?
    A. Employers are not required to accommodate the needs of pregnant employees.
    B. Pregnancy is a disability requiring special accommodation.
    C. Women must be assignment less strenuous tasks during pregnancy.
    D. Employers must treat pregnant employers the same as non-pregnant employees with similar abilities or inabilities.

    ANSWER: D, 183

19. The Equal Pay Act, enacted in 1963, requires employers to
    A. pay similar wage rates for similar work without regard to gender.
    B. establish pay rates based upon merit rather than seniority.
    C. conduct wage and salary surveys to ensure pay equity.
    D. ensure that older employees are not discriminated against in compensation.

    ANSWER: A, 184

20. The courts have ruled that a female employee with the same job title as a male
    A. must be paid the same salary and benefits as the male.
    B. must be paid the same unless the male employee has more seniority.
    C. may be paid less than the male employee if the job is less demanding.
    D. is not eligible for leave under the Family and Medical Leave Act.

    ANSWER: C, 184

21. According to the concept of _____, the pay for jobs requiring comparable levels of knowledge, skill, and ability should be similar even if actual duties differ significantly.
    A. equal pay
    B. pay equity
    C. comparable pay
    D. pay fairness

    ANSWER: B, 184

22. A 1998 study of men's and women's salaries found that
    A. the differences have almost been eliminated.
    B. college educated women earn about the same as college educated men.
    C. the income of full-time working women is about 90 percent of men's.
    D. pay disparity is greatest for lower skilled, less-educated women as compared with lower-skilled, less-educated men.

    ANSWER: D, 184

23. With regard to the concept of pay equity,
    A. it is not required by federal law.
    B. The Labor Department requires pay equity for public-sector employees.
    C. the federal government has legislated that jobs with comparable levels of knowledge, skills, and abilities be paid similarly.
    D. the Supreme Court has ruled that jobs requiring different skills, tasks, and responsibilities should not be paid the same.

    ANSWER: A, 184

24. The Paycheck Fairness Act, proposed by President Clinton in 1999, would
    A. mandate equal pay for equal work.
    B. require pay equity for federal contractors and subcontractors.
    C. allow women to sue employers for unlimited damages, in addition to the back pay available under other laws.
    D. establish a commission to automatically index minimum wage to inflation.

    ANSWER: C, 184

25. The *Arizona Governing Committee v. Norris* decision held that, in regard to retirement benefits,
    A. women with working spouses may receive less in retirement benefits.
    B. men and women who contribute equally to pension plans must receive equal monthly payments.
    C. both sexes must contribute equally to the plan.
    D. organizations must look at actuarial tables by sex to determine pensions.

    ANSWER: B, 184-185

26. Nepotism refers to
    A. favoritism in hiring.
    B. a discriminatory policy.
    C. an organization specifically selecting a protected class individual.
    D. the practice of allowing relatives to work for the same employer.

    ANSWER: D, 185

27. Policies of reassigning women from hazardous jobs to lower-paying jobs because of health-related concerns, including birth defects sustained during pregnancy,
    A. have been ruled illegal by the Supreme Court.
    B. are recommended as a way of reducing worker compensation premiums.
    C. are usually left for supervisors to decide on a case-by-case basis.
    D. are recommended as good corporate policy.

    ANSWER: A, 186

28. The _____ refers to discriminatory practices that have prevented women and other protected-class members from advancing to executive-level jobs.
    A. old boys network
    B. pyramid effect
    C. glass ceiling
    D. glass walls

    ANSWER: C, 186

78   Chapter 6

29. Statistics reveal that women tend to have better opportunities to progress in
    A.   multinational companies.
    B.   smaller firms.
    C.   the Federal Government.
    D.   family owned businesses.

    ANSWER: B, 186

30. A problem whereby women have tended to advance to senior management in a limited number of functional areas has been referred to as
    A.   the old boys network.
    B.   a pyramid effect.
    C.   glass ceiling.
    D.   glass elevators.

    ANSWER: D, 187

31. The Age Discrimination in Employment Act protects individuals over the age of
    A.   40.
    B.   50.
    C.   65.
    D.   70.

    ANSWER: A, 187

32. The Age Discrimination in Employment Act
    A.   permits mandatory retirement at age 65.
    B.   permits mandatory retirement at age 70.
    C.   forbids mandatory retirement in most circumstances.
    D.   regulates early retirement plans.

    ANSWER: C, 187

33. What is the legal position regarding mandatory retirement?
    A.   There can be no mandatory retirement age.
    B.   Mandatory retirement is permitted if age is a job-related occupational qualification.
    C.   A company can set its own maximum age, based on company tradition.
    D.   ADEA-protected individuals may not be fired.

    ANSWER: B, 187

34. Why have many organizations offered early retirement plans?
    A.   They are the most legal way to downsize.
    B.   The older employees are often unable to adjust to new technology.
    C.   It is one way to "get around" the ADEA.
    D.   They reduce employment costs in the higher salary brackets.

    ANSWER: D, 188

35. Which of the following was a concern of the Older Workers Benefit Protection Act of 1990?
    A. older workers may not give away their right to sue for age discrimination unless certain criteria exist
    B. pension plans must be administered fairly regardless of an employee's age
    C. medical insurance cannot be denied to retirees
    D. the companies must fund benefits in a financially-sound account

    ANSWER: A, 188

36. Which of the following best describes those covered by the Americans with Disabilities Act?
    A. all employers with 25 or more employees
    B. all federal, state, and local government employees
    C. all employers with 15 or more employees, including state and local governments
    D. all private and public sector employers

    ANSWER: C, 189

37. Title I of the ADA prohibits employment-related discrimination against
    A. pregnant women.
    B. persons with disabilities.
    C. disabled Vietnam-era veterans.
    D. individuals unable to perform certain essential job functions.

    ANSWER: B, 189

38. According to U.S. government estimates, _____ Americans have some sort of disability.
    A. less than 10 million
    B. approximately 20 million
    C. approximately 30 million
    D. almost 50 million

    ANSWER: D, 189

39. Which of the following would be considered disabled persons under the ADA?
    A. people with AIDS
    B. pregnant women
    C. current users of illegal drugs
    D. compulsive gamblers

    ANSWER: A, 190

40. The fundamental job duties of an employment position, not including marginal functions of the position, are called
    A. reasonable accommodations.
    B. minimum job requirements.
    C. essential job functions.
    D. primary job duties.

    ANSWER: C, 192

Chapter 6

41. _____ is the modification or adjustment to a job or work environment that enables a qualified individual with a disability to enjoy equal employment opportunity.
    A. Creating access
    B. Reasonable accommodation
    C. Job modification
    D. Permitting essential job functioning

    ANSWER: B, 192

42. If making reasonable accommodation for a disabled person imposes significant difficulty or expense on an employer, the employer
    A. may reduce the salary of the disabled person to compensate.
    B. will have to make the accommodation anyway.
    C. will be responsible for finding alternate work for the disabled person.
    D. can claim undue hardship.

    ANSWER: D, 192

43. In *TWA v. Hardison*, the Supreme Court ruled that an employer must make reasonable accommodation for
    A. an employee's religious beliefs.
    B. a disabled person.
    C. an employee infected with HIV.
    D. the domestic partner of an employee.

    ANSWER: A, 193

44. Which of the following is true with respect to the physical appearance of employees?
    A. Attractiveness may be a valid selection criterion.
    B. Obesity may be considered as an employment variable.
    C. Court decisions have allowed dress codes as long as they are applied uniformly.
    D. Minorities with health problems are exempt from certain appearance policies.

    ANSWER: C, 195

45. Which of the following statements is true about obesity and employment discrimination?
    A. Overweight people are protected from discrimination under the Civil Rights Act of 1991.
    B. Under the ADA, obese individuals may qualify as having a covered disability when they are perceived as having a disability.
    C. Discrimination against obese individuals is prohibited by Title VII of the 1964 Civil Rights Act.
    D. No special legal protection is provided based upon obesity.

    ANSWER: B, 195

46. With regard to sexual orientation and gay rights
    A. transvestites are considered disabled under the ADA.
    B. federal law protects against discrimination based on sexual orientation.
    C. sex discrimination covers people who have had gender-altering operations.
    D. the Supreme Court has not decided whether gay men and lesbians have rights under the equal protection amendment to the U.S. Constitution.

    ANSWER: D, 196

47. Which of the following is a requirement of the Vietnam-Era Veterans Readjustment Act of 1974?
    A. affirmative action for Vietnam-era veterans by federal contractors and subcontractors
    B. non-discrimination against Vietnam-era veterans
    C. employers with more than 15 employees must undertake affirmative action in hiring Vietnam-era veterans
    D. Vietnam-era veterans must be treated the same as other job applicants

    ANSWER: A, 196

48. All employers with _____ employees are required to keep certain records that can be requested by the EEOC.
    A. any number of
    B. at least 5
    C. 15 or more
    D. 25 or more

    ANSWER: C, 197

49. Which of the following employers must file the Annual Reporting Form EEO-1 with the EEOC?
    A. all employers
    B. all employers with 100 or more employees, except state and local governments
    C. all federal contractors
    D. all employers with 15 or more employees

    ANSWER: B, 197

50. In order to effectively defend itself against a charge of discrimination in the recruiting and selection of members of protected classes, organizations should maintain
    A. exit interview summaries.
    B. job evaluation data.
    C. objective applications.
    D. applicant flow data.

    ANSWER: D, 197

82 Chapter 6

51. A charge must be filed with the EEOC within _____ of when the alleged discriminatory action occurred.
    A. 180 days
    B. 12 months
    C. 30 days
    D. 2 years

    ANSWER: A, 200

52. When is a "right-sue-letter" issued?
    A. when an employer believes that it has been falsely charged with unlawful discrimination
    B. when the EEOC believes that it has a prima facie case of discrimination
    C. when the EEOC decides that it will not bring suit on behalf of the complainant
    D. when a person files a complaint with the EEOC

    ANSWER: C, 200

53. Which of the following preemployment inquiries may be discriminatory?
    A. whether the applicant has ever worked under a different name
    B. date of high school graduation
    C. whether the applicant is a citizen of the United States
    D. what branch of the military the applicant served in

    ANSWER: B, 202

54. Which of the following inquiries would usually not be discriminatory?
    A. whom to contact in case of an emergency
    B. photographs with application or resume
    C. number and types of arrests
    D. names of relatives already employed by the employer

    ANSWER: D, 203

55. A(n) _____ is issued by the president of the United States to provide direction to government departments on a specific issue or area.
    A. executive order
    B. presidential directive
    C. veto
    D. bill

    ANSWER: A, 204

56. Which agency is responsible for enforcing nondiscrimination in government contracts?
    A. The Equal Employment Opportunity Commission
    B. The Executive Orders Group
    C. The Office of Federal Contract Compliance Programs
    D. The U.S. Contracts and Agreements Agency

    ANSWER: C, 204

57. Who is required to have an affirmative action plan?
    A. all government contractors
    B. an employer with at least 50 employees and over $50,000 in government contracts
    C. all government agencies
    D. an employers with at least 20 employees

    ANSWER: B, 204

58. The purpose of a(n) _____ is to identify problem areas in the employment of protected-class members and initiate goals and steps to overcome these problems.
    A. EEOC audit
    B. workforce analysis
    C. job group analysis
    D. affirmative action plan

    ANSWER: D, 204

59. _____ identifies the number of protected-class members available to work in the appropriate labor markets in given jobs.
    A. An availability analysis
    B. A labor market survey
    C. A labor-trends analysis
    C. An affirmative action analysis

    ANSWER: A, 206

60. Identifying the number of protected-class members employed and the types of jobs they hold in an organization is the purpose of a(n)
    A. equal opportunity investigation.
    B. availability determination.
    C. utilization analysis.
    D. affirmative action assessment.

    ANSWER: C, 206

True and False

61. The original purpose of the Civil Rights Act of 1964 was to establish affirmative action programs.

    ANSWER: False, 176
    The original purpose of the act was to address race discrimination.

62. "Undocumented workers" is the term used when referring to illegal aliens.

    ANSWER: True, 176

63. The Immigration Reform and Control Act makes it illegal for an employer to discriminate in recruiting, hiring, or termination based on an individual's national origin or citizenship.

    ANSWER: True, 176

64. The purpose of the Immigration Reform and Control Act is to penalize illegal aliens who work in the United States, rather than to penalize the employers.

    ANSWER: False, 176
    The act requires that employers who knowingly hire illegal aliens be penalized, not the employees.

65. The Courts have generally upheld attempts by employers to ban employees from speaking foreign languages at all times in work areas.

    ANSWER: False, 177
    EEOC guidelines state that employers may require workers to speak only English at certain times or in certain situations, but the business necessity of the requirements must be justified.

66. Sexual harassment can occur among nonemployees who have business contacts with employees.

    ANSWER: True, 178

67. Withholding a raise from someone who refuses to date you is an example of *quid pro quo* harassment.

    ANSWER: True, 180

68. In *Harris v. Forklift Systems, Inc.*, the Supreme Court ruled that a complainant must suffer some tangible loss or damage before sexual harassment can be proven.

    ANSWER: False, 180
    The Supreme Court ruled that a hostile environment may constitute sexual harassment even though the employee suffered no tangible employment action.

69. The Equal Pay Act prohibits employers from having different pay rates based on race.

    ANSWER: False, 184
    The Equal Pay Act prohibits differences in pay based on sex.

70. Generally, employer anti-nepotism policies have been outlawed by the courts.

    ANSWER: False, 185
    The courts have upheld anti-nepotism policies.

71. According to the concept of pay equity, the pay for jobs requiring comparable levels of knowledge, skill, and ability should be similar even if actual duties differ significantly.

    ANSWER: True, 184

72. Employers may not restrict pregnant women from working at jobs that could cause birth defects.

ANSWER: True, 186

73. The Older Workers Benefit Protection Act (OWBPA) was passed to safeguard the Social Security benefits for retired workers.

ANSWER: False, 188
The act was passed to ensure that equal treatment for older workers occurs in early retirement or severance situations.

74. A rehabilitated drug user is not considered a disabled person under the ADA.

ANSWER: False. 190
While current users of illegal drugs are not classified as disabled, alcoholics and rehabilitated drug users are.

75. The ADA does not require an employer to hire a disabled person who is unable to perform all the requirements of the job.

ANSWER: False, 192
ADA guidelines require employers to identify essential job functions of each position. These do not include marginal functions of the position.

76. Teaching a supervisor sign language is considered a reasonable accommodation.

ANSWER: True, 192

77. The Civil Rights Acts of 1964 and 1991 permit religious schools to use religion as a selection variable for teachers.

ANSWER: True, 193

78. Obesity may be considered as a disability under the ADA.

ANSWER: True, 195

79. The courts have ruled that an employer may prohibit male employees from have long hair but not female employees.

ANSWER: True, 195

80. Federal employment laws prohibit discrimination based on sexual orientation.

ANSWER: False, 196
Although some states and cities have passed laws making it unlawful to discriminate based on sexual orientation, there are no federal laws.

Chapter 6

Essay

81. What is sexual harassment? How has sexual harassment been defined by the Courts? What actions can an organization take to minimize the probability of sexual harassment charges being filed?

    ANSWER: 178-183
    Sexual harassment - any action that is sexually directed, unwanted, subject the worker to adverse employment conditions or create a hostile work environment. It may be *quid pro quo* or hostile environment harassment, and is not limited to male/female behavior. Organizations may limit liability by producing evidence that it took reasonable care to prohibit sexual harassment.

82. Discuss in some detail two gender-based discrimination issues, other than sexual harassment. What, if any, legislation exists to address these issues?

    ANSWER: 183-187
    Discrimination in pay and benefits, discrimination in jobs and careers. Legislation includes Equal Pay Act (1963), Pregnancy Discrimination Act (1978), Glass Ceiling Act (1991), Family and Medical Leave Act (1993).

83. What are the major requirements of the Americans with Disabilities Act? What has been the impact of the ADA on both employers and individuals with disabilities? What actions should an employer take to insure compliance with the ADA?

    ANSWER: 189-193
    Employers with 15 or more employees are to make reasonable accommodation for individuals with disabilities. Jobs must be analyzed to identify essential job functions. Using the EEOC guidelines almost 50 million Americans have some sort of disability.

84. What records should an employer maintain to comply with all EEO and Affirmative Action requirements? How can good record-keeping assist an employer in defending a charge of illegal discrimination?

    ANSWER: 196-199
    Records - EEO policy statement, annual reporting form, applicant flow data form, plus all employment-related records. Good records can provide evidence that no unlawful discrimination occurred.

85. Describe the purpose and history of affirmative action. What is an Affirmative Action Plan? Who must have one?

    ANSWER: 204-207
    Executive orders 11246, 11375, and 11478 require federal government contractors and subcontractors to take affirmative action to overcome the effects of past discriminatory practices. Employers with at least 50 employees and over $50,000 in government contracts must have an AAP. An AAP identifies problem areas and goals and steps to overcome those problems.

Chapter 7

Analyzing and Identifying Jobs

Multiple Choice

1. Analyzing work done in organizations must be based on _____, not just _____.
    A. legal analysis; job descriptions
    B. facts and data; personal perceptions of managers and supervisors
    C. managerial experience; employee perceptions
    D. job demands; personal experience of employees and supervisors

    ANSWER: B, 214

2. Which of the following was identified as the most basic building block of HR management?
    A. recruitment and selection
    B. training and development
    C. strategic planning
    D. job analysis

    ANSWER: D, 214

3. Job analysis is a systematic way to
    A. gather and analyze information about the content and human requirements of jobs, and the context in which jobs are performed.
    B. analyze the distinct, identifiable work activities involved in a specific job classification.
    C. evaluate the quality of job performance of employees.
    D. evaluate the strategic determination of the relative worth of jobs.

    ANSWER: A, 214

4. A _____ is a grouping of similar positions having common tasks, duties, and responsibilities.
    A. job family
    B. position category
    C. job
    D. KSA

    ANSWER: C, 214

87

88   Chapter 7

5. _____ is(are) a collection of tasks, duties, and responsibilities performed by one person.
    A.   A job
    B.   A position
    C.   KSAs
    D.   Job analysis

    ANSWER: B, 214

6. If there are two persons working as cashiers in a small grocery store, there are two _____ but just one _____.
    A.   jobs; position
    B.   tasks; duty
    C.   duties; tasks
    D.   positions; job

    ANSWER: D, 214

7. The primary thrust of _____ is to mesh the productivity needs of the organization with the needs of the individuals performing the various jobs.
    A.   job design
    B.   organizational development
    C.   job analysis
    D.   job satisfaction

    ANSWER: A, 214-215

8. A key aim for _____ is to provide individuals meaningful work that fits effectively into the flow of the organization.
    A.   job analysis
    B.   time and motion studies
    C.   job design
    D.   organizational development

    ANSWER: C, 215

9. The primary purpose of _____ is to get a clear understanding of what is done on a job and what capabilities are needed to do it.
    A.   time and motion studies
    B.   job analysis
    C.   job design
    D.   organizational development

    ANSWER: B, 215

10. The focus in high technology industries is less on _____, and more on _____.
    A.   people; process
    B.   job analysis; job design
    C.   managing subordinates; cooperating as a task-force member
    D.   performing specific tasks and duties; attaining results

    ANSWER: D, 215

Analyzing and Identifying Jobs 89

11. Which of the following statements is true for fast-moving organizations in the high-technology industries?
    A. A job description is becoming an obsolete concept.
    B. Without a current job description, it is more difficult to assess performance.
    C. Job descriptions are critical for maintaining stability.
    D. Job descriptions need to be written collaboratively by group members and supervisors.

    ANSWER: A, 215

12. Which of the following studies the workflow, activities, context, and output of a job?
    A. job design
    B. organizational development
    C. work analysis
    D. job specification analysis

    ANSWER: C, 215

13. A distinctive, identifiable work activity composed of motions is a
    A. duty.
    B. task.
    C. job.
    D. position.

    ANSWER: B, 216

14. A _____ is a larger work segment composed of several tasks that are performed by an individual.
    A. position
    B. job
    C. responsibility
    D. duty

    ANSWER: D, 216

15. _____ are obligations to perform certain tasks and duties.
    A. Responsibilities
    B. Jobs
    C. Job descriptions
    D. Positions

    ANSWER: A, 216

16. Basic characteristics that can be linked to enhanced performance by individuals or teams, are called
    A. duties.
    B. responsibilities.
    C. competencies.
    D. tasks.

    ANSWER: C, 217

Chapter 7

17. The competency approach to job analysis considers
    A. the tasks, duties, knowledge, and skills associated with a job.
    B. how the knowledge and skills are used.
    C. the qualifications of the job holder.
    D. how performance will be assessed.

    ANSWER: B, 217

18. In most cases, the best source of job analysis information on what actually is done on a job is the
    A. HR department.
    B. job analyst.
    C. position's supervisor.
    D. employee.

    ANSWER: D, 219

19. Why is relying on supervisors for job analysis information not always advisable?
    A. They might not know what their employees actually do on the job.
    B. They have a unique perspective of the job.
    C. They might tend to inflate the importance of the job.
    D. They might feel threatened providing top management with this type of information.

    ANSWER: A, 219

20. Who is usually responsible for writing the actual job description?
    A. the job analyzer
    B. the job holder's direct supervisor
    C. the HR unit
    D. the employee holding the job

    ANSWER: C, 220

21. Who is responsible for identifying performance standards based on analysis information?
    A. the employee
    B. managers
    C. HR unit
    D. job analysts

    ANSWER: B, 220

22. In a typical division of job analysis responsibilities, a manager would
    A. prepare and coordinate job analysis procedures.
    B. write job descriptions and specifications.
    C. seek assistance from experts for difficult or unusual analyses.
    D. request new job analysis as jobs change.

    ANSWER: D, 220

23. A job description identifies
    A. the tasks, duties, and responsibilities of a job.
    B. the knowledge, skills, and abilities an individual needs to do the job satisfactorily.
    C. what the job accomplishes and what performance is considered satisfactory.
    D. the education, experience, and work skill requirements of a job.

    ANSWER: A, 221

24. A job _____ identifies what is done, why it is done, where it is done, and briefly, how it is done.
    A. analysis
    B. specification
    C. description
    D. performance standard

    ANSWER: C, 221

25. Performance standards should flow directly from
    A. job specifications.
    B. a job description.
    C. KSAs.
    D. the essential elements of the job.

    ANSWER: B, 221

26. _____ tell what the job accomplishes and how performance is measured in key areas of the job description.
    A. Competencies
    B. Job specifications
    C. Job standards
    D. Performance standards

    ANSWER: D, 221

27. Job specifications list
    A. the knowledge, skills, and abilities an individual needs to do the job satisfactorily.
    B. what the job accomplishes and how performance is measured in key areas of the job description.
    C. the tasks, duties, and responsibilities of a job.
    D. the education, experience, and work skill requirements of a job.

    ANSWER: A, 221

28. An example of a _____ for a secretary would be "types 50 words per minute with no more than two errors."
    A. job description
    B. KSA
    C. job specification
    D. performance standard

    ANSWER: C, 221

29. An accurate _____ might include education, experience, work skill requirements, personal abilities, and mental and physical requirements.
    A. job description
    B. job specification
    C. job standard
    D. performance standard

    ANSWER: B, 221

30. A job family is a grouping of _____ having similar characteristics.
    A. positions
    B. tasks
    C. employees
    D. jobs

    ANSWER: D, 221

31. What is the purpose of an organizational chart?
    A. to depict the relationships among jobs in an organization
    B. to illustrate the grouping of jobs having similar characteristics
    C. to display the communication patterns in the organization
    D. to facilitate succession planning

    ANSWER: A, 221

32. Dual reporting relationships exist in
    A. smaller organizations.
    B. traditional organizational charts.
    C. matrix organizations.
    D. hierarchical organizational charts.

    ANSWER: C, 224

33. Job analysis provides the foundation for many HR activities, including
    A. environmental scanning.
    B. compensation.
    C. input to grievance procedures.
    D. reengineering.

    ANSWER: B, 224

34. EEO guidelines require a sound and comprehensive job analysis to
    A. ensure pay equity.
    B. reduce the number of grievances filed.
    C. prepare "right-to-sue" letters.
    D. validate recruiting and selection criteria.

    ANSWER: D, 225

Analyzing and Identifying Jobs   93

35. The performance appraisal process should tie to the _____ and performance standards.
    A. job description
    B. job specification
    C. supervisor expectations
    D. selection and placement

    ANSWER: A, 226

36. The 1978 Uniform Selection Guidelines make it clear that HR requirements must _____ if employers are to defend their actions as a business necessity.
    A. apply to all employees
    B. not discriminate against protected-class members
    C. be tied to specific job-related factors
    D. be limited to actual on-the-job behaviors

    ANSWER: C, 226

37. Employers are now placing increased emphasis on developing and maintaining current and accurate job descriptions as a result of the passage of the
    A. Civil Rights Act of 1991.
    B. Americans with Disabilities Act.
    C. Family and Medical Leave Act.
    D. Equal Pay Act.

    ANSWER: B, 226

38. One result of the ADA is that many employers have had to revise their job specifications to
    A. permit the hiring of disabled individuals.
    B. limit the amount of time spent on any one job function.
    C. increase a supervisor's flexibility in assigning work.
    D. reflect the prerequisite KSAs.

    ANSWER: D, 226

39. _____ are the fundamental job duties of the employment position that an individual with the disability holds or desires.
    A. Essential functions
    B. Minimum requirements
    C. Primary requirements
    D. Essential KSAs

    ANSWER: A, 227

40. Marginal functions are those duties that are part of a job
    A. that a disabled person cannot perform.
    B. that most disabled individuals can perform with minor assistance.
    C. but are incidental or ancillary to the purpose and nature of a job.
    D. and essential to its operation.

    ANSWER: C, 227

Chapter 7

41. If a disabled applicant is qualified for the fundamental job duties, the employer is obligated to
    A. hire that individual first.
    B. make reasonable accommodations.
    C. treat the disabled applicant like any other job candidate.
    D. redesign the other aspects of the job.

    ANSWER: B, 227

42. Job analysis can be a threatening experience for both managers and employees in part because job analysis can
    A. highlight discrepancies between a manager's expectations and those of the employee.
    B. indicate that the job is no longer necessary for the organization to achieve its goals.
    C. illustrate that the employee has a poor record of performing the essential job functions.
    D. identify the difference between what currently is being performed in a job and what should be done.

    ANSWER: D, 228

43. Because job analysis information is often used for compensation purposes, employees and managers have a tendency to
    A. inflate the importance and significance of their jobs.
    B. cooperate with the job analyst.
    C. resent this examination of their jobs.
    D. use this as an opportunity to complain about their supervisors.

    ANSWER: A, 228

44. Which of the following was identified as an organizational problem that often occurs as part of the job analysis process?
    A. a managerial conflict between what should be done and what is done
    B. a focus on the job, rather than on the incumbent doing the job
    C. title inflation
    D. an over emphasis on the legal concerns

    ANSWER: C, 228

45. One problem that occurs when conducting a job analysis is
    A. using the job description only as a broad outline of a job's responsibilities.
    B. an overemphasis on the current employee.
    C. modesty when describing a job's importance.
    D. a willingness to redesign jobs to increase the employees' job satisfaction and involvement.

    ANSWER: B, 229

46. Job analysis data can be gathered using the following methods:
   A.   interviews, historical data, questionnaires.
   B.   questionnaires, experimentation, observations.
   C.   observations, market data, experimentation.
   D.   observations, interviews, questionnaires.

   ANSWER: D, 230

47. With respect to observation as a job analysis technique,
   A.   the method is limited because many jobs do not have complete and easily observed job cycles.
   B.   the manager or job analyst should make only one observation to avoid contamination of results.
   C.   avoid repetitive jobs. Concentrate on "knowledge work."
   D.   observation must be continuous not based on sampling.

   ANSWER: A, 230

48. The work sampling type of observation
   A.   gives a more detailed picture of the job.
   B.   is better received by the workers since it is less disruptive to their work schedules.
   C.   determines the content and pace of a typical workday through statistical sampling of certain actions.
   D.   is better for complex and non-repetitive jobs.

   ANSWER: C, 230

49. Which of the following is true about the use of group interviews to gather job analysis information?
   A.   They are relatively inexpensive given the information obtained.
   B.   Group interviews are probably most appropriate for difficult-to-define jobs.
   C.   They are less likely to result in "job inflation."
   D.   Through its open structure, a group interview obtains in-depth insights into the job.

   ANSWER: B, 231

50. What is the major advantage of the questionnaire method of gathering data on jobs?
   A.   A checklist is uncomplicated and easy for the employees to complete.
   B.   The anonymity of questionnaires permit employees to give the most valid information.
   C.   You obtain such a large body of data that follow-up observations and discussion are unnecessary.
   D.   Information on a large number of jobs can be collected inexpensively in a relatively short period of time.

   ANSWER: D, 231

96 Chapter 7

51. The functional job analysis (FJA) method examines the three components of
    A.   data, people, and things.
    B.   clerical, professional, and technical job elements.
    C.   activities, knowledge, and skills.
    D.   interpersonal, executive, and information job elements.

    ANSWER: A, 232

52. The _____ is a standardized data source provided by the U.S. Department of Labor.
    A.   Job Information Guide
    B.   Occupational Title Index
    C.   Dictionary of Occupational Titles
    D.   Dictionary of Job Titles

    ANSWER: C, 232

53. How is the Dictionary of Occupational Titles (DOT) useful to a manager or HR specialist?
    A.   a defense in an EEOC audit
    B.   a starting point when confronted with preparing a large number of job descriptions
    C.   to compare technological similarities of different jobs
    D.   to conduct wage classifications

    ANSWER: B, 232

54. The Position Analysis Questionnaire (PAQ) focuses on the _____ elements that describe behaviors necessary to do the job.
    A.   market-oriented
    B.   job-oriented
    C.   organization-oriented
    D.   worker-oriented

    ANSWER: D, 232

55. Which of the following is a characteristic of computerized job analysis?
    A.   a reduction in the time and effort involved in writing job descriptions
    B.   difficulty in identifying mismatches between job scores and pay survey data
    C.   production of technical reports which make it difficult to identify specific knowledge, skills, and abilities required in the job
    D.   results cannot be used to develop job evaluation weights

    ANSWER: A, 234

56. The _____ section of the job description gives the job title, reporting relationships, department, location, and date of analysis.
    A.   general summary
    B.   essential functions
    C.   identification
    D.   essential duties

    ANSWER: C, 239

Analyzing and Identifying Jobs

57. Clear, precise statements on the major tasks, duties, and responsibilities performed are contained in the _____ section of the job description.
    A. general summary
    B. essential functions and duties
    C. identification
    D. specification requirements

    ANSWER: B, 240

58. The purpose of _____ are to give the qualifications needed to perform the job satisfactorily.
    A. essential function statements
    B. performance standards
    C. job standards
    D. job specifications

    ANSWER: D, 240

59. When writing job specifications, it should be remembered that the current incumbent's job qualifications _____ the minimum KSAs required to perform the job satisfactorily.
    A. often exceed
    B. are usually below
    C. should closely match
    D. have no relation to

    ANSWER: A, 241

60. In writing job specifications in light of the ADA, it is crucial to
    A. clearly list all possible accommodations.
    B. list all the KSAs which might be required for job performance.
    C. clearly identify the physical and mental dimensions of each job.
    D. identify the kinds of jobs that could be performed by disabled persons.

    ANSWER: C, 242

True and False

61. Without the foundation of job analysis, it is difficult for an organization to defend its recruiting and selection procedures, performance appraisal system, employee disciplinary actions, and pay practices.

    ANSWER: True, 214

62. Job analysis refers to organizing tasks, duties, and responsibilities into a productive unit of work.

    ANSWER: False, 214
    Job analysis is a systematic way to gather and analyze information about the content and human requirements of jobs, and the context in which jobs are performed.

Chapter 7

63. Although the terms "job" and "position" are often used interchangeably, there is a slight difference in emphasis.

    ANSWER: True, 214

64. Attention is being paid to job design primarily to influence job performance rather than job satisfaction.

    ANSWER: False, 214-215
    Job design is concerned with meshing the productivity needs of the organization with the needs of the individuals performing the various jobs.

65. For fast-moving organizations in high-technology industries, a job description is essential for providing stability and direction for the employee.

    ANSWER: False, 215
    For such jobs, a job description is becoming an obsolete concept.

66. A task is a distinct, identifiable work activity composed of motions, whereas a duty is a larger work segment composed of several tasks that are performed by an individual.

    ANSWER: True, 216

67. Unlike the traditional approach to analyzing jobs, the competency approach considers the tasks, duties, knowledge, and skills associated with a job.

    ANSWER: False, 217
    The competency approach considers how the knowledge and skills are used.

68. A job description tells what a job accomplishes and what performance is considered satisfactory in each area of the job.

    ANSWER: False, 221
    A job description identifies the tasks, duties, and responsibilities of a job. Performance standards indicate what a job accomplishes.

69. The primary purpose of job analysis is to comply with government laws and regulations.

    ANSWER: False, 224
    Legal compliance is just one of the purposes of job analysis.

70. A sound and comprehensive job analysis is required by EEO guidelines for validation of recruiting and selection criteria.

    ANSWER: True, 225

71. Job analysis information is useful in identifying possible job hazards and working conditions associated with jobs.

    ANSWER: True, 226

Analyzing and Identifying Jobs 99

72. It is common in unionized environments for job descriptions to be very "loose" about what tasks are and are not covered in a job. This gives the union greater discretion during negotiations.

    ANSWER: False, 226
    Specific job descriptions can reduce the number of grievances filed by workers.

73. The ADA requires that organizations identify the essential functions of jobs.

    ANSWER: True, 227

74. Having identified the essential job functions through a job analysis, an employer escapes the necessity of making any accommodation for individuals with disabilities.

    ANSWER: False, 227
    An employer must be prepared to make reasonable accommodations for disabled persons.

75. Job analysis can help determine whether someone should be classified as exempt or nonexempt under wage/hour laws.

    ANSWER: True, 228

76. One job analysis method requires that employees "observe" their own performance by keeping a diary of their job duties, noting how frequently they are performed and the time for each duty.

    ANSWER: True, 230

77. The position analysis questionnaire (PAQ) focuses on "worker-oriented" elements that describe behaviors necessary to do the job, rather than on "job-oriented" elements that describe the technical aspects of the work.

    ANSWER: True, 232

78. The job specification should list the knowledge, skills, and abilities of the ideal candidate.

    ANSWER: False, 241
    Job specifications should reflect what is necessary for satisfactory job performance, not what the ideal candidate should have.

79. The current incumbent's job qualifications are usually a good indication of what is necessary to perform the job satisfactorily.

    ANSWER: False, 241
    Actually, the current incumbent's job qualifications often exceed the minimum KSAs required.

80. The written job specifications are the foundation for evaluating individuals with disabilities for employment.

    ANSWER: True, 242

Chapter 7

Essay

81. Discuss the statement: "Job analysis is the most basic function of human resource management."

    ANSWER: 214, 224-227
    Job analysis involves collecting information on the characteristics of a job that differentiates it from other jobs. It is necessary for all HR activities, and is necessary for defense in a EEO suit.

82. What impact has the Americans with Disabilities Act had on the job analysis process?

    ANSWER: 226-228
    Employers need job analysis to identify the essential functions of each job, including the physical demands and environmental condition of jobs. Employers must make reasonable accommodation for individuals with disabilities.

83. Describe four common job analysis methods. What are the advantages and limitations of each method?

    ANSWER: 230-234
    Common methods are observations, interviews, questionnaires, and specialized methods of analysis. Combinations of these methods are frequently used.

84. Describe the stages in the job analysis process.

    ANSWER: 234-237
    The stages are planning, preparation and communication, conducting the job analysis, developing job descriptions and job specifications, and maintaining and updating job descriptions and job specifications.

85. Illustrate how job descriptions and job specifications are essential in both avoiding and defending an EEO suit.

    ANSWER: 226-228
    The 1978 Uniform Selection Guidelines makes it essential that selection criteria be tied to specific job-related factors, and the Americans with Disabilities Act requires that selection be based on essential job functions. Detailed, well-written job descriptions and job specifications should clearly identify these factors.

Chapter 8

Recruiting in Labor Markets

Multiple Choice

1. "The process of matching appropriate people with appropriate jobs," is a definition of
    A. HR planning.
    B. staffing.
    C. recruiting.
    D. selection.

    ANSWER: B, 250

2. The process of generating a pool of qualified applicants for organizational jobs is called
    A. requisitioning.
    B. acquiring.
    C. pre-selecting.
    D. recruiting

    ANSWER: D, 250

3. If the number of available candidates equals the number of people to be hired
    A. there is no real selection.
    B. there can be perfect matching of jobs with people.
    C. the staffing process has been successful.
    D. the labor market is "tight."

    ANSWER: A, 250

4. _____ are the external sources from which organizations attract employees.
    A. Labor pools
    B. Recruitment sites
    C. Labor markets
    D. Applicant pools

    ANSWER: C, 250

Chapter 8

5. A(n) _____ labor market exists when the demand for employees exceeds the supply of people with the appropriate qualifications.
   A. loose
   B. tight
   C. ideal
   D. buyers'

   ANSWER: B, 250

6. Which of the following were **NOT** listed as ways to identify labor markets?
   A. geographic area
   B. type of skill
   C. blue collar
   D. income level

   ANSWER: D, 250

7. The _____ includes all individuals available for selection, if all possible recruitment strategies are used.
   A. labor force population.
   B. manpower pool.
   C. applicant pool.
   D. applicant population.

   ANSWER: A, 251

8. The group available for selection using a particular recruiting approach is called the
   A. manpower pool.
   B. labor force population.
   C. applicant population.
   D. applicant pool.

   ANSWER: C, 251

9. Recruiting decisions that affect the nature of the applicant population include all of the following except
   A. recruiting method.
   B. affirmative action plan.
   C. recruiting message.
   D. applicant qualifications required.

   ANSWER: B, 251

10. The _____ pool consists of all persons who are actually evaluated for selection.
    A. selection
    B. recruitment
    C. manpower
    D. applicant

    ANSWER: D, 251

11. The advantages of internal recruiting include
    A. better assessment of abilities.
    B. no need for an expensive management development program.
    C. cheaper and faster than training professionals.
    D. inbreeding.

    ANSWER: A, 253

12. Which of the following is given as an advantage of external recruiting?
    A. better assessment of abilities
    B. shorter adjustment or orientation time
    C. may bring industry insights
    D. having to hire only at entry level

    ANSWER: C, 253

13. The disadvantages of external recruiting include
    A. need for a stronger management-development program.
    B. may cause morale problems for internal candidates not selected.
    C. inbreeding.
    D. no group of political supporters in organization already.

    ANSWER: B, 253

14. Which of the following is given as a disadvantage of recruiting internally?
    A. may not select someone who will "fit" the job
    B. difficult to assess abilities
    C. can only hire at entry level
    D. need for strong management-development program

    ANSWER: D, 253

15. Which of the following was not listed as a disadvantage of internal recruiting?
    A. longer adjustment or orientation time
    B. inbreeding
    C. possible morale problems of those not promoted
    D. political infighting for promotions

    ANSWER: A, 253

16. In which of the following organizations would promotion from within be more suitable?
    A. a business with government contracts
    B. a high-tech business
    C. an organization in an environment that changes slowly
    D. an organization that makes use of independent contractors

    ANSWER: C, 253

Chapter 8

17. _____ makes use of recruiting sources and workers who are not traditional employees.
    A. Flextime
    B. Flexible staffing
    C. Part-time hiring
    D. External recruiting

    ANSWER: B, 254

18. Which of the following was not given as an example of flexible staffing?
    A. temporary workers
    B. independent contractors
    C. employee leasing
    D. internships

    ANSWER: D, 254

19. The use of temporary workers may make sense in which of the following situations?
    A. The work is subject to seasonal or other fluctuations.
    B. The organization wants to reduce its benefits costs.
    C. The industry has a history of high turnover.
    D. Government regulations make it too expensive to hire permanent employees.

    ANSWER: A, 254

20. Workers who perform specific services on a contract basis are called
    A. flexible staff.
    B. internal contractors.
    C. independent contractors.
    D. temporary workers.

    ANSWER: C, 254

21. A(n) _____ takes over the staff of a small business and writes the paychecks, pays the taxes, prepares and implements HR policies, and keeps all the required records for a fee.
    A. employment agency
    B. employee leasing company
    C. payroll executive
    D. trade hire firm

    ANSWER: B, 255

22. Which of the following is a problem associated with employee leasing?
    A. The manager abdicates supervisory authority to the leasing firm.
    B. The client firm is not able to treat the costs associated with the leased employees as a business expense for tax purposes.
    C. Typically the leasing contracts are long term, resulting in reduced flexibility for the client firms.
    D. The leased workers may sue the client firm for work-related injuries if there has been negligence by the client.

    ANSWER: D, 255

23. One of the advantages for employees of leasing companies is
   A. they may receive better benefits than they would otherwise get in many small businesses.
   B. they are not required to pay social security taxes.
   C. they can be regarded as self employed for IRS purposes.
   D. they usually receive many interesting assignments in a variety of start-up businesses.

   ANSWER: A, 255

24. In larger organizations, recruiting often begins when a manager
   A. asks that an advertisement be placed in appropriate media.
   B. reviews the files for candidates interviewed in the past.
   C. submits a requisition to the HR unit.
   D. makes contact with the appropriate employment agency.

   ANSWER: C, 255

25. What documents should be reviewed in the early stages of the recruiting process?
   A. applicable government regulations
   B. job description and job specifications
   C. EEO and affirmative action plans
   D. salary and benefits budgets

   ANSWER: B, 255

26. The HR representative and the manager must review _____ so that both have clear and up-to-date information of the job duties and specific qualifications desired of an applicant.
   A. the human resource plan
   B. both the organizational and the HR strategies
   C. the performance appraisal documents
   D. the job description and job specifications

   ANSWER: D, 255

27. When there is underrepresentation of protected-class members in relation to the labor markets utilized by the employer,
   A. disparate impact occurs.
   B. an affirmative action plan (AAP) is required.
   C. there is *prima facie* evidence of unlawful employment discrimination.
   D. all recruiting must be monitored by the EEOC.

   ANSWER: A, 256

28. When an organization has an underrepresentation of a particular protected class, _____ has been considered a violation of Title VII of the Civil Rights Act.
   A. campus recruiting
   B. employment advertising
   C. word-of-mouth referral
   D. hiring only at the entry level

   ANSWER: C, 257

29. One key to successfully recruiting employees with disabilities is
    A. redesigning all job to accommodate individuals with disabilities.
    B. well-designed jobs.
    C. establishing a separate pay scale that recognizes the individual's capabilities.
    D. to review the total compensation package (pay and benefits) to ensure that individuals with disabilities are not discriminated against.

    ANSWER: B, 258

30. Which of the following approaches is credited with successfully diversifying workforces?
    A. the development of an affirmative action plans
    B. establishing quotas for hiring from each protected-class group
    C. the appointment of an HR professional specifically to oversee the hiring of a diverse workforce
    D. using recruiting sources that target the appropriate types of applicants

    ANSWER: D, 258

31. Recruiting efforts may be viewed as either continuous or
    A. intensive.
    B. sporadic.
    C. targeted.
    D. continual.

    ANSWER: A, 259

32. _____ efforts to recruit have the advantage of keeping the employer in the recruiting market.
    A. Targeted
    B. Intensive
    C. Continuous
    D. Sporadic

    ANSWER: C, 259

33. _____ recruiting may take the form of a vigorous recruiting campaign aimed at hiring a given number of employees, usually within a short time period.
    A. Targeted
    B. Intensive
    C. Continuous
    D. Sporadic

    ANSWER: B, 259

34. Which of the following is a typical responsibility of the HR unit in the recruiting process?
    A. determine KSAs needed from applicants
    B. anticipate needs for employees to fill vacancies
    C. provide information about job requirements
    D. forecasts recruiting needs

    ANSWER: D, 259

35. In larger organizations, managers are usually responsible for _____ in the recruiting process.
    A. determining the KSAs needed from applicants
    B. forecasting recruiting needs
    C. planning and conducting recruiting efforts
    D. auditing and evaluating recruiting activities

    ANSWER: A, 259

36. Which of the following statements regarding job posting and bidding is <u>false</u>?
    A. It gives each employee an opportunity to move to a better job within the organization.
    B. Job generally are posted before any external recruiting is done.
    C. It makes it difficult for supervisors to develop employees long term.
    D. In a unionized organization, job posting and bidding often is spelled out in the labor agreement.

    ANSWER: C, 260

37. Which of the following was identified as a drawback of promoting from within?
    A. There may not be any current employees qualified for promotion.
    B. Performance on one job may not be a good predictor of performance on another.
    C. Additional training and development expenses must be incurred.
    D. Supervisors often are reluctant to recommend their better employees for promotion.

    ANSWER: B, 261

38. What is true about recruiting friends and family of current employees?
    A. Workers recruited through current employee had a high rate of turnover.
    B. Current employee referrals can reduce the risk of EEO scrutiny.
    C. Current employees are reluctant to refer their family and friends.
    D. Many qualified people can be reached at low cost.

    ANSWER: D, 261

39. What is the principle advantage for hiring former employees?
    A. their performance is known
    B. most managers are eager to take back a former employee
    C. they usually cost less in terms of salary and benefits
    D. their friends usually like to have an old colleague back

    ANSWER: A, 262

40. The advantage of computerized internal talent banks is that
    A. they permit employers to comply more easily with the numerous EEO rules.
    B. the EEOC guidelines recommend non-biased, automated systems.
    C. they allow recruiters to identify potential candidates more quickly than manually sorting numerous stacks and files of resumes.
    D. job candidates have more confidence in systems that minimize the possibility of personal bias.

    ANSWER: C, 262

41. Another name for computerized internal talent banks is
    A. internal agency lists.
    B. applicant tracking systems.
    C. personnel assessment records.
    D. recruiting asset sheets.

    ANSWER: B, 262

42. In a cooperative program,
    A. the HR unit and operating managers conduct joint interviews.
    B. employees cooperate with the HR unit in recruiting friends for job openings.
    C. the college placement center assists in identifying suitable job candidates.
    D. students work part time and receive some school credits.

    ANSWER: D, 263

43. Which of the following is not a major determinant when deciding at which college an employer will conduct interviews?
    A. faculty attitudes towards the employer's industry
    B. college reputation
    C. organizational budget constraints
    D. cost of available talent

    ANSWER: A, 263

44. In addition to a high GPA, which of the following attributes do recruiters seem to value most highly in college graduates?
    A. extracurricular activities
    B. family connections and networking possibilities
    C. poise and appearance
    D. part-time work experience

    ANSWER: C, 264

45. Which of the following statements is true regarding college recruiting?
    A. College recruiting is one of the least expensive recruitment methods.
    B. A candidate's impression of the recruiter affects hire rates.
    C. Recruiters overestimate the importance of extrinsic rewards such as pay and benefits.
    D. The cost of training decreases due to educational preparedness.

    ANSWER: B, 264

46. External recruiting sources include
    A. job posting and bidding
    B. friends of current employees.
    C. former employees.
    D. labor unions.

    ANSWER: D, 265

47. In some industries, such as _____, unions have traditionally supplied workers to employers.
    A. construction
    B. publishing
    C. law enforcement
    D. entertainment

    ANSWER: A, 265

48. Unions can work to an employer's advantage through
    A. less competition for skilled workers.
    B. establishing wage scales for job candidates.
    C. cooperative staffing programs.
    D. closed shop agreements.

    ANSWER: C, 265

49. What is the primary advantage of recruiting from trade and competitive sources?
    A. The firm can obtain competitive secrets.
    B. Recruits from these sources will spend less time in training because they already know the industry.
    C. Individuals hired from competitors have enhanced motivation because they have decided to take another position in the same industry.
    D. Salaries offered will be more competitive.

    ANSWER: B, 267

50. Executive search firms are split into two groups. _____ firms charge a fee only after a candidate has been hired by a client company.
    A. Contract
    B. Commission
    C. Retainer
    D. Contingency

    ANSWER: D, 268

51. One advantage of having an executive search firm on retainer is that
    A. search firms are ethically bound not to approach employees of client companies in their search efforts for another client.
    B. it establishes an on-going professional relationship which enables positions to be filled more efficiently.
    C. search firms give their clients first refusal of an outstanding candidate.
    D. in the long run, this is less expensive.

    ANSWER: A, 268

52. Which of the following is true about Internet recruiting?
    A. more expensive than traditional media
    B. used primarily for high-tech jobs
    C. improves the chances of contacting people not actively seeking work
    D. regarded as a replacement for newspaper advertising

    ANSWER: C, 268

53. Of the following recruiting resources, applicants are most likely to consider
    A. employment agencies.
    B. newspapers.
    C. word of mouth.
    D. friends and relatives.

    ANSWER: B, 269

54. Which of the following statements is true about using the Internet for recruiting?
    A. It is used by less than 10 percent of organizations.
    B. Internet recruiting has not lived up to expectations.
    C. Most managers prefer traditional, face-to-face recruiting methods.
    D. About 37% of companies now use the Internet for recruiting and the rate is increasing.

    ANSWER: D, 268

55. Evaluating the success of recruiting efforts is important because
    A. that is the only way to find out whether the efforts are cost effective in terms of time and money spent.
    B. it provides input to the HR unit's compensation system.
    C. that is one way to measure the firm's reputation on the college campuses.
    D. it indicates how the employer measures-up against competitors.

    ANSWER: A, 268

56. The _____ equals the number hired divided by the number of applicants.
    A. yield ratio
    B. success rate
    C. selection rate
    D. hit rate

    ANSWER: C, 269

57. _____ measures of recruiting effectiveness includes information on job performance, absenteeism, cost of training, and turnover by recruiting source.
    A. Cost/benefit
    B. Long-run
    C. The yield-ratio
    D. Time elapsed

    ANSWER: B, 270

58. A _____ is a comparison of the number of applicants at one stage of the recruiting process to the number at the next stage.
    A. selection rate
    B. success ratio
    C. hit rate
    D. yield ratio

    ANSWER: D, 270

59. Which of the following would be classified as an indirect cost of recruiting?
    A. involvement of operating managers
    B. recruiters' salaries
    C. agency fees
    D. length of time from contact to hire

    ANSWER: A, 271

60. In evaluating recruiting costs and benefits, direct costs include
    A. length of time from contact to hire.
    B. costs of leaving the position unfilled while waiting for a replacement.
    C. recruiters' salaries.
    D. involvement of operating managers.

    ANSWER: C, 271

True and False

61. Recruitment involves selecting among candidates for a position.

    ANSWER: False, 250
    Recruitment is the process of generating a pool of qualified applicants from which the employees are selected.

62. The term "labor market" refers to all individuals looking for a position in the same geographic area.

    ANSWER: False, 250
    Labor markets are the external sources from which organizations attract employees.

63. The applicant population includes all individuals who are available for selection in all possible recruitment strategies are used.

    ANSWER: False, 251
    This is the definition of "labor force population." The application population is a subset of the labor force population.

64. If a promotion-from-within policy is followed exclusively, it has the disadvantage of perpetuating old ways of operating.

    ANSWER: True, 252

65. Internal recruiting is faster and less expensive than having to train professionals recruited externally.

    ANSWER: False, 253
    Internal recruiting has the disadvantage of requiring organizations to operate expensive management-development programs.

112 Chapter 8

66. For organizations operating in environments that change slowly, promotions from within may be more suitable that emphasizing external recruiting.

    ANSWER: True, 253

67. Using flexible staffing arrangements enables employers to generate a high degree of employee loyalty by guaranteeing long-term job tenure.

    ANSWER: False, 254
    Just the opposite may result. Flexible staffing allows an employer to avoid some of the costs of full-time benefits.

68. Independent contractors include those who perform specific services on a contract basis.

    ANSWER: True, 254

69. Organizations using leased employees can encounter legal problems, especially regarding work-related injuries.

    ANSWER: True, 255

70. Disparate impact occurs when there is underrepresentation of protected-class members in relation to the labor markets utilized by the employer.

    ANSWER: True, 256

71. When an organization has an underrepresentation of a particular protected class, word-of-mouth referral is recommended as a means of recruiting previously underrepresented protected-class employees.

    ANSWER: False, 257
    Word-of-mouth recruiting has been considered a violation of Title VII of the Civil Rights Act if it perpetuates underrepresentation.

72. If outside agencies are used, equal employment and affirmative action concerns of the actual employers still must be met.

    ANSWER: True, 257

73. Employers are required to modify the workplace and supply needed equipment to accommodate the special needs of disabled persons.

    ANSWER: False, 258
    Employers are only required to make reasonable accommodation for persons with disabilities. Not every disability lends itself to every job, even with accommodation.

74. To successful diversify their workforce, employers are encouraged to advertise in minority-oriented publications and participate in job fairs sponsored by certain racial/ethnic organizations.

    ANSWER: True, 259

75. In a unionized organization, job posting and bidding can be quite formal.

    ANSWER: True, 260

76. Promotions from within are preferred since an employees performance on his/her current job is a good predictor of performance on the new job.

    ANSWER: False, 261
    Performance on one job may not be a good predictor of performance on another, because different skills may be required.

77. Utilizing current employee referrals is usually one of the least effective methods of recruiting.

    ANSWER: False, 261
    Actually it is one of the most effective methods of recruiting because many qualified people can be reached at a low cost.

78. A major limitation listed by employers who have used internal computer databases has been that they increase recruiting costs associated with advertising expenditures, search-firm fees, and internal processing and record retention expenses.

    ANSWER: False, 262
    Actually employers have found that computerized databases have reduced there recruiting costs.

79. An organization with a strong union may have less flexibility than a nonunion company in deciding where a newly hired person will be placed.

    ANSWER: True, 265

80. Executive search firms are ethically bound not to approach employees of client companies in their search efforts for another client.

    ANSWER: True, 268

Essay

81. Discuss the statement: *"The decisions that are made about recruiting help dictate not only the kinds and numbers of applicants, but also how difficult or successful recruiting efforts may be."*

    ANSWER: 252-253
    Planning decisions include: how many employees needed, when needed, KSAs needed, and special qualifications. Recruiting strategy decisions include: where and whom to recruit, and what the job requirements will be. Other decisions involve advertising choices and recruiting activities.

Chapter 8

82. What are the advantages and limitations of focusing on current employees to fill open positions?

    ANSWER: 252-253
    Seen as a reward for good work, serving as a motivator, a better assessment of abilities, causes a succession of promotions, and at times may be less costly. But perpetuate old ways of operating, EEO concerns, causes possible morale problems of those not promoted, may lead to political infighting, and there is a need for management-development programs.

83. Describe some of the flexible staffing alternatives available to employers. Why are some organizations examining these alternatives?

    ANSWER: 253-255
    Alternatives include temporary employees, independent contractors, and professional employer organizations or leased employees. These alternatives are attractive because of the high costs of government mandates regulations, and to avoid some of the costs of full-time benefits.

84. What are some of the legal restrictions on how organizations can recruit employees? How can an employer effectively use the recruiting process to achieve a more diverse workforce?

    ANSWER: 256-259
    EEOC guidelines forbid references to age or gender in advertising. If there is underrepresentation of protected-class members affirmative action may be required. A diverse workforce may be attracted by directing advertising to minority publications, and by working with associations representing older or disabled individuals.

85. Describe some of the external sources of job candidates.

    ANSWER: 262-268
    Schools, colleges, and universities, including cooperative programs, - useful for entry-level jobs. Employment agencies and labor unions. Media sources - newspapers, magazines, television, radio, and billboards, including minority publications. Professional and trade associations. Competitors' employees.

Chapter 9

Selecting and Placing Human Resources

Multiple Choice

1. The process of choosing individuals who have relevant qualifications to fill jobs in organizations is called
    A. recruitment.
    B. selection.
    C. staffing.
    D. placement.

    ANSWER: B, 278

2. Fit between the applicant and the organization affects both the employer's willingness to make a job offer and
    A. the compensation package offered to the potential employee.
    B. a possible impact on the organization's culture.
    C. the willingness of the current employees to welcome the new employee.
    D. an applicant's willingness to accept a job.

    ANSWER: D, 278

3. _____ involves fitting a person to the right job.
    A. Placement
    B. Selection
    C. Staffing
    D. Orientation

    ANSWER: A, 278

4. More than anything else, selection of human resources should be seen as a(n)
    A. public relations activity.
    B. HR unit responsibility.
    C. matching process.
    D. operating management responsibility.

    ANSWER: C, 278

Chapter 9

5. The most frequent reason why companies reject applicants is
   A. lack of working experience.
   B. lack of work skills and motivation.
   C. drug and alcohol abuse.
   D. deficiency in basic academic skills.

   ANSWER: B, 278

6. If it is done properly, _____ can provide the basis for identifying appropriate KSAs.
   A. selection
   B. recruitment
   C. test validation
   D. job analysis

   ANSWER: D, 279

7. If an employer hires at the entry level and promotes from within for most jobs, KSAs might be less important than
   A. general ability to learn and conscientiousness.
   B. integrity.
   C. qualifications and motivation.
   D. IQ.

   ANSWER: A, 279

8. A(n) _____ is a characteristic that a person requires to do the job successfully.
   A. validator
   B. essential element
   C. selection criterion
   D. predictor

   ANSWER: C, 280

9. Measurable indicators of the selection criteria are called
   A. performance standards.
   B. predictors.
   C. essential elements.
   D. validators.

   ANSWER: B, 280

10. Validity refers to
    A. the strength of the correlation between a test score and a predictor.
    B. the reliability with which the predictor actually tests the desired construct.
    C. whether the applicant will achieve approximately the same score in a test-retest situation.
    D. the correlation between a predictor and job performance.

    ANSWER: D, 281

Selecting and Placing Human Resources

11. _____ is(are) the extent to which a predictor repeatedly produces the same result, over time.
    A. Reliability
    B. Test validity
    C. Accuracy
    D. Multiple hurdles

    ANSWER: A, 281

12. In the _____ approach, a minimum cutoff is set on each predictor, and each minimum level must be passed.
    A. single predictor
    B. test validity
    C. multiple hurdles
    D. combined

    ANSWER: C, 281

13. In order to protect itself from legal problems related to selection, it is suggested that an employer has a written policy which defines exactly
    A. the employer's selection function.
    B. who is an applicant.
    C. the role of the interview.
    D. what is a job opening.

    ANSWER: B, 283

14. It is recommended that an organization retains all applications for
    A. one year.
    B. ten years.
    C. five years.
    D. three years.

    ANSWER: D, 283

15. Until the impact of EEO regulations became widespread, selection was often carried out _____ in many organizations.
    A. in a rather unplanned manner
    B. with a concentration on the "bottom line"
    C. by employment specialists
    D. by senior management

    ANSWER: A, 283

16. In smaller organizations, managers insist on selecting their own people because
    A. these jobs are usually filled through recommendations from friends.
    B. it tends to be cheaper.
    C. managers believe no one can choose their employees better than they can.
    D. there is usually no employment office.

    ANSWER: C, 283

118 Chapter 9

17. In the typical selection interface, the HR unit will be responsible for
    A. making the final selection decision.
    B. obtaining background and reference information.
    C. interviewing final candidates.
    D. requisitioning employees with specific qualifications.

    ANSWER: B, 284

18. Team staffing presents an interesting selection variation. Which of the following approaches was recommended for hiring new team members?
    A. Team members should vote for their top choice.
    B. The HR department should select and assign all team member.
    C. The team's supervisor should select the new team member.
    D. Hiring decision should be made by consensus.

    ANSWER: D, 284

19. What is the purpose of a job preview/interest screen?
    A. to see if the applicant is likely to match any jobs available in the organization
    B. to obtain information for an EEO report
    C. to provide a realistic job preview
    D. to encourage potential job candidates to complete application forms

    ANSWER: A, 286

20. The purpose of a _____ is to inform job candidates of the organizational realities of a job, so that they can more accurately evaluate their own job expectations.
    A. practical overview initiation
    B. accurate structured interview
    C. realistic job preview
    D. valid orientation assessment

    ANSWER: C, 287

21. Employers should be careful not to misrepresent or oversell their jobs during the selection process by conducting
    A. organizational job previews.
    B. realistic job previews.
    C. internship overviews.
    D. honest career assessment previews.

    ANSWER: B, 288

22. A review of research on realistic job previews found that
    A. they have little if any impact on employee turnover.
    B. they significantly reduce employee dissatisfaction and ultimately employee turnover.
    C. they reduce the size of the applicant pool.
    D. they do tend to result in applicants having lower job expectations.

    ANSWER: D, 288

Selecting and Placing Human Resources 119

23. Which of the following is a basic purpose of the application form?
    A. It is a basic employee record for applicants who are hired.
    B. It is an initial record for the organization's EEO/affirmative action plans.
    C. It provides a defense in an employment discrimination case.
    D. It is a record of the employer's desire to hire someone to fill an open position.

    ANSWER: A, 288

24. What action can an employer take if, after hiring an applicant, it is discovered that the applicant lied on the applicant form?
    A. Since the statute of limitations for wrongful hiring is six months, the employee can be fired only of the lie is discovered within six months of the hiring decision.
    B. The employee can be fired once it is discovered that he/she had lied on the applicant form.
    C. The employee can be fired if it can be shown that the employer would not have hired the applicant if it had known that the applicant had lied.
    D. The employee can be fired only if there are performance-related reasons.

    ANSWER: C, 288

25. Which of the following would not be considered an illegal question on an application form?
    A. number and ages of dependents
    B. felony convictions
    C. date of high school graduation
    D. who to contact in case of emergency

    ANSWER: B. 288

26. What should employers do in order to comply with the EEOC requirements of reporting the race and sex of applicants?
    A. Collect the data after the hiring decision has been made.
    B. Gather the information on the application blank.
    C. Make a visual assessment during the initial selection process and record the race and sex of applicants on a separate document.
    D. Ask the applicant to provide EEOC reporting data on a separate form.

    ANSWER: D, 290

27. In _____, numeric values are placed on possible responses to application-form items, and the responses of applicants are scored, totaled, and compared.
    A. weighted application forms
    B. scored application forms
    C. in-depth interviews
    D. preparatory interviews

    ANSWER: A, 290

Chapter 9

28. If an organization uses resumes or vitae in place of application forms,
    A. the employer will obtain more complete information about the candidate.
    B. it might be able to use certain "illegal information" which was included by the applicant.
    C. the resume must still be treated as an application form for EEO purposes.
    D. the employer should assume that the information included is less accurate.

    ANSWER: C, 290

29. The Immigration Reform and Control Act of 1986, requires employers to
    A. contact the Immigration Service if an illegal alien applies for a job.
    B. determine whether the job applicant is a U.S. citizen, registered alien, or illegal alien, within 72 hours of hiring.
    C. obtain proof of citizenship before making a hiring decision.
    D. send copies of all documents submitted by employees to the Social Security Administration.

    ANSWER: B, 292

30. What is a "test" as defined by the Uniform Selection Guidelines issued by the EEOC?
    A. all paper and pencil assessments that evaluate job skills
    B. only job assessments that have been validated
    C. all preemployment inquiries
    D. any employment requirement

    ANSWER: D, 292

31. Learned skills are assessed by
    A. ability tests.
    B. knowledge tests.
    C. aptitude tests.
    D. behavioral tests.

    ANSWER: A, 292

32. Tests that measure general ability to learn or acquire a skill are called
    A. ability tests.
    B. knowledge tests.
    C. aptitude tests.
    D. behavioral tests.

    ANSWER: C, 292

33. _____ tests require an applicant to perform a simulated job task.
    A. Vestibule
    B. Work sample
    C. Behavioral
    D. Assessment center

    ANSWER: B, 292

34. An "in basket" test is an example of a(n) _____ test.
    A. assessment center
    B. aptitude
    C. mental ability
    D. work sample

    ANSWER: D, 293

35. _____ tests measure reasoning capabilities.
    A. Mental ability
    B. Aptitude
    C. Assessment center
    D. Knowledge

    ANSWER: A, 293

36. A(n) _____ is a selection and development device composed of a series of evaluative exercises and tests.
    A. evaluative career assessment
    B. multi-faceted selection process
    C. assessment center
    D. "in basket"

    ANSWER: C, 293

37. Which of the following statements is true with regard to personality tests?
    A. The courts have banned the use of personality tests for privacy reasons.
    B. Predictive validities have tended to be lower for personality tests used as predictors of performance on the job.
    C. Personality tests cannot predict the interpersonal aspects of job success.
    D. Personality tests are rarely used today as a selection device.

    ANSWER: B, 294

38. The personality trait of _____ is the extent to which a person is achievement-oriented, careful, hardworking, organized, and responsible.
    A. extroversion
    B. openness/experience
    C. stability
    D. conscientiousness

    ANSWER: D, 294

39. The personality trait of _____ predicts success in jobs requiring social interaction, such as many sales jobs.
    A. extroversion
    B. openness/experience
    C. emotional stability
    D. conscientiousness

    ANSWER: A, 294

40. Psychological testing requires that _____ when used in selection.
    A. a trained psychologists oversees the process
    B. informed consent be obtained from the candidate
    C. a solid link be made with job relatedness
    D. full disclosure be made

    ANSWER: C, 294

41. The Employee Polygraph Protection Act
    A. prohibits government agencies from using polygraph tests.
    B. bars polygraph use for preemployment screening purposes by most employers.
    C. prohibits employers from using polygraph tests to investigate theft.
    D. permits the use of polygraphs, but only when administered by a trained expert.

    ANSWER: B, 294

42. The purpose of a(n) _____ is to identify information on a candidate and clarify information from other sources.
    A. polygraph test
    B. application form
    C. reference check
    D. selection interview

    ANSWER: D, 296

43. _____ is the ability to pick the same qualities again and again in applicants.
    A. Reliability
    B. Validity
    C. Rater experience
    D. Predictor correlation

    ANSWER: A, 296

44. In a structured interview,
    A. all candidates meet in the same room with the same interviewer.
    B. computers are used to devise a set of questions.
    C. a set of standardized questions are asked of all job applicants.
    D. each candidate appears before a panel of interviewers.

    ANSWER: C, 296

45. Research on interviews has consistently found that one approach is more reliable and valid than the others. What is this approach?
    A. situational interview
    B. structured interview
    C. stress interview
    D. panel interview

    ANSWER: B, 297

46. In what type of interview might an applicant be asked the following: "How did you handle a situation where there were no rules or guidelines on employee discipline?"
    A. stress
    B. negative
    C. aggressive reaction
    D. behavioral description

    ANSWER: D, 298

47. The _____ uses general questions from which other questions are developed.
    A. nondirective interview
    B. stress interview
    C. flow interview
    D. interface

    ANSWER: A, 299

48. The interviewer assumes an extremely aggressive and insulting posture in a
    A. situational interview.
    B. negative interview.
    C. stress interview.
    D. aggressive reaction interview.

    ANSWER: C, 299

49. Several interviewers interview a candidate at the same time in a
    A. situational interview.
    B. panel interview.
    C. stress interview.
    D. structured interview.

    ANSWER: B, 299

50. The _____ problems occur when interviewers form an early impression and spend the balance of an interview looking for evidence to support it.
    A. bias
    B. halo effect
    C. devil's horns
    D. snap judgment

    ANSWER: D, 301

51. An interview problem which occurs when an interviewer allows a prominent characteristic to overshadow other evidence is called
    A. the halo effect.
    B. bias perception.
    C. negative emphasis.
    D. the dominant trait error.

    ANSWER: A, 302

124   Chapter 9

52. _____ occurs when the candidate gives the interviewer responses that are socially acceptable rather than factual.
    A. Padding
    B. Prevarication
    C. Cultural noise
    D. Judgmental responding

    ANSWER: C, 302

53. Applicants frequently misrepresent their qualifications and backgrounds. Surveys have shown that the most common false information relates to
    A. academic credentials.
    B. length of prior employment.
    C. credit history.
    D. marital and family situation.

    ANSWER: B, 303

54. Which of the following is of the least value to a potential employer?
    A. academic transcripts
    B. law enforcement reports
    C. credit history
    D personal references

    ANSWER: D, 304

55. Which of the following is a basic provision of the Federal Privacy Act of 1974?
    A. A government entity must have a signed, written release from a person before it can give information about that person to someone else.
    B. All employers, both public and private sector, must have a signed, written release from a person before it can give information about that person to someone else.
    C. Government agencies must give permission before employers may seek certain critical information.
    D. An organization must have written permission from an applicant before it can seek information about that applicant from other sources.

    ANSWER: A, 305

56. Under the Fair Credit Reporting Act,
    A. the use of credit reports for employment purposes is forbidden.
    B. a government entity must have a signed, written release from a person before it can give information about that person to someone else.
    C. an employer must disclose that a credit check is being made and obtain written consent from the person being checked.
    D. credit agencies are liable for damages if false credit information is disclosed.

    ANSWER: C, 305

Selecting and Placing Human Resources

57. An employers may be sued for _____ if a worker commits violent acts on the job.
    A. insufficient validity
    B. negligent hiring
    C. criminal acquiescence
    D. criminal liability

    ANSWER: B, 305

58. Which of the following questions would be proper in regard to the Americans with Disabilities Act?
    A. Do you have any physical or other limitations?
    B. Have you ever filed for workers' compensation?
    C. How many times were you absent due to illness in the past two years?
    D. How would you perform the essential tasks of the job for which you applied?

    ANSWER: D, 307

59. Which of the following statements is true with regards to medical examinations?
    A. A company may require applicants to take a drug test.
    B. All preemployment medical exams are prohibited.
    C. Medical exams can be given only after a candidate reaches the short list.
    D. Companies may only ask job applicants questions about their current medical condition, not past problems.

    ANSWER: A, 306

60. Which of the following is true about genetic testing?
    A. Genetic testing minimizes a company's liability for workplace illnesses.
    B. The public approves of the use of genetic testing for risk screening.
    C. Genetic testing permits employers to exclude individuals from certain jobs if they have genetic conditions that increase their health risks.
    D. Federal law prohibits the use of genetic tests to screen applicants.

    ANSWER: C, 308

True and False

61. With good selection tests, it is generally possible to tell exactly what the applicant can and wants to do.

    ANSWER: False, 278
    The task of selection is difficult because it is not always possible to tell exactly what the applicant can and wants to do.

62. The primary reason why organizations reject job applicants is because they lack work experience.

    ANSWER: False, 278
    The primary reason is a deficiency in work skills and motivation.

63. Job analysis can provide the basis for identifying appropriate KSAs if it is done properly.

    ANSWER: True, 279

64. In selection, a predictor is a characteristic that a person requires to do the job successfully.

    ANSWER: False, 280
    A selection criterion is a characteristic that a person requires to do the job successfully. A predictor is a measurable indicator of that criterion.

65. An arithmetic test given to potential bank tellers would be seen as a valid predictor if it helped improve the quality of the work done by the tellers hired.

    ANSWER: True, 281

66. Reliability is the ability of a test to produce the same results again and again in applicants.

    ANSWER: True, 281

67. It is advisable to use as many predictors as possible, within financial constraints, in order to select the most qualified candidate.

    ANSWER: False, 282
    Having too many predictors, especially those with lower accuracy rates, may actually harm the quality of selection decisions.

68. Employment interviewers have been greatly assisted by a list of taboo questions which has been generated by the EEOC.

    ANSWER: False, 283
    There is no standard list of taboo questions.

69. Unless an organization has a written policy defining conditions that make a person an applicant, any persons who call or send unsolicited resumes might later claim they were not hired because of illegal discrimination.

    ANSWER: True, 283

70. To be successful, teams should be involved in selecting their teammates.

    ANSWER: True, 284

71. The Uniform Guidelines of the EEOC define application forms as employment tests.

    ANSWER: True, 288

72. In order to fulfill EEOC requirements for reporting on the race and sex of applicants, it is recommended that optional questions about race and sex be included in application forms.

    ANSWER: False, 290
    The application form cannot contain these questions. It is recommended that applicants provide EEOC reporting data on a separate form which is filed separately and not used in any other HR activity.

73. The Immigration Reform and Control Act of 1986 states that employers can assume that documents submitted by new employees, such as U.S. passports, birth certificates, original Social Security cards, and driver's licenses are genuine.

    ANSWER: False, 292
    Employers are responsible to make sure that the documents "reasonably appear on their face to be genuine."

74. Aptitude tests measure reasoning capabilities.

    ANSWER: False, 292
    Aptitude tests measure general ability to learn or acquire a skill.

75. In a behavioral description interview, applicants are required to give specific examples of how they have handled a problem in the past.

    ANSWER: True, 296

76. Just because someone is personable and likes to talk, there is no guarantee that the person will be a good interviewer.

    ANSWER: True, 299

77. One negative fact may influence the selection decision more than any amount of positive information.

    ANSWER: True, 302

78. Personal references are a useful indication of an applicant's character.

    ANSWER: False, 304
    No applicant would request a recommendation from someone who would give a negative one. Greater reliance should be placed on work-related references.

79. Federal law provides immunity for employers who, in good faith, provide information on a current or past employee to another employer.

    ANSWER: False, 305
    There is no federal protection. Some states have passed laws providing legal immunity for employers providing information to other employers.

80. Employees cannot use the Fourth Amendment (relating to search and seizure) to challenge drug testing in the private sector.

    ANSWER: True, 307

128 Chapter 9

Essay

81. What is an applicant? Why must an employer develop a policy defining "applicant?"

    ANSWER: 282-283
    An employer must not discriminate against an applicant for any reasons that are against the law, and must keep detailed records on applicant flow. An individual submitting an unsolicited resume may be considered an applicant if the employer does not define at what point an inquiry becomes an application for employment.

82. Briefly describe the steps in a typical selection process. What are the legal considerations, if any, at each step?

    ANSWER: 285-308
    Reception and job preview - define who is an applicant. Application form - can only ask questions that are job related. Testing - all tests must be valid and job related. Interviewing - most widely used and least valid test. Cannot ask nonjob-related questions. Background investigation - Privacy Act, Fair Credit Reporting Act. Conditional job offer. Medical exam/drug test - Other than drug tests, most medical exams may violate the ADA. Job placement.

83. You have been appointed college recruiter for an investment bank. What selection testing would you administer?

    ANSWER: 288-308
    Application form requesting academic and work achievements. Assessment center to assess skills and management potential. Psychological test for ability to work under stress. Honesty test, interview, background investigation, drug test.

84. Discuss the statement: *"Interviews are the most widely used, but the least valid, selection method."* What are some of the uses and problems associated with employment interviews?

    ANSWER: 296-303
    An interviewer can integrate all information obtained from application forms, tests, and reference checks, and investigate any conflicting information that may have emerged. The interview has high intrarater reliability and face validity. It can be the final step before a hiring decision is made. Problems include low interrater reliability and poor validity, snap judgment, negative emphasis, halo effect, and biases.

85. Would you recommend that employers conduct background investigations and medical examinations of job applicants? What are some of the legal issues involved?

    ANSWER: 303-308
    Background investigations can be used to verify information given on application forms and identify any criminal records. Medical examinations should only be used to check for drug use. The Privacy Act, the Fair Credit Reporting Act, and the ADA limit what can be investigated.

Chapter 10

Training Human Resources

Multiple Choice

1. A growing number of employers have recognized that training is
    A. an expensive necessity.
    B. an investment in the human capital of the organization.
    C. an expense that can be cut when times get tough.
    D. primarily associated with orienting new employees to the organization and their jobs.

    ANSWER: B, 316

2. Which is the best way to determine if training is cost effective?
    A. identify attitude changes following the training programs
    B. assess any reductions in voluntary turnover
    C. measure improvements in performance resulting from training
    D. compare costs and benefits associated with training

    ANSWER: D, 316

3. How is training affected as organizations restructure and implement strategic changes?
    A. Training becomes more important.
    B. Training budgets are cut.
    C. Employee development budgets increase as training budgets stabilize.
    D. Generally there is no impact on training and development.

    ANSWER: A, 317

4. _____ is a process whereby people acquire capabilities to aid in the achievement of organizational goals.
    A. Reinforced learning
    B. Orientation
    C. Training
    D. Employee development

    ANSWER: C, 317

5. In a limited sense, _____ provides employees with specific, identifiable knowledge and skills for use on their present jobs.
   A. employee development
   B. training
   C. orientation
   D. learning

   ANSWER: B, 317

6. Training is distinguished from development, in that
   A. equal employment opportunity laws and regulations apply primarily to training not development.
   B. training is used mostly for management positions.
   C. development provides people with specific, identifiable knowledge and skills for use on their present jobs.
   D. development is broader in scope, focusing on individuals gaining new capabilities useful for both present and future jobs.

   ANSWER: D, 317

7. In a typical division of training responsibilities, the HR unit
   A. prepares skill-training materials.
   B. monitors training needs.
   C. conducts on-the-job training.
   D. participates in organizational change efforts.

   ANSWER: A, 318

8. With respect to training, the HR unit
   A. has a more short-term view of employee careers and development than operating managers.
   B. should conduct on-the-job training.
   C. serves as a source of expert training assistance and coordination.
   D. is the best source of technical info used in skill training.

   ANSWER: C, 317

9. In a typical division of training responsibilities, which of the following would be a primary responsibility of operating managers?
   A. conduct or arrange for off-the-job training
   B. monitor training needs
   C. prepare skill-training materials
   D. provide input and expertise for organizational development

   ANSWER: B, 318

10. Of the following types of training, which is more likely to be conducted in-house rather than by external training resources?
    A. new equipment operation
    B. sexual harassment
    C. train-the-trainer
    D. new employee orientation

    ANSWER: D, 319

11. Which of the following is true about on-the-job training?
    A. It tends to be viewed as being very applicable to the job.
    B. It is more expensive as compared to classroom training.
    C. It is less disruptive to the work flow.
    D. Supervisors are better prepared to teach their own subordinates.

    ANSWER: A, 318

12. _____ occurs internally through interactions and feedback among employees.
    A. Vestibule training
    B. Employee development
    C. Informal training
    D. New employee orientation

    ANSWER: C, 319

13. _____ involves the use of vendors to train employees.
    A. On-the-job development
    B. Outsourcing
    C. Informal training
    D. Certification

    ANSWER: B, 320

14. Training is an area targeted by EEO laws and regulations. One area of concern involves
    A. the method by which mentors are chosen.
    B. the content of training programs.
    C. the cost of training programs.
    D. the practices used to select individuals for inclusion in training programs.

    ANSWER: D, 320

15. The ability to learn must be accompanied by
    A. intention to learn.
    B. to right attitude.
    C. appropriate time.
    D. organizational support.

    ANSWER: A, 321

16. An employee's _____ is determined by answers to questions like "What's in it for me?"
    A. ability to learn
    B. Gestalt learning
    C. motivation to learn
    D. valence

    ANSWER: C, 321

Chapter 10

17. People vary in their beliefs about their ability to learn things through training. People with high self-efficacy seem to do better with
    A. one-on-one training.
    B. conventional training.
    C. mentoring.
    D. computer-assisted programs.

    ANSWER: B, 321

18. Giving trainees an overall view of what they will be doing prior to dividing the instructions into small elements is part of
    A. behavior modification.
    B. vestibule training.
    C. assessment evaluation.
    D. Gestalt learning.

    ANSWER: D, 321

19. _____ refers to providing trainees information about the processes and strategies that can lead to training success.
    A. Attentional advice
    B. Active practice
    C. Motivation to learn
    D. Reinforcement

    ANSWER: A, 321

20. When people repeat responses that give them some type of positive reward and avoid actions associated with negative consequences, they are demonstrating the law(s) of
    A. modification.
    B. behavior.
    C. effect.
    D. learning

    ANSWER: C, 321

21. Behavior modification uses the theories of psychologist
    A. Abraham Maslow.
    B. B.F. Skinner.
    C. Frederick Winslow Taylor.
    D. Peter Drucker.

    ANSWER: B, 322

22. Behavior modification postulates that
    A. "not all behavior should be reinforced."
    B. "values are relative"
    C. "learning is doing."
    D. "learning is changing what we do."

    ANSWER: D, 322

23. Which of the following best describes the concept of negative reinforcement?
    A. An individual works to avoid an undesirable consequence.
    B. Action taken to repel a person from an undesired action.
    C. The absence of an expected response to a situation.
    D. An undesirable consequence following an inappropriate action.

    ANSWER: A, 322

24. Research suggests that for most training situations, _____ is most effective.
    A. punishment of the undesirable behavior
    B. behavior modification
    C. positive reinforcement of the desired behavior
    D. negative reinforcement

    ANSWER: C, 322

25. The learning concept of _____ indicates that people learn best if reinforcement is given as soon as possible after training.
    A. behavior modeling
    B. immediate confirmation
    C. positive reinforcement
    D. active practice

    ANSWER: B, 322

26. The most elementary way in which people learn is _____, or copying someone else's behavior.
    A. behavior modification
    B. positive reinforcement
    C. cognitive practice
    D. behavior modeling

    ANSWER: D, 322

27. _____ occurs when trainees perform job-related tasks and duties during training.
    A. Active practice
    B. Whole learning
    C. Transfer of training
    D. Positive reinforcement

    ANSWER: A, 323

28. _____ occurs when several practice sessions are spaced over a period of hours or days.
    A. Alternate practice
    B. Active practice
    C. Spaced practice
    D. Massed practice

    ANSWER: C, 323

Chapter 10

29. For memorizing tasks, _____ is usually the more effective training design.
    A. cognitive practice
    B. massed practice
    C. alternative practice
    D. spaced practice

    ANSWER: B, 323

30. Two conditions must be met for effective transfer of training, including
    A. positive reinforcement for applying the skills on the job.
    B. the trainees must be able to recall the training as needed.
    C. the trainees must understand the practical application of the training.
    D. use of the learned material must be maintained over time on the job.

    ANSWER: D, 323

31. One way to aid transfer of training to job situations is to ensure that
    A. the training is as much like the jobs as possible.
    B. positive reinforcement occurs.
    C. immediate confirmation is provided.
    D. the trainees are able to see the "big picture."

    ANSWER: A, 323

32. "The planned introduction of new employees to their jobs, coworkers, and the organization" is a definition of
    A. employee development.
    B. organizational entry.
    C. orientation.
    D. socialization.

    ANSWER: C, 324

33. In a small organization without an HR department, new employee orientation becomes the responsibility of
    A. the new employer him/herself.
    B. the new employee's supervisor or manager.
    C. a well-written employee handbook.
    D. the new employee's coworkers.

    ANSWER: B, 324

34. The overall goal of _____ is to help new employees learn about the organization as soon as possible, so that they can begin contributing.
    A. mentoring
    B. training and development
    C. active practice
    D. orientation

    ANSWER: D, 324

35. Which of the following was not given as a specific purpose of the orientation process?
    A. establishment of employee expectations
    B. creation a favorable impression
    C. productivity enhancement
    D. turnover reduction

    ANSWER: A, 324

36. When does orientation to the organization begin?
    A. when the job offer is made
    B. when the job offer is accepted
    C. during the recruiting and selection processes
    D. when the new employee first reports for work

    ANSWER: C, 325

37. If a well-planned formal orientation is lacking,
    A. productivity will be adversely affected.
    B. the new employee may be oriented solely by the work group.
    C. the employee will not gain an accurate picture of how the firm really works.
    D. the "buddy" system becomes more important.

    ANSWER: B, 327

38. Which of the following can be a gauge of the success of orientation or any other type of training?
    A. the total cost of the orientation or training program
    B. the degree of job satisfaction reported by the employees who participated in the training
    C. the improvement in employee productivity following the orientation or training
    D. the amount of learning that occurs and is transferred to the job

    ANSWER: D, 330

39. In the _____ phase of a training system, planners determine the need for training and specify the objectives of the training effort.
    A. assessment
    B. implementation
    C. evaluation
    D. accomplishment

    ANSWER: A, 330

40. The _____ phase in a training system focuses on measuring how well the training accomplished what its originators expected.
    A. assessment
    B. implementation
    C. evaluation
    D. accomplishment

    ANSWER: C, 331

Chapter 10

41. Departments or areas with high turnover, high absenteeism, low performance, or other deficiencies can be pinpointed through which level of a training needs assessment?
    A. task analysis
    B. organizational analysis
    C. individual analysis
    D. group analysis

    ANSWER: B, 332

42. During _____ analysis, the requirements of jobs are compared with the knowledge, skills, and abilities of employees to identify training needs.
    A. organizational
    B. group
    C. individual
    D. task

    ANSWER: D, 332

43. The most common type of training at all levels in an organization is
    A. on-the-job training.
    B. classroom instruction.
    C. simulation exercises.
    D. role playing.

    ANSWER: A, 334

44. Which of the following is a problem with on-the-job training (OJT)?
    A. uncontrolled environment
    B. professional trainers not managers do the training
    C. can disrupt regular work
    D. emphasis is on learning not doing

    ANSWER: C, 335

45. In _____ training, a training site is set up to be identical to the work site.
    A. assessment-center
    B. simulation
    C. in-basket
    D. programmed

    ANSWER: B, 335

46. In a simulation setting, trainees can learn _____ but be away from the pressures of the production schedule.
    A. in a classroom
    B. on-the-job
    C. after regular working hours
    D. under realistic conditions

    ANSWER: D, 335

47. _____ combine(s) job training with classroom instruction.
    A. Internships
    B. Trade education
    C. Simulations
    D. Vestibule training

    ANSWER: A, 336

48. Apprenticeships are used most often to train people for jobs in
    A. management development.
    B. technology-related areas.
    C. skilled crafts.
    D. the construction industry.

    ANSWER: C, 336

49. _____ training focuses less on physical skills than on attitudes, perceptions, and interpersonal issues.
    A. Vestibule
    B. Behaviorally experienced
    C. Managerial development
    D. Cooperative

    ANSWER: B, 336

50. Which of the following may be classified as a type of behaviorally experienced training?
    A. internships
    B. programmed instruction
    C. simulations
    D. diversity training

    ANSWER: D, 337

51. Computer simulations where the trainee makes management decisions and gets feedback on success are
    A. business games.
    B. computer-assisted instructions.
    C. role playing exercises.
    D. job instruction training.

    ANSWER: A, 337

52. _____ is an unstructured attempt to show how others see you, providing insight into interpersonal skills.
    A. Diversity training
    B. Role playing
    C. Sensitivity training
    D. An assessment center

    ANSWER: C, 337

Chapter 10

53. Computer-assisted instruction (CAI) lends itself to which type of training?
    A. sequencing
    B. drill and practice
    C. demonstrations
    D. experiments

    ANSWER: B, 338

54. _____ allows trainees to "see" the training situations and react to them using computer interactive technology.
    A. Vestibule training
    B. New Age training
    C. A simulator
    D. Virtual reality

    ANSWER: D, 338

55. Which of the following is a major advantage of all forms of computer-assisted instruction?
    A. It allows self-directed instruction.
    B. It takes place off-the-job.
    C. Computer literacy is enhanced.
    D. It combines text, graphics, sound, and animation.

    ANSWER: A, 338

56. _____ to evaluate training, HR professionals in an organization gather data on training and compare it to data on training at other organizations in their industry and size.
    A. In the results approach
    B. Using the reaction level of trainees
    C. To do benchmarking
    D. To use a cost/benefit analysis

    ANSWER: C, 340

57. When a university asks students to complete an instructor-evaluation survey, it is evaluating training at the _____ level.
    A. results
    B. reaction
    C. learning
    D. behavior

    ANSWER: B, 340

58. The _____ level of evaluation involves measuring the effect of training on job performance through interviews of trainees and their coworkers and observing job performance.
    A. reaction
    B. learning
    C. results
    D. behavior

    ANSWER: D, 341

59. The difficulty with evaluating results by measuring the effect of training on the achievement of organizational objectives is
    A. pinpointing whether it actually was training that caused the changes in results.
    B. that organizational results are not clearly quantifiable.
    C. the criteria is hard to obtain.
    D. being able to interpret subjective performance measures.

    ANSWER: A, 342

60. A problem with the pre/post measure of evaluating training, is
    A. the difficulty of constructing a good test.
    B. being able to eliminate cultural discrimination.
    C. knowing if the training was responsible for the change.
    D. being able to intervene in the workplace at the appropriate times.

    ANSWER: C, 342

True and False

61. Since most of the benefits of training are intangible (such as attitude changes and safety awareness), it is rarely possible to evaluate the effectiveness of training programs.

    ANSWER: False, 316
    A comparison of the costs and benefits of training, which can often be measured, is the best way to determine if training is cost effective.

62. Using a variety of statistical analyses, researchers found that managerial training produces a greater return on investment than sales or technical training.

    ANSWER: False, 317
    Just the opposite was found - sales/technical training has a greater effect than managerial training.

63. A distinction may be made between training and development, with training being broader in scope and focusing on individuals gaining new knowledge and skills useful for both present and future jobs.

    ANSWER: False, 317
    Actually it is development that is broader in scope with a longer-term focus.

64. Fair employment laws and regulations also apply to training.

    ANSWER: True, 320

140 Chapter 10

65. The concept of reinforcement is based on the law of confirmation, which states that people tend to repeat behaviors that receive a positive confirmation.

    ANSWER: False, 321
    The concept of reinforcement is based on the law of effect which states that people tend to repeat responses that give them some type of positive reward.

66. Behavior modification uses the theories of B.F. Skinner, who stated that "learning is not doing; it is changing what we do."

    ANSWER: True, 322

67. In the design of a training program, negative reinforcement occurs when action is taken to repel a person from an undesired action.

    ANSWER: False, 322
    Punishment is action taken to repel a person from an undesired action. Negative reinforcement occurs when an individual works to avoid undesirable consequences.

68. Behavior modeling is the most elementary way in which people learn, and it is one of the best.

    ANSWER: True, 322

69. For effective transfer of learning to occur, the use of the learned material must be maintained over time on the job.

    ANSWER: True, 323

70. The primary purpose of an orientation program is to provide information on how to do the job.

    ANSWER: False, 324
    This is only one of many purposes of orientation which also includes productivity enhancement, turnover reduction, and creating an favorable first impression.

71. To provide legal protection for employers, employees should be asked to sign a statement that they have been informed of pertinent rules and procedures during orientation.

    ANSWER: True, 327

72. Orientation should be viewed as a never-ending process of introducing both old and new employees to the current state of the organization.

    ANSWER: True, 329

73. It is essential that objectives for training be related to the budgetary priorities identified in the organizational analysis.

    ANSWER: False, 334
    Training objectives and priorities are set to close the gap between where an organization is with its employee capabilities and where it needs to be.

74. On-the-job training is by far the most commonly used form of training, because it is provides little or no disruption to regular work.

    ANSWER: False, 335
    While OJT is the most common form of training, it can disrupt regular work.

75. Simulation is a training approach where trainees can learn under realistic conditions but be away from the pressures of the production schedule.

    ANSWER: True, 335

76. Internships are a form of training used most often to train people for jobs in skilled crafts, such as carpentry, plumbing, photoengraving, typesetting, and welding.

    ANSWER: False, 336
    An internship is a form of on-the-job training that combines job training with classroom instruction. It is used for a range of jobs from trade to professional. Apprenticeships are primarily used for skilled crafts.

77. Behaviorally experienced training is a form of on-the-job training that usually combines job training with classroom instruction in trade schools, high schools, colleges, or universities.

    ANSWER: False, 336
    This is a description of internships. Behaviorally experiences training deals less with physical skills than with attitudes, perceptions, and other interpersonal skills.

78. Diversity training seeks to shape attitudes about a work environment with differing kinds of employees.

    ANSWER: True, 337

79. An employee participating in an in-basket exercise would be required to deal with a series of memos or letters in a rapid fashion.

    ANSWER: True, 337

80. Virtual reality can be used to "place" police officers, training them when to use weapons when chasing suspects in darkened and crowded areas.

    ANSWER: True, 338

Essay

81. U.S. employers are spending at least $50 million on training annually. How can an organization determine if its training expenditures are cost effective?

    ANSWER: 316-317, 340
    While some benefits (such as attitude changes) are hard to quantify, the best approach involves a comparison of costs and benefits. Figure 10-1 identifies some of the costs and benefits of training, many of which can be quantified. Benchmarking training is one way of comparing costs with the benefits received.

82. What are some of the legal issues associated with training? What actions should an employer take to comply with EEO laws and regulations?

    ANSWER: 320
    EEO laws and regulations apply to training. They are concerned with criteria used to select individuals for inclusion in a training program. The criteria must be job related and not unfairly limit the participation of protected-class members. However, training is a cost, and courts have upheld the practice whereby some firms require trainees to sign promissory notes to repay the training costs if the trainee left the firm within a specified time period.

83. What learning principles would you consider in designing a training program?

    ANSWER: 320-324
    Learning is a continual process and only occurs when the information is received, understood, and internalized in such a way that some change or conscious effort has been made to use the information. The ability to learn must be accompanied by intention to learn. The principles of reinforcement and behavior modification apply. Transfer of learning requires that the learning be applied on the job, and its use maintained over time.

84. What is the purpose of an orientation program? What should be the format and content of an effective orientation?

    ANSWER: 324-329
    Orientation is the planned introduction of new employees to their jobs, coworkers, and the organization. For employers, the purpose is to enhance productivity, reduce turnover, and inform new employees about the nature of the organization. For new employees it can help create a favorable impression and enhance interpersonal acceptance. Effective orientation is an ongoing process that begins with presenting new employees with needed information,

85. What is cooperative training? Describe its usefulness.

    ANSWER: 336
    Internships and apprenticeships are the two most widely used methods of cooperative training. They mix classroom training and on-the-job experience. They help the trainee get first-hand job experience and enables the employer to assess possible future job candidates.

Chapter 11

Human Resource Development and Careers

Multiple Choice

1. Which of the following is true regarding the current role of employee development?
    A. There is an increased role for qualified middle managers.
    B. Project-based work is growing, making careers a series of projects, not steps upward in a given organization.
    C. High-tech firms prefer to "grow" rather than hire qualified managers.
    D. Many firms are reducing their dependence on core competencies while increasing their need for managers with both technical and managerial expertise.

    ANSWER: B, 350

2. Development results from
    A. the training that employees receive.
    B. mentors assigned to new employees.
    C. the simple process of getting older and wiser.
    D. experience and the maturity that comes with it.

    ANSWER: D, 350

3. The focus of _____ is learning specific behaviors and actions, while _____ focuses on understanding information, concepts, and context.
    A. training; development
    B. knowledge; training
    C. development; training
    D. training; knowledge

    ANSWER: A, 351

4. _____ can be thought of as growing capabilities that go beyond those required by the current job; representing efforts to improve employees' ability to handle a variety of assignments.
    A. Career planning
    B. Succession planning
    C. Development
    D. Employability

    ANSWER: C, 350

Chapter 11

5. What impact does the development process have on individuals' careers?
   A. The employees' career goals are subordinated to the organization's goals.
   B. The individuals' careers gain focus and evolve.
   C. The employees become more valuable to their organizations.
   D. Individual careers will flourish and generate more success.

   ANSWER: B, 350

6. Which of the following is not a basic requirement to be met if HR development is to provide a sustained competitive advantage?
   A. The developed workforce produces more positive economic benefit for the organization than an undeveloped workforce.
   B. The abilities of the workforce provide an advantage over competitors.
   C. The abilities of the workforce are not easily duplicated by a competitor.
   D. The costs of developing the workforce do not exceed the economic benefits.

   ANSWER: D, 352

7. Which of the following statements best describes current trends regarding the hiring of technical and professional people?
   A. Hiring is based on the amount of skill development the candidates have already achieved.
   B. Employers prefer to develop rather than "buy" their human resources.
   C. There is a growing shortage of managers with technical backgrounds.
   D. There is no consensus on what is the "best" way to develop technicians for managerial positions.

   ANSWER: A, 352

8. Which of the following was not identified as an important management capability?
   A. action orientation
   B. ethical values
   C. communication skills
   D. technical skills

   ANSWER: C, 352

9. Development should begin with
   A. an appraisal of the performance of all managers.
   B. the HR plans of an organization.
   C. a review of current training and development practices.
   D. the career plans of current employees.

   ANSWER: B, 353

10. What is an assessment center?
    A. A place specifically established for selection screening.
    B. A procedure for evaluating training and development programs.
    C. The centralized employee performance appraisal system.
    D. A collection of instruments and exercises designed to diagnose a person's development needs.

    ANSWER: D, 355

11. Which of the following statements is true about assessment centers?
    A. Traits like leadership, initiative, and supervisory skills are more accurately assessed.
    B. The assessment center is a place where employment testing is centralized.
    C. Unfortunately, assessment centers have the same built-in biases as other selection techniques.
    D. Assessment centers are used primarily for selecting management trainees.

    ANSWER: A, 355

12. The advantages of assessment centers include
    A. the "typical" manager can serve as an assessor.
    B. they are used as a way of avoiding difficult promotion decisions.
    C. they help identify employees with potential in a large organization.
    D. they are not as expensive as traditional selection techniques.

    ANSWER: C, 355

13. The problems with assessment centers include
    A. they are subject to the same biases inherent in interview situations.
    B. some managers may use the assessment center as a way to avoid difficult promotion decisions.
    C. a clever participant can fake the results.
    D. the conclusions reached usually are not valid.

    ANSWER: B, 355

14. The biggest problem with psychological testing lies in
    A. the limited validity of these types of tests.
    B. how the tests are scored.
    C. the administration costs.
    D. interpreting the results.

    ANSWER: D, 355

15. Which of the following is true regarding psychological testing?
    A. Such testing is appropriate only when the testing and feedback process is closely supervised by a qualified professional throughout.
    B. The EEOC has banned the use of these tests by private-sector employers.
    C. Psychological testing is never appropriate for developing employees.
    D. Psychological tests are valid predictors of motivation, reasoning abilities, interpersonal response traits, and job preferences.

    ANSWER: A, 356

16. What is the purpose of replacement charts?
    A. To provide legal cover for an employer needing to replace an employee.
    B. To prepare a collection of instruments and exercises designed to diagnose a person's development needs.
    C. To ensure that the right individuals are available at the right time, and that they have had sufficient experience to handle the targeted jobs.
    D. To help train and development recruiters in the HR department.

    ANSWER: C, 356

17. _____ can be part of the development process by specifying the nature of development each employee needs to be prepared for the identified promotions.
    A. Succession plans
    B. Replacement charts
    C. Career pathing
    D. Needs assessment

    ANSWER: B, 356

18. Which of the following is the oldest on-the-job development technique?
    A. assistant-to
    B. job rotation
    C. committee assignments
    D. coaching

    ANSWER: D, 357

19. _____ is/are the daily training and feedback given to employees by immediate supervisors.
    A. Coaching
    B. Committee assignments
    C. Development exercises
    D. Job rotation

    ANSWER: A, 357

20. Which of the following is a limitation of committee assignments as a development method?
    A. It can be a broadened experience.
    B. There is no guarantee that the trainee can perform the assignment well.
    C. Committee assignments can become time-wasting activities.
    D. Doing the work gets priority over learning.

    ANSWER: C, 358

21. When opportunities for promotion are scarce, what is an especially good way to keep employees motivated?
    A. coaching
    B. job rotation
    C. assistant-to position
    D. committee assignments

    ANSWER: B, 359

22. As a development technique, the best lateral moves do which of the following?
    A. Ensure trainees have an opportunity to deal with interesting assignments.
    B. Provide a monetary incentive for taking on new work.
    C. Provide a continual process of learning.
    D. Move the person into the core business.

    ANSWER: D, 359

23. Which of the following is true about the use of job rotation as a development method?
    A. Managerial time is lost when the trainees must become acquainted with different people and techniques in each new unit.
    B. The trainees report that constant job changes reduce their level of motivation.
    C. Rotation reduces the potential for learning new skills.
    D. Job rotation is only appropriate when the organization is growing and can provide increasingly new responsibilities.

    ANSWER: A, 359

24. Assistant-to positions are useful for development if
    A. a team of upper management people act as mentors to each individual.
    B. mature individuals are selected for participation.
    C. the assignments are challenging or interesting.
    D. there is no money for outside development activities.

    ANSWER: C, 359

25. Advantages of off-the-job-site development techniques?
    A. less disruptive of daily operations.
    B. meeting with other people who are concerned with somewhat different problems and come from other organizations may provide new perspectives on old problems.
    C. a variety of available programs provided by a variety of educational institutions can provide a cornucopia of development possibilities.
    D. less expensive than on-the-job methods.

    ANSWER: B, 359

26. The lecture system has the following disadvantage.
    A. Only a limited amount of information can be covered in a lecture.
    B. The lecturer may be constantly interrupted by questions.
    C. It is an expensive training and development technique.
    D. Lectures encourage passive listening.

    ANSWER: D, 359

27. Which of the following is true of classroom instruction?
    A. Results depend on the ability of the instructor and the subject matter.
    B. The lecture system discourages passive listening.
    C. Classrooms promote opportunities to ask questions and seek clarification.
    D. Its effectiveness is independent of the size of the group.

    ANSWER: A, 359

28. The main problem with human relations training programs is
    A. the costs associated with conducting the programs.
    B. the unwillingness of supervisors to admit that they need such training.
    C. the difficulty in measuring their effectiveness.
    D. the heavy use of role-playing exercises which supervisors dislike.

    ANSWER: C, 360

Chapter 11

29. What is the most common reason why new managers fail after being promoted?
    A. lack of internal political savvy
    B. poor teamwork with subordinates and peers
    C. deficiency of technical skills
    D. inability to balance work and family demands

    ANSWER: B, 361

30. _____ provide a medium through which the trainee can study the application of management or behavioral concepts.
    A. Management seminars
    B. Psychological analyses
    C. Assistant-to positions
    D. Case studies

    ANSWER: D, 360

31. _____ is a development technique requiring the trainee to assume a role in a given situation and act out behaviors associated with that role.
    A. Role playing
    B. Simulations
    C. Play acting
    D. Assistant-to positions

    ANSWER: A, 360

32. Which of the following development techniques requires the participant to analyze a situation and decide the best course of action based on the data given?
    A. case study
    B. psychological analysis
    C. simulation
    D. role-playing

    ANSWER: C, 360

33. A _____ is paid time off the job to develop and rejuvenate oneself.
    A. leave of absence
    B. sabbatical
    C. wilderness-survival course
    D. simulated leave

    ANSWER: B, 361

34. Which of the following is a disadvantage of paid sabbaticals?
    A. The executives often work so hard during the sabbatical, that they burnout upon their return.
    B. It is not a viable option for business organizations.
    C. Executives often use the sabbatical to look for another job.
    D. The nature of the learning experience is not within the control of the organization and is left somewhat to chance.

    ANSWER: D, 362

Human Resource Development and Careers

35. Wilderness excursions, as a management development technique,
    A. can create a sense of teamwork via the shared-risk experiences.
    B. are an activity enjoyed by everybody involved.
    C. help work groups reevaluate goals.
    D. are a fad with very little value for management development.

    ANSWER: A, 362

36. Managers learn by behavior modeling, which is defined as
    A. reinforcing the desirable behaviors exhibited.
    B. setting an example for junior managers.
    C. copying someone else's behavior.
    D. articulate reflection.

    ANSWER: C, 364

37. In the context of management development, _____ is best accomplished when it involves a relationship between two managers for a period of time as they perform their jobs.
    A. behavioral modeling
    B. coaching
    C. human relations training
    D. assistant-to development

    ANSWER: B, 364-365

38. _____ is a relationship in which managers at the midpoints in their careers aid individuals in the first stages of their careers.
    A. Human relations training
    B. Management coaching
    C. Management modeling
    D. Mentoring

    ANSWER: D, 365

39. During the cultivation stage of mentoring, the older manager
    A. provides challenging work, coaching, visibility, protection, and sponsorship for the younger manager.
    B. realizes the younger manager is someone who is "coachable."
    C. gains self-confidence, new attitudes, values, and styles of operation.
    D. demonstrates success at developing management talent as they move apart.

    ANSWER: A, 365

40. The glass ceiling refers to
    A. mentors describing the experiences of top management to a younger manager.
    B. the "window" through which the outside world can see inside the organization.
    C. the situation is which women fail to progress to top management positions.
    D. senior managers illustrating the opportunities for younger managers to progress in the organization.

    ANSWER: C, 366

Chapter 11

41. Which of the following statements is true regarding mentoring?
    A. Young minority managers find white managers are willing to help them.
    B. Mentoring is seen as a way for women to crack the "glass ceiling."
    C. Women are less willing to be mentors than men.
    D. Mentoring is seen as a one-way-street, with the younger manager getting all the benefits from the relationship.

    ANSWER: B, 366

42. Which of the following has been identified as a problem with mentoring?
    A. The relationship between mentor and protégé may become more social than work related.
    B. Successful managers do not have the time to be effective mentors.
    C. Women are reluctant to serve as mentors.
    D. Young minority managers report difficulty finding older white mentors.

    ANSWER: D, 366

43. When an individual learns new methods and ideas in a development course and returns to a work unit that is still bound by old attitudes and methods,
    A. encapsulated development occurs.
    B. negative reinforcement is experienced.
    C. lost transference occurs.
    D. non transference has ensued.

    ANSWER: A, 366

44. A(n) _____ is a sequence of work-related positions a person occupies throughout life.
    A. occupation
    B. job
    C. career
    D. profession

    ANSWER: C, 367

45. Why of the following best describes why people pursue careers?
    A. to sustain life
    B. to satisfy deeply individual needs
    C. to achieve personal achievement
    D. an identification with the Protestant Work Ethic

    ANSWER: B, 367

46. A career plan in which an individual enters the sales department of an organization as a sales counselor, then is promoted to account director, to sales manager, and finally to vice-president of sales, would be an example of
    A. lifetime employment.
    B. career transitions.
    C. individual-centered career planning.
    D. organization-centered career planning.

    ANSWER: D, 367

47. Individual-centered career planning focuses on
    A. the individual's goals and skills.
    B. the career ladder for that employee.
    C. the replacement chart.
    D. the internal opportunities for career advancement.

    ANSWER: A, 368

48. In recent years, many people have found themselves in career transition, that is, in need of finding other jobs. This has been caused by
    A. moonlighting.
    B. challenges to their ethical values.
    C. organizational retrenchment and downsizing.
    D. corporate growth and international expansion.

    ANSWER: C, 368

49. Individual characteristics that affect how people make career choices include
    A. physical and cognitive traits.
    B. interests, self-image, personality, and social backgrounds.
    C. self-identity and self-disclosure.
    D. a desire for certain individual and organizational rewards.

    ANSWER: B, 368

50. How a person chooses a specific organization is often a function of
    A. the socioeconomic status and the education and occupation level of the person's parents.
    B. the personal orientation and personal needs of the individual.
    C. the salary and other compensation offered by the organization.
    D. the availability of a job when the person is looking for work.

    ANSWER: D, 368

51. The "dream jobs" of young people change over time. Which of the following were listed as dream jobs by 13-17 year-old boys in the 1990s but not in the 1970s?
    A. businessman
    B. lawyer
    C. athlete
    D. engineer

    ANSWER: A, 369

52. Which of the following is a recent characteristic of career planning?
    A. The number of middle-management positions will continue to grow.
    B. Small businesses will provide fewer and fewer jobs each year.
    C. The typical career will include many different positions, transitions, and organizations.
    D. Large companies will be the source of increased career opportunities.

    ANSWER: C, 369

Chapter 11

53. Many theorists in adult development describe the first half of life as the young adult's quest for
    A. personal integrity.
    B. competence and a way to make a mark in the world.
    C. possessions and personal wealth.
    D. challenge and risk taking.

    ANSWER: B, 369

54. During the first half of life, the young adult seeks happiness primarily through
    A. the development of integrity, values, and well-being.
    B. contributions to society.
    C. a series of highly structured experiences.
    D. external achievements and the acquisition of skills and goods.

    ANSWER: D, 369

55. During the second half of life, the individual's career interests involve
    A. the need for integrity, values, and well-being.
    B. retirement planning and income maintenance.
    C. learning new skills.
    D. external achievements as measured by wealth and achievements.

    ANSWER: A, 370

56. Adult development theorists believe that
    A. lives and careers are predictably linear.
    B. from early childhood, people have preordained careers.
    C. lives and careers must be viewed as cycles of structure and transition.
    D. a person's career is the manifestation of the inner values affecting that person's life.

    ANSWER: C, 370

57. Which of the following was <u>not</u> identified as a common emotional adjustment faced by retirees?
    A. a need to belong
    B. a renewed need for security
    C. territoriality or personal "turf"
    D. pride in achievement

    ANSWER: B, 370

58. In order to reward talented technical people who do not want to move into management, many companies have established
    A. portable career paths.
    B. phased retirement plans.
    C. the position of technical-professional.
    D. dual career ladders.

    ANSWER: D, 372

59. Which of the following statements is true about dual-career couples?
    A. Dual-career couples have more to lose when relocating.
    B. Their numbers are decreasing as more women opt for the "mommy track."
    C. Part-time work, flextime, and work-at-home arrangements are generally unacceptable options for most couples.
    D. Dual-career couples are increasingly more mobile as a result of the dual income.

    ANSWER: A, 373

60. Which of the following is true regarding moonlighting?
    A. Moonlighting typically involves a second job for the underpaid blue-collar worker.
    B. Moonlighting should be acceptable, since it does not compromise the primary company's work, nor does it seem to reduce job performance.
    C. Moonlighting can be a career development strategy for some professionals.
    D. Federal law prevents an employer from prohibiting moonlighting activities.

    ANSWER: C, 374

True and False

61. Development involves growing capacities that go beyond those required by the current job.

    ANSWER: True, 350

62. As a consequence of merger and acquisition activities, the "new career" is one in which the organization manages an individual's career development.

    ANSWER: False, 351
    Actually the emphasis in the "new career" is on self-development, development managed by the individual not the organization.

63. In contrast to most employees, workers in fast-paced Silicon Valley are more loyal to their employers than to their own careers and technology.

    ANSWER: False, 351
    Just the opposite is true. Workers in Silicon Valley change jobs at a rate of twice the national average.

64. Trends indicate that employers prefer to "buy" rather than "make" scarce employees in today's labor market.

    ANSWER: True, 352

154   Chapter 11

65. The HR development process should begin with a detailed analysis of the current operations of the organization.

    ANSWER: False, 353
    Development should begin with the HR plans of an organization.

66. Assessment centers are specially equipped training facilities that are used to evaluate individual employees.

    ANSWER: False, 355
    Assessment centers are not places as much as they are collections of instruments and exercises designed to diagnose a person's development needs.

67. Psychological testing can furnish useful information to employers about such factors as motivation, reasoning abilities, leadership styles, interpersonal response traits, and job preferences.

    ANSWER: True, 355

68. In closely-held Family firms (those that are not publicly traded on stock exchanges), most CEOs arrange for the business to be sold following their retirement or death.

    ANSWER: False, 356
    Many CEOs plan to pass the business on to a family member. Thus succession planning is important.

69. The purpose of replacement charts is to document who will temporarily take over responsibilities if the person in charge is unavailable.

    ANSWER: False, 356
    Their purpose is to ensure that the right individuals are available at the right time, and that they have had sufficient experience to handle the targeted jobs.

70. Coaching is the daily training and feedback given to employees by immediate supervisors.

    ANSWER: True, 357

71. A substantial amount of managerial time is lost when job rotation is used as a management development technique.

    ANSWER: True, 359

72. The problem with human relations training programs is the difficulty in measuring their effectiveness.

    ANSWER: True, 360

73. Role playing is a development technique that requires the participant to analyze a situation and decide the best course of action based on the data given.

    ANSWER: False, 360
    This is a description of simulations or business games.

74. Behavior modeling is defined as copying someone else's behavior.

    ANSWER: True, 364

75. Mentoring may be a useful way to attack the "glass ceiling" since it was found that women with mentors move up faster than those without mentors.

    ANSWER: True, 366

76. Encapsulated development occurs when an individual learns new methods in a development course and is able to incorporate what was learnt upon returning to the work unit.

    ANSWER: False, 366
    Just the opposite. Encapsulated development occurs when the individual returns to a work unit that is still bound by old attitudes and methods.

77. Organization-centered career planning focuses on finding opportunities for career growth within the organizational structure.

    ANSWER: False, 367
    It focuses on jobs and on constructing career paths that provide for the logical progression of people between jobs in an organization.

78. The objective of phased retirement is to reduce the shock that sudden retirement poses for some individuals.

    ANSWER: True, 371

79. Dual career paths have been established by many large companies to deal with the problems faced by dual-career couples.

    ANSWER: False, 372
    Dual career paths have been established to enable technical and professional workers to advance in their organizations without having to move into management.

80. Moonlighting is defined as work outside a person's regular employment that takes 12 or more additional hours per week.

    ANSWER: True, 374

156 Chapter 11

Essay

81. Define HR development. What is the difference between development and training? What variables enter into the decision to "buy" rather than "make" scarce employees in today's labor market?

    ANSWER: 350-352
    HR development represents efforts to improve employees' ability to handle a variety of assignments. As contrasted to training, development involves growing capabilities that go beyond those required by the current job. Developing (or making) human resources is expensive and many firms prefer to buy if the resources are available. However buying does not contribute to the three basic requirements for sustained competitive advantage through human resources.

82. Discuss the concept of lifelong learning as it applies to HR development.

    ANSWER: 352-353
    Lifelong learning is a recognition that learning and development do not occur only once during a person's lifetime. Many professions require continuing education for certification. For skilled and semi-skilled employees, it involves training to expand existing skills.

83. What is an assessment center? What role can an assessment center play in an organization's HR development process?

    ANSWER: 355
    An assessment center is not a place but rather a collection of instruments and exercises designed to diagnose a person's development needs. They are useful as a selection tool to identify managerial potential. They can overcome many of the biases inherent in interviews, supervisor ratings, and written tests.

84. Describe a typical mentoring relationship. How can mentoring aid women and minorities in their career advancement?

    ANSWER: 365-366
    Mentoring is a relationship in which managers in the midpoints of their careers aid individuals in the first stages of their careers. Technical, interpersonal, and political skills can be conveyed. Historically, most mentoring relationships have involved white males. Mentoring has been found to be useful in countering the glass ceiling, which is assumed to prevent many protected-class members from advancing in their organizations.

85. Describe the unique problems faced by dual-career couples. What can an employer do to address these problems?

    ANSWER: 372-374
    Problems include family issues, recruiting, and transfers. Actions to address family issues include part-time work, flex-time, and work-at-home arrangements. For recruitment and relocation, the employer can join an employer network, pay employment agency fees, or hire the spouse.

Chapter 12

Performance Management and Appraisal

Multiple Choice

1. A _____ system consists of the processes used to identify, encourage, measure, evaluate, improve, and reward employee performance.
    A. performance appraisal
    B. performance management
    C. organizational analysis
    D. organizational feedback

    ANSWER: B, 380

2. Performance management is part of the link between the organizational
    A. culture and performance.
    B. goal setting and actions.
    C. performance and individual rewards.
    D. strategy and results.

    ANSWER: D, 380

3. Performance is essentially
    A. what an employee does or does not do.
    B. limited to what can be effectively measured.
    C. what a supervisor says it is.
    D. the quantity and qualify of output.

    ANSWER: A, 381

4. What are job criteria?
    A. the most important duties and tasks of jobs
    B. expected levels of performance
    C. important elements of a job on which performance is measured
    D. the essential elements of a job

    ANSWER: C, 381

Chapter 12

5. _____ define what the organization is paying an employee to do.
   A. Performance measures
   B. Job criteria
   C. Essential job elements
   D. Expected performance levels

   ANSWER: B, 381

6. _____ information identifies a subjective character trait such as pleasant personality, initiative, or creativity.
   A. Results-based
   B. Behaviorally-anchored
   C. Personality-factor
   D. Trait-based

   ANSWER: D, 381

7. Which basis for performance evaluation is the least defensible in a court of law?
   A. trait-based
   B. results-based
   C. behavior-oriented
   D. productivity-based

   ANSWER: A, 381

8. Which type of information on performance is the most difficult to identify?
   A. trait-based
   B. results-based
   C. behavior-based
   D. productivity-based

   ANSWER: C, 382

9. Which of the following is true about behavior-based information used for evaluating job performance?
   A. The aim is to identify the one behavior which will lead to job success.
   B. Behavior-based information has the advantage of clearly specifying the behaviors management wants to see.
   C. Behavior-based information is the easiest to develop.
   D. Behavior-based information looks at what the employee has done or accomplished.

   ANSWER: B, 382

10. Results-based information, used for evaluation performance,
    A. focuses on specific behaviors that lead to job success.
    B. identifies character traits that result from job success.
    C. determines how well the employees do their jobs.
    D. considers what the employee has done or accomplished.

    ANSWER: D, 382

11. A results-based approach works very well for jobs in which
    A. measurement is easy and appropriate.
    B. performance criteria are multidimensional.
    C. team work is emphasized.
    D. employees need little or no supervision.

    ANSWER: A, 382

12. Performance measures are said to be _____ if they leave out some important job duties.
    A. subjective
    B. contaminated
    C. deficient
    D. unnecessary

    ANSWER: C, 382

13. When measuring performance, if some irrelevant criteria are included, the criteria are said to be
    A. subjective.
    B. contaminated.
    C. deficient.
    D. unnecessary.

    ANSWER: B, 382

14. Counting the number of insurance claims that a clerk processes each week is a(n) _____ measure of performance.
    A. quality
    B. subjective
    C. acceptable
    D. objective

    ANSWER: D, 382

15. A supervisor's rating of an employee's customer service performance would be an example of a(n) _____ measure.
    A. subjective
    B. objective
    C. deficient
    D. acceptable

    ANSWER: A, 382

16. _____ define the expected level of performance.
    A. Job criteria
    B. Job analyses
    C. Performance standards
    D. Essential elements

    ANSWER: C, 382

Chapter 12

17. Performance _____ define what satisfactory job performance is.
    A. measures
    B. standards
    C. appraisals
    D. objectives

    ANSWER: B, 382

18. Requiring that bank tellers balance at the end of each day is an example of a(n) _____ standard of performance.
    A. objective
    B. subjective
    C. acceptable
    D. nonnumerical

    ANSWER: D, 383

19. _____ is the process of evaluating how well employees perform their jobs when compared to a set of standards, and then communicating that information to those employees.
    A. Performance appraisal
    B. Job evaluation
    C. Appraisal interview
    D. Supervisor rating

    ANSWER: A, 384

20. With respect to an organization with a strong union, which of the following statements is false?
    A. Only salaried, nonunion employees usually receive performance appraisals.
    B. Unions emphasize seniority over merit.
    C. HR specialists take on increased responsibilities for evaluation.
    D. Unions equate experience with qualifications.

    ANSWER: C, 384

21. Which of the following best reflects most managers' attitudes towards conducting appraisals?
    A. It is an activity they look forward to.
    B. Not all appraisals are positive, and discussing ratings with poorly performing employees may not be pleasant.
    C. It highlights their own deficiencies as a supervisor.
    D. They are comfortable with their role of "playing God" with employees' raises and careers.

    ANSWER: B, 384

22. The two general uses of performance appraisal, which are often in conflict, are
    A. salary administration and discipline.
    B. training and development.
    C. coaching and career planning.
    D. administrative and development.

    ANSWER: D, 384

23. Which of the following would be an example of the administrative role of performance appraisal?
    A. measuring performance for the purpose of rewarding employees
    B. identifying weaknesses to determine coaching needs
    C. identifying the organization's training needs
    D. communicating feedback to the employee

    ANSWER: A, 384

24. In addition to compensation administration, performance appraisal
    A. predicts management success.
    B. helps assess the potential of an employee.
    C. is a primary source of information and feedback for employees.
    D. identifies promotional opportunities.

    ANSWER: C, 384

25. What is the role of appraisal in compensation administration?
    A. It is the direct determinant of most compensation increases.
    B. It is the link between productivity and rewards.
    C. It has very little input into most compensation programs.
    D. It is perceived by employees as the critical factor in pay raises.

    ANSWER: B, 384

26. Why are performance appraisals necessary when organizations terminate, promote, or pay people differently?
    A. They help explain the connection between merit and seniority.
    B. They provide developmental information to the employees.
    C. They are an important input to the strategic planning process.
    D. They are a crucial defense if employees sue over such decisions.

    ANSWER: D, 385

27. Which of the following best describes the manager's role in the developmental aspect of performance appraisal?
    A. coach
    B. father/mother
    C. teacher
    D. judge

    ANSWER: A, 385

28. What is the purpose of developmental feedback?
    A. to compare individuals
    B. to prepare candidates for promotion
    C. to change or reinforce individual behavior
    D. to provide examples of acceptable and unacceptable performance

    ANSWER: C, 385

162 Chapter 12

29. How can teams be useful in the appraisal process?
    A. Teams are equipped to handle administrative appraisal.
    B. Teams can provide developmental feedback to members.
    C. Teams can provide useful input in downsizing situations.
    D. Teams are better able to allocate rewards based on merit.

    ANSWER: B, 386

30. A(n) _____ is conducted as part of the day-to-day working relationship between a manager and an employee.
    A. HR functionary
    B. systematic appraisal
    C. HR evaluation
    D. informal appraisal

    ANSWER: D, 386

31. Which of the following statements is true regarding informal appraisals?
    A. Frequent informal feedback to employees can prevent surprises later when the formal evaluation is communicated.
    B. When time is an issue, informal appraisals are not as appropriate.
    C. On-the-spot examinations of a piece of work are an unacceptable practice.
    D. The day-to-day working relationship between a manager and an employee would be disrupted by regular informal appraisals.

    ANSWER: A, 386

32. A(n) _____ is used when the contact between manager and employee is formal, and a system is in place to report managerial impressions and observations on employee performance.
    A. HR functionary
    B. HR evaluation
    C. systematic appraisal
    D. informal appraisal

    ANSWER: C, 387

33. In the typical division of appraisal responsibilities, the HR unit is responsible for
    A. rating performance of employees.
    B. designing and maintaining the formal system.
    C. reviewing appraisals with employees.
    D. providing regular informal appraisals.

    ANSWER: B, 388

34. In the appraisal process, managers are typically responsible for
    A. making sure the reports are in on time.
    B. training the raters.
    C. designing the formal appraisal system.
    D. reviewing appraisals with employees.

    ANSWER: D, 388

35. The most frequently used pattern for conducting formal appraisals is
    A. once a year, around anniversary date.
    B. once a year, in December or January.
    C. twice a year.
    D. quarterly.

    ANSWER: A, 387

36. The timing of performance appraisals and pay discussions should be different because
    A. for maximum reinforcement value, the pay discussion should be conducted at a later time.
    B. most supervisors don't know how much their employees are paid.
    C. employees often focus more on the pay amount than on what they need to improve.
    D. each of these activities fall under different HR managers, and need different coordination times.

    ANSWER: C, 388

37. Traditional ratings of employees by supervisors is based on the assumption that
    A. employees are more receptive to criticism from their immediate supervisors.
    B. the immediate supervisor is the person most qualified to evaluate the employee's performance realistically, objectively, and fairly.
    C. they have regular day-to-day opportunities for informal appraisals.
    D. supervisors are more aware of their subordinates' desires and goals.

    ANSWER: B, 388

38. Which of the following applies to the concept of employees rating superiors and managers?
    A. Supervisors strongly oppose the concept.
    B. It decreases internal group conflict since employees now have an outlet for their grievances.
    C. It results in managers catering to employee whims, causing them to be less effective.
    D. It can be the basis for coaching as part of a career development effort for the managers.

    ANSWER: D, 390

39. In which of the following situations would peer ratings be most appropriate?
    A. The supervisor does not have the opportunity to observe each employee's performance, but other work group members do.
    B. A group of salespeople meets regularly as a committee to talk about one another's customer relations achievements.
    C. The manager is too busy to meet with each subordinate for a formal appraisal interview.
    D. The members of the work group are drawn from a diverse population.

    ANSWER: A, 390

164 Chapter 12

40. Total quality management (TQM) emphasizes
    A. individual accountability for the quality of work outcomes.
    B. quality of outputs over total quantity.
    C. team performance rather than individual performance.
    D. a balance between quality and quantity of outcomes.

    ANSWER: C, 390

41. _____ is a self-development tool that forces employees to think about their strengths and weaknesses and set goals for improvement.
    A. Supervisory appraisal
    B. Self-appraisal
    C. Team evaluation
    D. Peer evaluation

    ANSWER: B, 391

42. Multisource, or _____, recognizes that the manager is no longer the sole source of performance appraisal information.
    A. team appraisal
    B. outside raters
    C. peer evaluation
    D. 360° rating

    ANSWER: D, 391

43. In which appraisal method is feedback obtained from various colleagues and constituencies and given to the manager?
    A. 360° appraisal
    B. supervisors rating their employees
    C. team members rating each other
    D. comprehensive appraisal

    ANSWER: A, 391

44. The 360° rating method appears to be more appropriate, and less threatening, for
    A. employee evaluation purposes.
    B. top management appraisal.
    C. development uses.
    D. the appraisal of mid-level managers.

    ANSWER: C, 393

45. The simplest methods for appraising performance are the
    A. behaviorally anchored rating scales (BARS).
    B. category rating methods.
    C. comparative methods.
    D. written methods.

    ANSWER: B, 393

46. The _____ allows the rater to mark an employee's performance on a continuum.
    A. ranking system
    B. checklist
    C. forced distribution
    D. graphic rating scale

    ANSWER: D, 393

47. Which of the following are characteristics of graphic rating scales?
    A. Descriptive words used may have different meanings to different people.
    B. Interrater reliability is high.
    C. Raters are forced to choose among several statements to describe an employee's performance.
    D. The descriptors can be modified to assign various weights to ratings.

    ANSWER: A, 394

48. Which performance appraisal method consists of listing all employees from highest to lowest in performance?
    A. checklist
    B. graphic rating scale
    C. ranking
    D. forced distribution

    ANSWER: C, 394

49. The forced distribution method of appraisal assumes that
    A. supervisors understand the theory of individual differences.
    B. the "bell-shaped curve" of performance exists in a given group.
    C. supervisors can make the necessary distinctions in their group.
    D. it is possible to compare each employee with each other employee in the group.

    ANSWER: B, 396

50. In the _____ method, the manager keeps a written record of both highly favorable and unfavorable actions in an employee's performance.
    A. checklist
    B. paired comparisons
    C. essay
    D. critical incident

    ANSWER: D, 397

51. In a(n) _____, an outsider interviews the manager about each employee's performance, then compiles the notes from each interview into a rating for each employee.
    A. field review
    B. external audit
    C. critical incident appraisal
    D. essay appraisal

    ANSWER: A, 397

Chapter 12

52. Attempting to assess an employee's behaviors instead of other characteristics is the purpose of
    A. critical incident techniques.
    B. a management by objectives system.
    C. behavioral rating approaches.
    D. job dimension methods.

    ANSWER: C, 397

53. What is the first step in constructing behavioral scales?
    A. determining a "standard of excellence" for each job dimension
    B. identifying the most important performance factors in an employee's job description
    C. assessing the performance of the current job holder(s)
    D. specifying the performance goals that each employee hopes to attain within an appropriate period of time

    ANSWER: B, 398

54. _____ specifies the performance goals that an individual hopes to attain within an appropriate length of time.
    A. Behavioral rating scales
    B. Strategic performance management
    C. The critical incident technique (CIT)
    D. Management by objectives (MBO)

    ANSWER: D, 399

55. Which of the following is a key assumption underlying Management by objectives?
    A. If what an employee is involved in planning and setting the objectives and determining the measure, a higher level of commitment and performance may result.
    B. If supervisors set clearly defined objectives, employees are motivated to increased levels of effort.
    C. Employees do better when they don't deviate from clear and precise goals.
    D. There should be an emphasis on penalties associated with not meeting goals.

    ANSWER: A, 399

56. The _____ occurs when a rater gives greater weight to recent events when appraising an individual's performance.
    A. contrast error
    B. halo error
    C. recency effect
    D. primacy effect

    ANSWER: C, 402

57. A _____ is committed when an appraiser rates all employees within a narrow range (usually the middle or average).
    A. contrast error
    B. central tendency error
    C. generalization error
    D. leniency error

    ANSWER: B, 402

58. The halo effect occurs when a manager
    A. lets his or her values and prejudices distort the rating.
    B. rates all subordinates in a narrow band in the middle of the rating scale.
    C. gives greater weight to recent occurrences when appraising performance.
    D. rates an employee high or low on all items because of one characteristic.

    ANSWER: D, 404

59. The "tendency to rate people relative to other people rather than to performance standards" is the definition of _____ error.
    A. contrast
    B. generalization
    C. halo
    D. central tendency

    ANSWER: A, 404

60. Which of the following was identified as an organizational tendency that diminishes the value of many appraisal systems?
    A. minimizing the time spent on discussing the results
    B. permitting HR personnel to revise forms based on AAP concerns
    C. distilling performance appraisals into a single number that can be used to support pay raises
    D. not allowing employees to participate in designing the appraisal forms

    ANSWER: C, 408

True and False

61. The primary purpose of a performance management system is to evaluate employee performance for administrative decision making.

    ANSWER: False, 380
    The purpose of a performance management system is broader than evaluation. It is also concerned with encouraging, improving, and rewarding performance.

62. Many court decisions have held that performance evaluations based on traits are too vague to use as the basis for performance-based HR decisions.

    ANSWER: True, 381

63. Subjective measures of performance tend to be more narrowly focused than objective measures. This may lead to the subjective measures being inadequately defined.

    ANSWER: False, 382
    Subjective measures are judgmental and thus more difficult to measure directly. However objective measures are limited to what can be directly counted and so tend to be narrowly defined.

64. Realistic, measurable, clearly understood performance standards benefit both the organization and the employees.

    ANSWER: True, 382-383

65. The two roles of performance appraisal, administrative decision making and development, are seen as generally complimentary.

    ANSWER: False, 384
    The two roles are in potential conflict. Evaluations leading to compensation, promotion, or layoff decisions, for example, may conflict with the counselor role of the manager.

66. A systematic appraisal is used when the contact between manager and employee is formal and a system is in place to report managerial impressions and observations on employee performance.

    ANSWER: True, 387

67. It is argued that the timing of performance appraisals and pay discussions should be different because managers may manipulate pay adjustments to justify performance ratings.

    ANSWER: False, 388
    The major reason for separating performance appraisals from pay discussions is so that the focus will be on improvement rather than the pay amount. There is the danger that managers may manipulate the ratings to justify the pay decision.

68. The most common method of performance appraisal involves employees being evaluated by their immediate supervisors.

    ANSWER: True, 388

69. One advantage of having supervisors and managers rated by their employees is that this type of rating program can help make the managers more responsive to employees.

    ANSWER: True, 390

70. Peer ratings are best used for administrative purposes, such as determining equitable pay increases, rather than for developmental purposes.

    ANSWER: False, 390
    Peer ratings are useful for development when supervisors do not have the opportunity to closely observe each team member's performance.

71. Self-appraisal is essentially a self-development tool that forces employees to think about their strengths and weaknesses and set goals for improvement.

    ANSWER: True, 391

72. The purpose of multisource or 360° feedback is to obtain reliable assessments of an employee's performance from a variety of sources.

    ANSWER: False, 392
    The purpose is not to increase reliability by soliciting like-minded views, rather it is to capture all of the differing evaluations that bear on the employee's different roles.

73. A graphic rating scale is an example of the category rating method.

    ANSWER: True, 393

74. The forced distribution method of performance appraisal lists all employees from highest to lowest in performance.

    ANSWER: False, 396
    The ranking method consists of listing all employees from highest to lowest.

75. The forced distribution method of appraisal assumes that the widely known bell-shaped curve of performance exists in a given group.

    ANSWER: True, 396

76. In the behavioral rating approaches to performance appraisal, the manager keeps a record of both favorable and unfavorable actions in an employee's performance.

    ANSWER: False, 397
    The behavioral approach assesses an employee's behaviors instead of other characteristics.

77. Management by objectives evaluates managers by the extent to which they have achieved organizational objectives.

    ANSWER: False, 399
    MBO specifies the goals that an individual hopes to attain within an appropriate length of time. Although these goals are derived from the overall goals of the organization, employees are appraised by the extent to which they meet their individual goals.

78. The recency effect occurs when a rater gives greater weight to recent events when appraising an individual's performance.

    ANSWER: True, 402

79. The Uniform Guidelines issued by the EEOC require that performance appraisals be job related and nondiscriminatory.

    ANSWER: True, 407

80. The overall aim of an effective system is to distill performance appraisal into a single number that can be used to support pay raises and other administrative decisions.

    ANSWER: False, 408
    A system that is focused on pay raises fails to fulfil the developmental role of performance management. They are too simplistic to give employees useful feedback or help managers pinpoint training and development needs.

Essay

81. Describe the role of performance appraisal in administrative decision making. What is the possible impact of poorly conducted appraisals?

    ANSWER: 384-385
    Performance appraisal is a process of evaluating how well employees perform their jobs. One purpose is for rewarding or otherwise making administrative decisions about employees. These include compensation, promotion, dismissal, downsizing, and layoff decisions. In the absence of good performance appraisal, ineffective, unfair, and possibly unlawful decisions may be made.

82. Describe the role of performance appraisal in the development of employees. What appraisal methods are appropriate for this role?

    ANSWER: 385-386, 397-401
    In the role of development, the manager operates as a counselor, not a judge. The emphasis is on identifying potential, and planning the employee's growth opportunities and direction. Development uses include identifying strengths, identifying areas for growth, developmental planning, and coaching and career planning. Appraisal methods useful for development include behavioral rating approaches and management by objectives.

83. What is multisource appraisal? Why are some organizations using this approach to performance appraisal?

    ANSWER: 391-393
    Multisource or 360° rating recognizes that the manager is not the sole source of performance appraisal information. Feedback is obtained from various colleagues and constituencies and given to the manager. It is primarily useful for development purposes.

84. Describe the possible sources of error in the performance appraisal process.

    ANSWER: 402-404
    Problems of varying standards occur when there are ambiguous criteria and subjective weightings. Recency effect occurs when greater weight is placed on recent events. Central tendency, leniency, and strictness errors occur when a manager rates all employees within a narrow range - at either extreme or at the middle of the range. Rater bias occurs when a rater's values or prejudices distort the rating. The halo effect occurs when a person is rated high or low on all items because of just one characteristic. The contrast error is the tendency to rate people relative to other people rather than to performance standards.

85. Discuss the characteristics of a legal appraisal system.

    ANSWER: 407
    The Uniform Guidelines issued by the EEOC and other federal enforcement agencies make it clear that performance appraisal must be job related and nondiscriminatory. Court decisions have in effect stated that the appraisal system must be based on job analysis, have evidence of validity, limit managerial discretion, and not have disparate impact.

Chapter 13

Compensation Strategies and Practices

Multiple Choice

1. Compensation is fundamentally about balancing human resource costs with
    A. the responsibility to meet employee needs.
    B. the ability to attract, retain, and reward employees.
    C. rewarding employees for outstanding performance.
    D. allocating scarce organizational resources.

    ANSWER: B, 416

2. Which of the following would be an example of an intrinsic reward?
    A. an additional vacation day as a reward for completing a special project
    B. additional medical insurance coverage
    C. country club memberships
    D. praise from a supervisor for completing a special project

    ANSWER: D, 416

3. Medical insurance, paid by the employer, is classified as _____ compensation.
    A. indirect
    B. direct
    C. variable
    D. intrinsic

    ANSWER: A, 416

4. Which of the following is identified as the basic compensation an employees receives?
    A. incentive
    B. benefits
    C. base pay
    D. motivator

    ANSWER: C, 416

174 Chapter 13

5. _____ are payments directly calculated on the amount of time worked.
   A. Salaries
   B. Wages
   C. Incentives
   D. Bonuses

   ANSWER: B, 416

6. People who are paid _____ receive payments that are consistent from period to period despite the number of hours worked.
   A. compensation
   B. base pay
   C. wages
   D. salaries

   ANSWER: D, 416

7. Which type of compensation is linked directly to performance accomplishments?
   A. variable pay
   B. motivators
   C. wages
   D. salary

   ANSWER: A, 417

8. A(n) _____ is an indirect reward given to an employee or a group of employees as a part of organizational membership.
   A. incentive
   B. perk
   C. benefit
   D. motivator

   ANSWER: C, 417

9. In a typical division of compensation responsibilities, the HR unit would be responsible for
   A. attempting to match performance with rewards.
   B. conducting job evaluations.
   C. recommending pay rates and pay increases.
   D. monitoring attendance and productivity for compensation purposes.

   ANSWER: B, 417

10. In a typical division of compensation responsibilities, operating managers
    A. develop and administer the compensation system.
    B. conduct wage surveys.
    C. develop wage and salary structures and policies..
    D. evaluate employee performance for compensation purposes.

    ANSWER: D, 417

11. In a division of compensation responsibilities, _____ typically conduct(s) job evaluations and wage surveys.
    A. HR specialists
    B. operating managers
    C. senior management
    D. outside consultants

    ANSWER: A, 417

12. Because so many organizational funds are spent on compensation-related activities, it is crucial for top management to
    A. conform to affirmative action guidelines.
    B. reexamine their compensation strategies annually.
    C. view the strategic fit of compensation with the strategies and objectives of the organization.
    D. ensure that compensation is tied directly to organizational, unit and individual performance.

    ANSWER: C, 418

13. Which of the following would be a recommended compensation practice for a new organization that wishes to create an innovative, entrepreneurial culture?
    A. offer high starting salaries to attract highly-talented employees
    B. offer bonuses and stock equity programs, and set base pay at modest levels
    C. establish a highly structured pay and benefits program
    D. establish pay levels consistent with the results of a salary survey

    ANSWER: B, 418

14. The two basic compensation philosophies, which should be seen as opposite ends of a continuum, are the _____ and the _____ orientations.
    A. merit; seniority
    B. exempt; non-exempt
    C. time; productivity
    D. entitlement; performance

    ANSWER: D, 418

15. Most employees receive the same or nearly the same percentage increase each year in an organization that has a(n) _____ orientation.
    A. entitlement
    B. "don't-rock-the-boat"
    C. fairness
    D. performance

    ANSWER: A, 418

16. Bonuses are determined very paternalistically in what type of organization?
    A. entrepreneurial
    B. strategic
    C. entitlement-oriented
    D. performance-oriented

    ANSWER: C, 419

Chapter 13

17. In an organization with a performance-oriented philosophy,
    A. employees can at least count on an annual cost-of-living raise.
    B. no one is guaranteed compensation just for adding another year's service.
    C. commissions and piece-rate incentives replace traditional salaries.
    D. fairness concerns dominate compensation decisions.

    ANSWER: B, 419

18. Which of the following would be a recommended compensation practice for a large, static organization?
    A. offer stock equity programs, while keeping pay at modest levels
    B. offer high starting salaries to attract highly-talented employees
    C. establish pay levels consistent with the results of a salary survey
    D. establish a highly structured pay and benefits program

    ANSWER: D, 419

19. _____ organizations are more likely to reward current performance and growth.
    A. Dynamic, rapidly changing
    B. Traditional, family-owned
    C. Merit-based
    D. Union-free

    ANSWER: A, 419

20. Organizations that have specifically stated policies about where they wish to be positioned in the labor market use a
    A. competitive-position strategy.
    B. bench marking strategy.
    C. quartile strategy.
    D. labor market strategy.

    ANSWER: C, 420

21. Employers may choose to use a _____ if there is an abundance of lower-skilled workers.
    A. third-quartile approach
    B. first-quartile approach
    C. competitive-pricing strategy
    D. foreign-worker strategy

    ANSWER: B, 420

22. A third-quartile approach is a(n)
    A. strategy to pay below market compensation.
    B. strategy based on merit.
    C. team-based approach.
    D. aggressive, above-market approach.

    ANSWER: D, 421

23. In skill-based pay systems, employee start at a base level of pay. They receive pay increases
    A. as they learn to do other jobs.
    B. based upon the quality of their production.
    C. based on the number of "pieces" produced.
    D. as they teach other employees how to do their jobs.

    ANSWER: A, 422

24. Which of the following was not listed as an organization-related outcome of a competency-based pay system?
    A. greater workforce flexibility
    B. increased effectiveness of work teams
    C. lower overall labor costs
    D. increased worker output per hour

    ANSWER: C, 423

25. Employee-oriented outcomes of competency-based pay systems include
    A. increased compensation.
    B. enhanced employee understanding of the organizational "big picture."
    C. reduced employee satisfaction.
    D. fewer bottlenecks in the work flow.

    ANSWER: B, 423

26. _____ is the practice of using fewer pay grades having broader ranges than traditional compensation systems.
    A. Scaling
    B. Variable scheduling
    C. Pay openness
    D. Broadbanding

    ANSWER: D, 423

27. Which of the following is a benefit of reducing the number of pay grades and broadening pay ranges?
    A. it is more consistent with the flattening of organizational levels.
    B. it recognizes the unidimensional nature of many of the newly-created jobs.
    C. it enhances the distinctions between various jobs.
    D. it increases the opportunities for upward mobility.

    ANSWER: A, 423

28. _____ is the perceived fairness of the relation between what a person does and what the person receives.
    A. Procedural justice
    B. Compensation satisfaction
    C. Equity
    D. Distributive justice

    ANSWER: C, 426

Chapter 13

29. In a discussion of equity, _____ are what a person brings to the organization, including age, educational level, experience, and productivity.
    A. outputs
    B. inputs
    C. outcomes
    D. judicials

    ANSWER: B, 426

30. Pay, benefits, recognition, achievement. prestige, and any intangible reward are the _____ one receives from a job.
    A. valances
    B. outputs
    C. inputs
    D. outcomes

    ANSWER: D, 426

31. The perceived fairness of the process and procedures used to make decisions about employees, including their pay, is called
    A. procedural justice.
    B. equity.
    C. distributive justice.
    D. supervisory protocol.

    ANSWER: A, 426

32. Two critical issues in determining _____ are how appropriate and fair is the process used to assign jobs to pay grades, and how are the pay ranges for those jobs established.
    A. equitable protocol
    B. supervisory protocol
    C. procedural justice
    D. distributive justice

    ANSWER: C, 426

33. _____ is the perceived fairness of the amounts given for performance.
    A. Procedural justice
    B. Distributive justice
    C. Compensation satisfaction
    D. Reward-performance perceptions

    ANSWER: B, 426

34. A crucial aspect of an open pay system is that
    A. the wages are competitive with the competition.
    B. employees can discuss their wages with each other, promoting positive competition.
    C. it is very easy to understand.
    D. managers be able to explain satisfactorily any pay differences that exist.

    ANSWER: D, 427

35. What is a likely outcome when an organization's compensation is viewed as lacking external equity?
    A. difficulty recruiting qualified and scarce-skilled employees
    B. lower than average turnover
    C. employees discussing their pay with other employees
    D. pressures for secrecy regarding pay and benefits

    ANSWER: A, 427

36. The major law affecting compensation is the
    A. National Compensation Fairness Act.
    B. Equal Pay Act.
    C. Fair Labor Standards Act.
    D. Wagner Act.

    ANSWER: C, 428

37. Which of the following is a major objective of the Fair Labor Standards Act?
    A. give labor unions the right to organize
    B. establish a minimum wage floor
    C. promote safe working conditions
    D. outlaw child labor

    ANSWER: B, 428

38. A lower minimum wage level is set for which of the following employee groups?
    A. minors, that is, children aged between 16 and 18 years
    B. disabled workers
    C. interns working in a cooperative training program
    D. "tipped" employees working in restaurants

    ANSWER: D, 429

39. _____ has been identified as the amount needed for a family of four to be supported by one worker so that the family income is above the officially identified poverty level.
    A. The living wage
    B. The minimum wage
    C. Comparable worth
    D. Pay equity

    ANSWER: A, 429

40. Under FLSA, what is the minimum age for employment, in nonhazardous occupations, with unlimited hours?
    A. 18 years.
    B. 17 years.
    C. 16 years.
    D. 15 years.

    ANSWER: C, 429

180   Chapter 13

41. Which of the following are not paid overtime under the Fair Labor Standards Act?
    A. hourly workers
    B. exempt employees
    C. salaried employees
    D. nonexempt employees

    ANSWER: B, 430

42. Under the FLSA, which of the following would be classified as a nonexempt employee?
    A. an outside sales person
    B. a public school teacher
    C. a supervisor with discretionary authority for independent action
    D. an administrative secretary spending at least 50 percent of the time doing routine clerical work

    ANSWER: D, 431

43. Which of the following is a true statement about the overtime provisions of the FLSA?
    A. Overtime pay is set at one-and-one-half times the regular pay rate for all hours in excess of 40 per week.
    B. All employees are entitled to overtime payments.
    C. The work week is defined as 168 hours beginning at 12:01 Monday morning.
    D. A manufacturing firm with a 4-day/10-hour schedule still must pay overtime for the two hours above 8 each day.

    ANSWER: A, 430

44. Compensatory time-off can be given in the private sector if
    A. the hourly wage is at least one and one-half times the minimum wage.
    B. it is the equivalent of the number of hours worked overtime.
    C. it is given at the rate of one and one-half times the hours worked over a 40 hour week.
    D. it is used up within the next three months by the employee.

    ANSWER: C, 431

45. The criteria for deciding independent contractor status, as identified by the IRS, include all of the following except
    A. can the individual incur a profit or loss, so that some economic risk is involved?
    B. can the individual quit at any time without incurring liability?
    C. does the individual offer the same or similar services to the general public and other firms on a regular basis?
    D. has the individual invested in and does he or she own the facilities and equipment used?

    ANSWER: B, 432

46. The Equal Pay Act amendment to the FLSA prohibits wage discrimination on the basis of
   A. race.
   B. job classification.
   C. seniority.
   D. sex

   ANSWER: D, 433

47. _____ is the concept that the pay for all jobs requiring comparable knowledge, skills, and abilities should be similar even if actual duties and market rates differ significantly.
   A. Pay equity
   B. Wage fairness
   C. Compensatory pay
   D. Socialized return

   ANSWER: A, 433

48. _____ is a court action in which a portion of an employee's wages is set aside to pay a debt owed a creditor.
   A. Alimony
   B. Creditor protection
   C. Garnishment
   D. Debt deduction

   ANSWER: C, 434

49. The purpose of wage and salary administration is to
   A. ensure that the pay checks are ready on time.
   B. provide pay that is both competitive and equitable.
   C. develop performance appraisal systems to provide input for pay increases.
   D. keep accurate records of absenteeism, tardiness, hours work, and vacation entitlement.

   ANSWER: B, 434

50. Organizations that choose to lead the market by paying above-market rates,
   A. usually have a strong union.
   B. are primarily in declining industries.
   C. are subject to investigation for monopolistic practices.
   D. are aided in attracting and retaining employees.

   ANSWER: D, 434

51. What is the effect of unions on a company's pay policy?
   A. Unionized employees generally have higher wage levels than nonunion workers.
   B. Nonunion workers are usually more satisfied with their pay.
   C. There is more flexibility under a contract for wage determination.
   D. There is very little effect, since all companies must remain competitive.

   ANSWER: A, 436

52. In a job evaluation, every job in an organization is examined and ultimately priced according to which of the following features?
    A. the seniority needed to advance to the next level in the hierarchy
    B. the educational qualifications needed for employment
    C. the relative importance of the job
    D. the job's level in the organizational hierarchy

    ANSWER: C, 437

53. A _____ job is one that is found in many organizations and performed by several individuals who have similar duties that are relatively stable and that require similar KSAs.
    A. key
    B. benchmark
    C. comparable
    D. red-circled

    ANSWER: B, 437

54. The major difficulty with the classification method of job evaluation is that
    A. it does not conform to EEO guidelines.
    B. it is not appropriate for large organizations.
    C. it is too cumbersome and statistical in nature that most supervisors do not understand it fully.
    D. subjective judgments are needed to develop the class descriptions and to place jobs accurately in them.

    ANSWER: D, 437

55. When using the point method of job evaluation, a _____ factor is used to identify a job value that is commonly present throughout a group of jobs.
    A. compensable
    B. consideration
    C. value-related
    D. KSA

    ANSWER: A, 438

56. Which of the following is a major drawback to the point method of job evaluation?
    A. It does not consider all components of a job.
    B. It is relatively complex.
    C. It cannot be established quickly.
    D. It can only be used by HR specialists.

    ANSWER: C, 438

Compensation Strategies and Practices

57. When an employer collects data on existing compensation rates for workers performing similar jobs at other organizations, a(n) _____ is being conducted.
    A. equity study
    B. pay survey
    C. compensation study
    D. competitive evaluation

    ANSWER: B, 441

58. Which of the following approaches is recommended for bringing a red-circled employee's pay into line.
    A. Transfer the employee to a lower paying job, while cutting the employee's pay to match the rate for the new job.
    B. Keep pay rates secret.
    C. Cut the employee's pay so it falls within the range.
    D. Freeze the employee's pay until the pay range can be adjusted upward to get the employee's pay rate back into the grade.

    ANSWER: D, 447

59. A person's _____ is that employee's current pay level divided by the midpoint of the pay range.
    A. compa-ratio
    B. average pay rate
    C. mid-grade mark
    D. market price

    ANSWER: A, 448

60. Which of the following is an advantage of a lump-sum increase (LSI) plan?
    A. LSI plans involve less administrative work.
    B. The unions support this concept of merit bonuses.
    C. An LSI plan heightens employees' awareness of what their performance merited.
    D. It increases the compounding effect of succeeding raises.

    ANSWER: C, 450

Chapter 13

True and False

61. Compensation is fundamentally about providing employees with the economic means necessary to meet individual and family living expenses.

    ANSWER: False, 416
    Compensation is an important factor affecting how and why people choose to work at one organization over others. It is concerns hiring, keeping, and rewarding performance of individuals. It is fundamentally about organizational competitiveness, not employee needs.

62. Benefits are indirect rewards given to an employee or a group of employees as a part of organizational membership.

    ANSWER: True, 417

63. In a typical division of compensation responsibilities, the HR unit is responsible for matching performance and rewards.

    ANSWER: False, 418
    Operating managers are responsible for matching performance and rewards.

64. An organization that follows an entitlement philosophy to compensation will find that, as employees continue their employment lives, the organization's costs will increase, regardless of employee performance.

    ANSWER: True, 419

65. Surveys have shown that most organizations are totally performance-oriented in all facets of their compensation practices.

    ANSWER: False, 419
    In fact, very few organizations are totally performance-oriented in their compensation practices. The entitlement philosophy is dominant with regards to benefits, bonuses, cost-of-living adjustments, and union negotiations.

66. A competency-based pay system rewards employees who are more versatile and have continued to develop their skills.

    ANSWER: True, 421

67. Broadbanding is most appropriate in a traditional, hierarchial organization where the managers have been conditioned to expect a broad range of benefits and pay grades.

    ANSWER: False, 424
    Broadbanding is the practice of using fewer pay grades having broader ranges than traditional compensation systems. Structured, traditional, hierarchial organizations lack the flexibility associated with broadbanding.

Compensation Strategies and Practices

68. Compensation practices are simplified as organizations shift to using work teams, because everyone on a team is paid the same amount.

    ANSWER: False, 425
    Just the opposite - paying everyone on teams the same amount, even though there are differing competencies and levels of performance, creates equity concerns for individual members.

69. Distributive justice refers to the perceived fairness of the amounts given for performance.

    ANSWER: True, 426

70. An increasing number of organizations are keeping pay information secret, thus avoiding disputes about paycheck fairness.

    ANSWER: False, 427
    A growing number of organizations are opening up their pay systems allowing employees to make more accurate equity comparisons. Closed systems create tensions as employees speculate about other employees' pay.

71. The Fair Labor Standards Act sets minimum wage standards and hours of work for all employees.

    ANSWER: False, 429-430
    The FLSA set minimum wage and overtime provisions for hourly and nonexempt employees. Salaried-exempt employees are not required to be paid the minimum wage and overtime.

72. The work week, as defined by the FLSA for overtime purposes, does not have to be a calendar week.

    ANSWER: True, 430

73. The Equal Pay Act of 1963 was passed to achieve pay equity..

    ANSWER: False, 433
    The Equal Pay Act addresses equal pay for equal work, not equitable pay for comparable work.

74. Federal law requires that the pay for all jobs requiring comparable knowledge, skills, and abilities should be similar, even if actual duties and market rates differ significantly.

    ANSWER: False, 433
    There is no federal law requiring pay equity, (also known as comparable worth.) Some states have laws requiring pay equity for public-sector jobs.

75. Job evaluation provides a systematic basis for determining the relative worth of jobs within an organization.

    ANSWER: True, 437

76. The point method of job evaluation is popular because it is a relatively simple system to use.

ANSWER: True, 438

77. Employers often use outside consultants to conduct pay surveys to avoid charges that the employers are attempting "price fixing" on wages.

ANSWER: True, 443

78. A green-circled employee is an incumbent who is paid above the range set for the job.

ANSWER: False, 447
A green-circled employee is paid below the range. Red-circles employees are paid above the range set for the job

79. Pay compression occurs when the range of pay differences among individuals with different levels of experience and performance in the organization become small.

ANSWER: True, 447

80. A maturity curve depicts the relationship between experience and pay rates.

ANSWER: True, 450

Essay

81. Discuss the different roles of base pay, variable pay, and benefits in a compensation package, illustrating the effect of each on employee behavior.

ANSWER: 416-418
Base pay, either wages or salaries, is based on the job or position held. Competitive rates impact hiring and retention. Variable pay, usually bonuses, incentives, or stock options, reward above-expectation performance. Benefits, including medical insurance, paid time off, and retirement pensions, are given as a part of organizational membership.

82. Is equity an important consideration on compensation? What is meant by equity?

ANSWER: 426-428
Equity is the perceived fairness of the relation between a person's inputs and outcomes. Inputs are what a person brings to the job including education, skills, experience, and productivity. Outcomes are what the person receives from the organization, including pay, benefits, and recognition. A sense of inequity occurs when there is a perceived imbalance between inputs and outcomes. Comparisons are made both within the organization and externally. Procedural and distributive justice contribute to the perceptions of equity.

Compensation Strategies and Practices 187

83. Would you recommend that an employer require that all salary information be kept confidential? Why or why not? What would be the impact of a secret pay system?

    ANSWER: 426-428
    Organizations sometimes choose to keep pay information secret in "closed" systems. This information includes how much people make, what raises have been received, and what pay grades and ranges exist in the organization. The rationale is often to hide any potential inequities. A growing number of organizations are opening up their pay systems to allow employees to make more accurate equity comparisons. Procedural and distributive justice require the system to be open.

84. What was the purpose of the Fair Labor Standards Act (FLSA) of 1938? Is it relevant to today's workforce?

    ANSWER: 428-432
    The FLSA has three major objectives: to establish a minimum wage floor, to discourage oppressive use of child labor, and to encourage limits on the number of weekly hours employees work through overtime provisions. Employees are classified as either exempt or nonexempt. Nonexempt employees must be paid overtime. The FLSA was passed when the majority of workers were males employed in manufacturing jobs. The Equal Pay Act of 1963 prohibits discrimination in compensation based on sex. The increasing numbers of computer-related jobs and independent contractors have led to some changes in the act. The concept of a "living wage" is being debated as an alternate to the minimum wage.

85. Why do organizations conduct job evaluations. Discuss four methods of performing a job evaluation.

    ANSWER: 437-440
    Job evaluation provides a systematic basis for determining the relative worth of jobs in an organization. Every job in the organization is examined according to the relative importance of the job, the KSAs needed to perform the job, and the difficulty of the job. Job evaluations are used to determine internal job worth. Job evaluation methods include ranking, classification, point, and factor comparison.

Chapter 14

Variable Pay and Executive Compensation

Multiple Choice

1. What is variable pay?
    A. techniques to motivate employees to work harder
    B. additional tangible rewards given to employees for performance beyond normal expectations
    C. psychic satisfaction provided for employees
    D. compensation that reflects the knowledge and skills employees bring to the job

    ANSWER: B, 458

2. "Compensation linked to individual, team, and/or organization performance" is a definition of
    A. compa-pay.
    B. benefits.
    C. executive perquisites.
    D. variable pay.

    ANSWER: D, 458

3. Which of the following is an assumption of variable-pay systems?
    A. Some jobs contribute more to organizational success than others.
    B. Time spent each day is the primary measure of short-term contributions.
    C. Differences in individual contributions to the organization are recognized through different base pay levels.
    D. Length of time with the organization is the primary differentiating factor among people.

    ANSWER: A, 458

4. Pay systems based on seniority or length of service assume that
    A. some jobs contribute more to organizational success than others.
    B. some people perform better than others.
    C. giving additional performance rewards to some people but not to others is divisive and hampers employees working together.
    D. people should be compensated for above average skill and experience.

    ANSWER: C, 458

190 Chapter 14

5. A feature of variable pay plans is that _____ do not increase the degree of cooperation among individuals.
    A.   benefit programs
    B.   individual incentives
    C.   ESOP plans
    D.   organizational incentives

    ANSWER: B, 459

6. Which of the following is classified as an individual variable pay plan?
    A.   gainsharing
    B.   labor-cost reduction
    C.   employee stock options
    D.   attendance bonuses

    ANSWER: D, 460

7. _____ is a type of organization-wide variable pay plan.
    A.   Profit sharing
    B.   Bonuses
    C.   Quality improvement
    D.   Gainsharing

    ANSWER: A, 460

8. Which type of plan works best when productivity is being directly measured and employees are not encouraged to cooperate with one another?
    A.   group
    B.   organizational
    C.   individual
    D.   societal

    ANSWER: C, 459

9. When an entire work group or team is rewarded for its performance,
    A.   the performance of the entire organization improves.
    B.   more cooperation among the members is required and usually forthcoming.
    C.   employees may withhold information from others and focus only on what is rewarded.
    D.   individual and team competition is reduced and all employees working together can generate financial gain.

    ANSWER: B, 459

10. What is the purpose of organizational incentives?
    A.   to sabotage efforts of competitor organizations
    B.   to aid in recruiting high-potential employees
    C.   to distribute fairly the excess profits of the organization
    D.   to reward people for the performance of the entire organization

    ANSWER: D, 459

11. An important factor in the success of any variable pay program is that
    A. it be consistent with both the culture and the financial resources of the organization.
    B. the employees want to participate.
    C. all jobs are well defined in terms of the procedures used.
    D. participation is throughout the organization.

    ANSWER: A, 461

12. Any incentive system requires an organizational climate of _____ between employees and managers.
    A. competition
    B. separation and demarcation
    C. trust and cooperation
    D. positive conflict

    ANSWER: C, 462

13. It is important to make sure that what is being rewarded ties to organizational objectives, because people tend to
    A. guess what they think management wants done.
    B. produce what is measured and rewarded.
    C. produce what is convenient.
    D. avoid doing unpleasant tasks.

    ANSWER: B, 462

14. Which of the following was identified as a problem that may limit the effectiveness of variable pay plans?
    A. organizations pay too much because performance isn't measured
    B. the wrong people get the rewards
    C. Theory X management style
    D. informal group pressures and sanctions

    ANSWER: D, 463

15. Successful variable pay plans, that clearly identify how much the variable pay plan provides to employees,
    A. separate the incentive payment from base salary.
    B. factor in an employee's seniority.
    C. provide everyone in the organization with regular bonuses.
    D. pay a large bonus at the end of the year when employees most need it.

    ANSWER: A, 463

16. Under the _____ system, wages are determined by multiplying the amount of units produced by the piece rate for one unit.
    A. Scanlon
    B. differential piece-rate
    C. straight piece-rate
    D. production commission

    ANSWER: C, 463

17. A differential piece-rate system pays employees
    A. one piece-rate wage for standard production, less if producing below quota.
    B. one piece-rate wage for units produced up to a standard output and a higher piece-rate wage for units produced over the standard.
    C. a higher rate per piece for employees with more experience and seniority.
    D. differential wages depending on the differing responsibilities in the production of each unit.

    ANSWER: B, 464

18. Bonuses are less costly than general wage increases, since
    A. they receive preferred tax privileges.
    B. less money can be given while still increasing employee satisfaction.
    C. they provide a bigger motivational "bang for the buck."
    D. they do not become part of employees' base wages.

    ANSWER: D, 464-465

19. A bonus recognizes performance by both the employee and
    A. the company.
    B. the economy.
    C. the work group.
    D. the team.

    ANSWER: A, 465

20. Special incentive programs that provide awards to individuals,
    A. are most popular in production line situations.
    B. seem to work best in the middle management ranks.
    C. focus on rewarding only high-performing individuals.
    D. reach out to give special thanks to the entire organization.

    ANSWER: C, 466

21. A _____ approach is useful when serving and retaining existing accounts is emphasized more than generating new sales and accounts.
    A. straight commission
    B. salary only
    C. salary plus commission
    D. salary draw

    ANSWER: B, 468

22. When an employee receives no compensation until a sale is totally completed, the compensation system is called
    A. lump sum.
    B. sales payoff.
    C. deferred salary.
    D. straight commission.

    ANSWER: D, 470

Variable Pay and Executive Compensation   193

23. A "draw" is
    A. an amount advanced to an employee and repaid from future commissions.
    B. a special incentive program used widely in sales-related jobs.
    C. a term to represent salary-plus-commission.
    D. a lump-sum payment or bonus at the end of the month.

    ANSWER: A, 470

24. The most frequently used form of sales compensation is the
    A. draw.
    B. straight commission.
    C. salary plus commission.
    D. differential commission.

    ANSWER: C, 470

25. Which of the following characteristics is true about team-based incentives?
    A. Union leaders are usually supportive of the concept.
    B. The presence of one or two poor performers can result in the group being denied an incentive payment.
    C. All groups are encouraged to work towards the organizational goals.
    D. There is no evidence that group incentives improve organizational productivity.

    ANSWER: B, 473

26. Group incentives work best when certain criteria are present. These include:
    A. significant independence exists among the work of the individual team members.
    B. management wants to reinforce individual responsibility for the performance outcomes.
    C. overall efficiency depends on plant-wide cooperation.
    D. difficulties exist in identifying exactly who is responsible for differing levels of performance.

    ANSWER: D, 473

27. _____ is defined as "the sharing with employees of greater-than-expected gains in profits and/or productivity."
    A. Gainsharing
    B. The Rucker Plan
    C. Profit sharing
    D. ESOP

    ANSWER: A, 474

28. The most crucial step when beginning a gainsharing plan is to
    A. calculate the value added formula.
    B. determine the "standard" cost of production.
    C. involve employees at all levels in the process.
    D. get the support of top management.

    ANSWER: C, 474

29. There are two crucial decisions that must be made by the gainsharing task force. These are: How much gain is to be shared with employees? and
    A. How is the "gain" to be divided up among the employees?
    B. What are the performance measures to be used?
    C. What are the minimum standards to be met?
    D. What action(s) should be taken if gains are less than expected?

    ANSWER: B, 474

30. What is an Improshare program?
    A. It is an organizational-wide profit-sharing plan.
    B. It is a group-incentive plan.
    C. It is similar to the Scanlon Plan in that cost savings are rewarded.
    D. It is similar to a piece-rate plan except that it rewards all workers in the organization.

    ANSWER: D, 475

31. In a(n) _____ plan, a standard is calculated and weekly bonuses are paid based on the extent to which the standard is exceeded.
    A. Improshare
    B. organizational-wide profit-sharing
    C. Rucker
    D. Scanlon

    ANSWER: A, 475

32. In which of the following types of organizations has the Scanlon Plan been implemented most often?
    A. large multinational organizations
    B. small family owned businesses
    C. smaller unionized industrial firms
    D. Large union-free organizations

    ANSWER: C, 475

33. The basic concept underlying the Scanlon plan is that
    A. individuals can be motivated through money.
    B. efficiency depends on teamwork and plant-wide cooperation.
    C. small teams can work more effectively than entire departments.
    D. workers want to be "owners."

    ANSWER: B, 475

34. In the Scanlon Plan, incentive rewards are paid to employees on the basis of
    A. increased production.
    B. increases in sales.
    C. profitability.
    D. improvements in pre-established ratios.

    ANSWER: D, 475

Variable Pay and Executive Compensation

35. Which of the following statements best describes the Scanlon Plan?
    A. Employees receive incentive compensation for reducing labor costs.
    B. It is an organization-wide profit sharing plan.
    C. Team members each receive identical reward based on the team's productivity.
    D. Employees receive incentive payments for exceeding predetermined levels of production.

    ANSWER: A, 475

36. The Rucker plan uses a _____ variable to establish an incentive.
    A. cost-of-raw-materials
    B. cost-efficiency
    C. value-added
    D. labor-overhead

    ANSWER: C, 476

37. A(n) _____ distributes a portion of the profits of the organization to employees.
    A. team-based incentive plan
    B. profit sharing plan
    C. gainsharing plan
    D. employee stock ownership plan (ESOP)

    ANSWER: B, 476

38. For a profit-sharing plan to be effective, management must
    A. increase innovative solutions to technical problems.
    B. recruit employees who are motivated primarily by money.
    C. stabilize profits so that the annual payoff is consistent.
    D. be willing to disclose financial and profit information to employees.

    ANSWER: D, 476-477

39. A(n) _____ is a plan whereby employees gain stock ownership in the organization for which they work.
    A. employee stock ownership plan
    B. employee shareholder plan
    C. shareholder bonus plan
    D. scanlon stock bonus plan

    ANSWER: A, 477

40. An organization establishes an ESOP by
    A. deducting a small amount from each employee's pay for the purchase of stock.
    B. providing upper management with a special bonus.
    C. using its stock as collateral to borrow capital from a financial institution.
    D. having its profits distributed with favorable tax treatment.

    ANSWER: C, 477

196 Chapter 14

41. Which of the following statements about ESOPs is false?
   A. The firm can receive favorable tax treatment of the earnings earmarked for use in the ESOP.
   B. Many employees opt-out of being involved in the company's ESOP.
   C. Employees are motivated to work harder because they have a "piece of the action."
   D. Employees place their financial future at greater risk.

   ANSWER: B, 477

42. New rules on ESOPs by the Financial Accounting Standards Board (FASB) require companies to
   A. list the stock transfers as an expense.
   B. first seek approval from the IRS before any future stock transfers are made.
   C. report the value of the stock options as income to the individual employees.
   D. report the value of the stock options they give employees.

   ANSWER: D, 478

43. An executive typically is defined as someone
   A. in the top two levels of an organization.
   B. earning more than $250,000 a year.
   C. whose salary puts them in the top quartile of the organization.
   D. in the top two positions in each of the functional areas.

   ANSWER: A, 478

44. "Ensuring that the total compensation packages for executives are competitive with compensation packages in other firms that might employ them" is one of the objectives of
   A. members of boards of directors.
   B. HR compensation committees.
   C. executive compensation.
   D. benefit administration.

   ANSWER: C, 478

45. Which of the following is an objective that influences executive compensation?
   A. Ensure that the total executive compensation package is attractive to potential management personnel.
   B. Tie the overall performance of the organization over a period of time to the compensation that is paid to executives.
   C. Minimize the total income tax liability.
   D. Promote loyalty among the executives to minimize the probability of executive attrition.

   ANSWER: B, 478

46. At the heart of most executive compensation plans is the idea that
    A. executives should be rewarded for their current performance.
    B. outstanding executives are hard to keep unless they are well compensated.
    C. base pay is not as important as the other benefits and perks.
    D. executives should be rewarded if the organization grows in profitability and value over a period of years.

    ANSWER: D, 478-479

47. On average, salaries make up about _____ of the typical top executive's annual compensation total.
    A. 40-60 percent
    B. 20 percent
    C. two-thirds
    D. ninety percent

    ANSWER: A, 479

48. A provision of the 1993 tax act prohibits a publicly traded company from
    A. providing special non-taxable benefits for the top executives.
    B. offering compensation to executives that defers income tax liability.
    C. deducting pay of more than $1 million for each of its top five officers unless that pay is based on performance criteria approved by outside directors and shareholders.
    D. deducting that portion of an executive's compensation that is more than ten times the compensation of the lowest paid full-time employee.

    ANSWER: C, 479

49. To be meaningful, annual bonus compensation must
    A. be competitive with what executives at similar firms receive.
    B. reflect some kind of performance measure.
    C. be awarded to all employees at the firm.
    D. reflect the employee's level of seniority in the firm.

    ANSWER: B, 479

50. Some organizations award executive bonuses based on subjective judgments of the CEO and the board of directors. Which statement best describes this approach?
    A. The executive is aware of the discretionary reasons for the bonus.
    B. A discretionary system permits the board to account for non-controllables.
    C. It is not always possible to have objective measures of performance.
    D. The absence of formal, measurable targets is a major drawback.

    ANSWER: D, 479

51. A(n) _____ is a plan that gives an individual the right to buy stock in a company, usually at a fixed price for a period of time.
    A. stock option
    B. appreciation right
    C. price discretion
    D. investment bonus

    ANSWER: A, 479

Chapter 14

52. Which of the following is used to emphasize the long-term growth and success of the organization?
    A. executive perquisites
    B. executive bonus plans
    C. stock options
    D. golden parachutes

    ANSWER: C, 479

53. What type of organizations grant "stock equivalences" to its executives?
    A. public sector organizations
    B. closely-held firms
    C. non-profit corporations
    D. publicly traded corporations

    ANSWER: B, 479

54. Where stock is closely held, firms may grant _____ to its executives.
    A. ownership options
    B. stock options
    C. family participation rights
    D. phantom stock

    ANSWER: D, 479

55. Why do some organizations offer deferred compensation to executives?
    A. to help executives with tax liabilities caused by incentive plans
    B. to emphasize long-term performance of the organization
    C. to place "golden handcuffs" on key executives
    D. to hide excessive one-time bonuses earned by executives

    ANSWER: A, 480

56. _____ are special benefits for executives that are usually noncash items.
    A. Stock options
    B. Enhanced benefits packages
    C. Perquisites
    D. Golden handcuffs

    ANSWER: C, 480

57. What is the usual composition of the compensation committee?
    A. a subgroup of the board of directors including officers of the firm
    B. a subgroup of the board of directors who are not officers of the firm
    C. executives from other companies
    D. compensation consultants without executive management involvement

    ANSWER: B, 480

Variable Pay and Executive Compensation

58. What is the role of a compensation committee?
    A. Assist the HR unit is developing overall pay and benefit programs for the organization.
    B. Develop a compensation package that ties overall compensation to performance.
    C. Make recommendations to the shareholders on the compensation formula for members of the board of directors.
    D. Make recommendations to the board of directors on overall pay policies, salaries for top officers, bonuses, and additional perks for executives.

    ANSWER: D, 480

59. Golden parachutes provide executives with
    A. protection and security in the event that they lose their jobs.
    B. special retirement packages, available only if the executives do not leave the firm before a specified date.
    C. a package of additional perks that is considered very generous.
    D. larger than usual bonus percentages against company profits.

    ANSWER: A, 484

60. A silver parachute is a severance and benefit plan to protect
    A. principal stock holders if the firm is sold.
    B. executives, but only from hostile takeovers.
    C. non-executives if their firms are acquired by other firms.
    D. unionized personnel from lay-offs.

    ANSWER: C, 484

True and False

61. The role of variable pay is to link bonuses with performance.

    ANSWER: False, 458
    Variable pay plans are attempts to tie additional rewards to performance beyond normal expectations.

62. Variable pay plans may be very successful if doing the job requires a great deal of cooperation among employees.

    ANSWER: False, 459
    Individual incentives decrease the degree of cooperation in teams.

63. When an entire work group or team is rewarded for its performance, more cooperation among the members is required and usually forthcoming.

    ANSWER: True, 459

Chapter 14

64. As the subjectivity of the criteria used for determining rewards becomes greater, the likelihood of a successful incentive program increases.

    ANSWER: False, 462
    Effective variable pay plans give employees clear information on how employees' performance will be evaluated.

65. People tend to produce what is measured and rewarded.

    ANSWER: True, 462

66. It is not always appropriate to link pay to performance.

    ANSWER: True, 463

67. Informal group pressure and sanctions commonly are used to restrict the amount that individuals produce, even if individual pay is reduced as a result.

    ANSWER: True, 463

68. Incentive payments should be paid as part of the individual's base salary.

    ANSWER: False, 463
    Successful variable pay plans clearly identify how much the variable plan provides to employees separate from their base amounts.

69. Piece-rate systems are not an appropriate when quality concerns are important.

    ANSWER: True, 464

70. Bonuses, as individual incentive compensation, are becoming less common because they increase an organization's overall payroll costs.

    ANSWER: False, 464-465
    Bonuses are increasing in popularity because they do not become part of the employees' base wages. They are less costly to employers than pay increases.

71. Many companies have introduced team-based incentives, finding that teams are eager to handle pay decisions for coworkers.

    ANSWER: False, 472
    Companies have found that in most cases team members are unwilling to make pay decisions about coworkers.

72. Unlike other organizational incentive plans, gainsharing is not dependent on the culture of the organization.

    ANSWER: False, 475
    The success or failure of all incentive programs begins with the culture of the organization.

73. Improshare is a piece-rate plan that rewards all workers in the organization.

    ANSWER: True, 475

74. The Scanlon plan is not a true profit-sharing plan, because employees receive incentive compensation for reducing labor costs, regardless of whether the organization ultimately makes a profit.

    ANSWER: True, 475

75. Organized labor continues to oppose profit-sharing plans in which employees' pay increases are tied to improved company performance.

    ANSWER: False, 476
    In recent years, unions have supported profit-sharing plans in which employees' pay increases are tied to improved company performance.

76. For profit sharing to work, management must be willing to disclose financial and profit information to the employees.

    ANSWER: True, 476-477

77. The primary objective of executive compensation plans is to minimize the tax consequences for the executive.

    ANSWER: False, 478
    The two objectives of executive compensation are to ensure that total compensation packages of executives are competitive with that of other firms, and to tie the overall performance of the organization to the compensation paid.

78. A provision of the 1993 tax act prohibits a publicly traded company from deducting that portion of an executive's pay that exceeds $1 million.

    ANSWER: False, 479
    The $1 million limit only applies if the pay is not based on performance criteria approved by outside directors and shareholders.

79. Perquisites offer substantial tax savings because many perks are not taxed as income.

    ANSWER: True, 480

80. Golden parachutes are typically included in employment contracts to give special compensation to executives if they are negatively affected in an acquisition or merger.

    ANSWER: True, 484

Essay

81. Contrast variable pay plans with a system based on seniority or length of service?

    ANSWER: 458
    Variable pay is additional compensation linked to individual, team, and/or organizational performance. These plans recognize that some jobs contribute more to organizational success than others, and that some people perform better than others. Systems based on seniority or length of service differentiate among people based on time spent each day and length of service, recognizing that it is not always possible to differentiate individual contributions.

82. Not all variable pay plans are successful. What conditions must be met for establishing a successful variable pay plan?

    ANSWER: 460-463
    Be consistent with organizational culture, resources, and objectives, make plans understandable, keep plans current, tie variable pay to desired performance, recognize individual differences, and separate variable pay from base pay.

83. Describe the various methods of compensating sales and marketing employees.

    ANSWER: 467-470
    Compensation paid to sales or marketing employees is partly or entirely tied to sales performance. Plans include salary only, straight commission, draw system, salary plus commission or bonuses. Each plan has different motivating potential.

84. Describe gainsharing and profit-sharing as organizational incentive systems. Discuss the impact of each system in improving performance.

    ANSWER: 474-477
    Gainsharing is the sharing with employees of greater-than-expected gains in profits and/or productivity. Employees are rewarded for doing more than the minimum acceptable level of performance. Profit sharing distributes a portion of organizational profits to employees. Both systems require that employees see the link between better performance and rewards.

85. How does executive compensation differ from the compensation packages provided for other employees in the organization? Describe some of the incentives available for executives.

    ANSWER: 478-485
    At the heart of most executive compensation plans is the idea that executives should be rewarded if the organization grows in profitability and value over a period of years. Executive salaries are often high and attention is paid to tax consequences. Publicly traded companies are prohibited from deducting pay of more than $1 million for top executives unless that pay is based on performance criteria. Executive pay is often set by outside compensation committees. Executive compensation often includes bonuses, stock options, benefits, perquisites, and golden parachutes in addition to salaries.

Chapter 15

Managing Employee Benefits

Multiple Choice

1. Which statement best describes changes in employee benefits during the past decade?
    A. The terms "health and welfare benefits" have been replaced by "fringe benefits."
    B. The terms "health and welfare benefits" and "fringe benefits" have become obsolete.
    C. Increased competition has forced many employers to reduce the number of benefits provided to employees.
    D. New IRS rules now require benefits to be taxed, making them less attractive as employment incentives.

    ANSWER: B, 491

2. Employee benefits are defined as
    A. a reward for employee loyalty.
    B. a right related to organizational membership.
    C. a performance-related form of compensation.
    D. a form of indirect compensation.

    ANSWER: D, 492

3. Unlike employers in many other countries, in the United States _____ has/have become a major provider of benefits for citizens.
    A. employers
    B. families
    C. Churches and other community organizations
    D. the national government

    ANSWER: A, 492

4. Benefits, such as health insurance and retirement contributions, must be viewed as
    A. the responsibility of each individual employee.
    B. a right of citizenship.
    C. part of the total compensation package.
    D. a governmental responsibility.

    ANSWER: C, 492

204   Chapter 15

5. _____ include(s) money paid directly and money paid indirectly.
   A. Employee benefits
   B. Total compensation
   C. Membership incentives
   D. Organizational rewards

   ANSWER: B, 492

6. Which of the following is considered a strategic goal of benefits by employers?
   A. significantly improve the quality of life for employees
   B. minimize the tax consequences for employees
   C. provide the benefits that are mandated by government
   D. compete for employees in tight labor markets

   ANSWER: D, 492

7. Which of the following is a consequence of more dual-career couples and single-parent families?
   A. benefits associated with work and family issues are having to be addressed
   B. on-site child-care centers are becoming a necessary benefit
   C. the government has mandated paid parental leave
   D. employers are reluctant to hire working mothers

   ANSWER: A, 492-493

8. One purpose of benefits is
   A. to capitalize on lower insurance premiums.
   B. to generate employee loyalty in an attempt to discourage union organizing activities.
   C. to attempt to protect employees and their dependents from financial risks associated with illness, disability, and unemployment.
   D. to comply with government mandates.

   ANSWER: C, 493

9. Which of the following factors as not given as having influenced the growth of benefits?
   A. tax advantages
   B. management's concern about corporate responsibility
   C. federal social legislation
   D. the Family and Medical Leave Act

   ANSWER: B, 493-494

10. Which is of the following was listed as a strategic concern about benefits that HR professionals should address?
    A. What benefits significantly improve the quality of life for employees?
    B. What are the tax consequences for employees of each benefit?
    C. What benefits are mandated by government?
    D. How much total compensation, including benefits, should be provided?

    ANSWER: D, 494

11. Those benefits which employers in the United States are required to provide by law are called _____ benefits.
    A. mandated
    B. required
    C. compulsory
    D. obligatory

    ANSWER: A, 494

12. Social Security, workers' compensation insurance, and Medicare are called
    A. employment benefits.
    B. government-sponsored benefits.
    C. legally mandated benefits.
    D. social benefits.

    ANSWER: C, 494

13. What are the requirements of the Consolidated Omnibus Budget Reconciliation Act (COBRA) with respect to health care?
    A. Employers with more than 50 employees must provide medical insurance for all full-time employees.
    B. Most employers must offer extended health-care coverage to employees after they leave the organization.
    C. Employer contributions to Medicare were raised to 2.9 percent of payroll.
    D. Employers offering medical insurance cannot exclude pre-existing conditions from coverage.

    ANSWER: B, 494

14. The Health Insurance Portability and Accountability Act (HIPAA) requires
    A. employers with more than 50 employees provide medical insurance for all full-time employees.
    B. insurance companies to offer coverage to contingent workers.
    C. that most employers offer extended health-care coverage to employees after they leave the organization.
    D. that most employees be able to obtain health-care insurance coverage if they were previously covered in a health plan.

    ANSWER: D, 494

15. One reason why employers face increasing pressure to provide benefits is
    A. federal and state governments want to shift many of the social costs for health care and other expenditures to employers.
    B. private industry can provide these services more efficiently than government.
    C. unions are becoming more aggressive in contract negotiations.
    D. the need to compete for quality employees in a tight labor market.

    ANSWER: A, 495

16. _____ benefits are provided by employers in order to compete for and retain employees.
    A. Involuntary
    B. Competitive-market
    C. Voluntary
    D. Labor-market

    ANSWER: C, 496

17. What is workers' compensation?
    A. the pay and benefits package provided to employees
    B. benefits provided to persons injured on the job
    C. law-suit judgments awarded to workers injured on the job
    D. what a worker receives in compensation for outstanding performance

    ANSWER: B, 496

18. To be eligible for workers' compensation, the worker must
    A. prove that the accident was caused by employer negligence.
    B. be employed by a federally insured employer.
    C. not have contributed to the cause of the injury.
    D. suffer a work-related injury or illness.

    ANSWER: D, 496

19. How is workers' compensation funded?
    A. by insurance purchased from a private carrier or state insurance fund
    B. by a tax levied by state governments based on size of payroll
    C. by a pool of organizations in the same industry
    D. through the Social Security Administration

    ANSWER: A, 496

20. In exchange for workers' compensation coverage, employees
    A. forfeit medical insurance coverage.
    B. can be required to attend safety-awareness seminars.
    C. give up the right of legal actions and awards.
    D. are required to pay a portion of the insurance premiums.

    ANSWER: C, 496

21. How is unemployment compensation administered?
    A. by the federal government.
    B. on a state-by-state basis.
    C. by the states, under U.S. Department of Labor guidelines.
    D. by a pool of companies engaged in similar industries.

    ANSWER: B, 497

22. How is an employer's cost for unemployment compensation determined?
    A. the type of business and its known seasonal fluctuations
    B. the number of covered employees
    C. the total cost of payroll
    D. the number of claims filed by workers who leave

    ANSWER: D, 497

23. What is a SUB program?
    A. It is a benefit, negotiated by a union, requiring an employer to contribute to a fund that supplements unemployment compensation.
    B. It provides for severance pay in those cases where the company closes down.
    C. Businesses with seasonal work that use subcontractors rather than hire and lay off people.
    D. It is a type of benefits program that supervisors have some discretion over.

    ANSWER: A, 497

24. _____ is a security benefit voluntarily offered by employers to employees who lose their jobs.
    A. Unemployment insurance
    B. Supplemental unemployment benefit
    C. Severance pay
    D. Family security

    ANSWER: C, 497

25. What is the principle requirement of the Worker Adjustment and Retraining Notification Act (WARN) of 1988?
    A. Employers are to give severance pay to workers who lose their jobs permanently.
    B. Most employers must give 60 days' notice if a mass layoff or facility closing is to occur.
    C. Workers are to be given full disclosure regarding and hazardous materials present at the work site.
    D. Workers under age 60 are entitled to a retraining allowance if their jobs are eliminated.

    ANSWER: B, 498

26. As a result of a 1986 amendment to the Age Discrimination in Employment Act (ADEA), most employees cannot be forced to retire
    A. before age 65.
    B. before age 67.
    C. before age 70.
    D. at any age.

    ANSWER: D, 498

208 Chapter 15

27. The _____ requires equal treatment of older workers in early retirement or severance situations.
    A. Older Workers Benefit Protection Act (OWBPA)
    B. Age Discrimination in Employment Act (ADEA)
    C. Employee Retirement Income Security Act (ERISA)
    D. Worker Adjustment and Retraining Notification Act (WARN)

    ANSWER: A, 499

28. The Older Worker Benefit Protection Act (OWBPA) sets forth some very specific conditions that must be met when older workers
    A. are fired for cause or laid off.
    B. denied coverage under an employers health insurance plan.
    C. sign waivers promising not to sue for age discrimination.
    D. apply for supplemental social security benefits.

    ANSWER: C, 499

29. Rule 106 issued by the Financial Accounting Standards Board (FASB)
    A. permits health-care benefits to be paid out of current yearly income.
    B. requires that firms establish accounting reserves for funding retiree health-care benefits.
    C. permits health costs to be taken from after-tax dollars.
    D. requires a pool of funds that is at least 60 percent of health-care liability costs.

    ANSWER: B, 500

30. Social security can be classified as a(n) _____ benefit.
    A. voluntary
    B. insurance
    C. social
    D. security

    ANSWER: D, 500

31. Which of the following benefits is not provided by the Social Security system?
    A. displacement
    B. disability
    C. survivor
    D. old age

    ANSWER: A, 500

32. How are Social Security benefits funded?
    A. employers are taxed on the amount of wages and salaries paid to employees
    B. a tax on employee wages and salaries, paid by the employee
    C. a tax on employee wages and salaries paid equally by employers and employees
    D. general tax revenues

    ANSWER: C, 500

33. Retirement benefits established and funded by employers and employees are
    A. mandated by the Employee Retirement Income Security Act (ERISA).
    B. called pension plans.
    C. often treated as "golden handcuffs."
    D. substitutes for Social Security.

    ANSWER: B, 501

34. Which of the following is not a requirement of the Employee Retirement Income Security Act (ERISA)?
    A. Accrued benefits must be given to employees when they retire or leave.
    B. Plans must meet minimum funding requirements.
    C. Employers must pay termination insurance to ensure employee pensions will be there even if the company goes out of business.
    D. Employers must offer retirement benefits for all full-time employees after five years' service.

    ANSWER: D, 502

35. In a contributory pension plan, the money for pension benefits is
    A. paid by both employees and employers.
    B. provided by the employer.
    C. deducted from the employees salary pre-tax.
    D. contributed from the pre-tax earnings of the employer.

    ANSWER: A, 502

36. In a _____ pension plan, all the funds are provided by the employer.
    A. defined-benefit
    B. defined-contribution
    C. non-contributory
    D. vested

    ANSWER: C, 502

37. In a _____ plan the employer makes an annual payment to an employee's pension account.
    A. non-contributory pension
    B. defined-contribution
    C. vested
    D. defined-benefit

    ANSWER: B, 502

38. _____ is the right of employees to receive benefits from their pension plans.
    A. Dispatchment
    B. Portability
    C. Social security
    D. Vesting

    ANSWER: D, 502

Chapter 15

39. _____ refers to a feature that allows employees to move their pension benefits from one employer to another.
    A. Portability
    B. Transference
    C. Vesting
    D. Carry-over

    ANSWER: A, 503

40. In *Arizona Governing Committee v. Norris*, the Supreme Court ruled that
    A. medical examinations may be required before an employee is enroled in a pension plan.
    B. all participants in a pension plan must be vested.
    C. pension plan administrators must use unisex mortality tables.
    D. employers cannot be required to provide pension benefits.

    ANSWER: C, 504

41. A special account in which an employee can set aside funds that will not be taxed until the employee retires is called
    A. a 401(k) plan
    B. an individual retirement account
    C. a super-saver account
    D. a Keogh plan

    ANSWER: B, 504

42. A 401(k) plan is an agreement in which
    A. an employee can set aside funds that will not be taxed until retirement.
    B. individualized pension plans are established for self-employed people.
    C. both the employee and employee contribute funds to a pension plan.
    D. a percentage of an employee's pay is withheld and invested in a tax-deferred account.

    ANSWER: D, 504

43. A(n) _____ is a special type of individualized pension plan for self-employed individuals.
    A. Keogh plan
    B. IRA
    C. defined-contribution
    D. 401(k) plan

    ANSWER: A, 505

44. Managed care consists of approaches that monitor and reduce _____ using restrictions and market system alternatives.
    A. child-care expenses
    B. elder-care costs
    C. medical costs
    D. domestic-partner expenses

    ANSWER: C, 506

45. A _____ is a health-care provider that contracts with an employer or an employer group to provide health-care services to employees at a competitive rate.
    A. contractual medical organization (CMO)
    B. preferred provider organization (PPO)
    C. public/private health organization (PPH)
    D. health maintenance organization (HMO)

    ANSWER: B, 506

46. A _____ is a managed care plan that provides services for a fixed period on a prepaid basis.
    A. contractual medical organization (CMO)
    B. preferred provider organization (PPO)
    C public/private health organization (PPH)
    D. health maintenance organization (HMO)

    ANSWER: D, 506

47. A _____ is an audit and review of the services and costs billed by health-care providers.
    A. utilization review
    B. practice analysis
    C. operational control
    D. procedural review

    ANSWER: A, 508

48. Why are utilization reviews conducted?
    A. Employers need cost/benefit analyses of services provided by their PPO.
    B. The government requires an annual audit of health-care expenditures.
    C. Many employers found that some of the health care provided by doctors and hospitals is unnecessary, incorrectly billed, or deliberately overcharged.
    D. Labor unions need accurate costing of benefits for contract negotiation purposes.

    ANSWER: C, 508

49. _____ try to encourage employees to have more healthy lifestyles.
    A. In-house dietitians
    B. Wellness programs
    C. Physical fitness programs
    D. Health counseling centers

    ANSWER: B, 508

50. Long-term disability insurance
    A. is a mandatory security benefit.
    B. allows employees to accrue sick leave for emergency needs.
    C. is rarely provided as part of an employer's benefit package.
    D. provides continuing income protection for employees who become disabled and unable to work.

    ANSWER: D, 510

51. Which of the following is not a requirement for employer-paid educational assistance to qualify as non-taxable income under section 127 of the IRS Code?
    A.   must be provided by an accredited educational institution
    B.   must be job related
    C.   must be expressly required
    D.   must be above minimum standards

    ANSWER: A, 511

52. The Family and Medical Leave Act of 1993, requires that employers allow eligible employees to take a total of _____ during any _____ period.
    A.   1 month's paid leave;   12-month
    B.   3 months' paid leave;   24-month
    C.   12 weeks' unpaid leave; 12-month
    D.   15 weeks' unpaid leave; 24-month

    ANSWER: C, 513

53. The FMLA defines a _____ as one requiring in-patient, hospital, hospice, or residential medical care or continuing physician care.
    A.   medical leave emergency
    B.   serious health condition
    C.   life threatening illness
    D.   covered health situation

    ANSWER: B, 513

54. The Family and Medical Leave Act (FMLA) of 1993 provides that
    A.   employees must be guaranteed a job following the leave, but the scope and status of the job may be different.
    B.   employees are entitled to take family leave after two years' employment.
    C.   the employee is required to return to work following the leave.
    D.   health benefits must be continued during the leave at the same level and conditions.

    ANSWER: D, 513

55. _____ provides employees with assistance in caring for elderly relatives.
    A.   Elder care
    B.   Family security
    C.   Care giving assistance
    D.   A day-care benefit program

    ANSWER: A, 515

56. As an abuse-control measure regarding holidays, employers commonly
    A.   provide workers with some flexibility as to the holidays they want off.
    B.   pay time-and-a-half to hourly employees who must work holidays.
    C.   require employees to work the last scheduled day before a holiday and the first scheduled workday after a holiday to be eligible for holiday pay.
    D.   permit the use of vacation days by employees who don't want to work on a holiday.

    ANSWER: C, 517

57. A(n) _____ plan combines all time-off benefits into a total number of hours or days that employees can take off with pay.
    A. well-pay
    B. earned-time
    C. leaves-of-absence
    D. time-off-benefit

    ANSWER: B, 518

58. What is the purpose of a flexible benefits plan?
    A. to allow employees to contribute pre-tax dollars to buy additional benefits
    B. to continuously update benefit options as employee needs and desires change
    C. to combine all time-off benefits into a total number of hours that employees can take off with pay
    D. to allow employees to select the benefits they prefer from groups of benefits established by the employer

    ANSWER: D, 519

59. A plan that allows employees to contribute pre-tax dollars to buy additional benefits is called a
    A. flexible spending account.
    B. benefit incentive plan.
    C. tax-deferred benefit option.
    D. cafeteria-style plan.

    ANSWER: A, 520

60. A problem with flexible benefits plans is _____, a situation in which only higher-risk employees select and use certain benefits.
    A. risk tendency
    B. augmented liability
    C. adverse selection
    D. self-selection

    ANSWER: C, 521

True and False

61. The term "total compensation" refers to the wages and salaries paid by employers to their employees.

    ANSWER: False, 492
    Total compensation also includes money paid indirectly, such as benefits.

62. Benefits generally are not taxed as income to employees.

    ANSWER: True, 493

63. Generally employers find it more cost effective to hire additional people rather than pay mandated overtime wages.

    ANSWER: False, 494
    As a result of the high cost of benefits employers prefer to have existing employees work overtime rather than hiring new employees.

64. Benefits mandated by the Fair Labor Standards Act include paid vacations and holidays after one years' full-time service.

    ANSWER: False, 495
    There is no government mandate regarding vacations or holidays.

65. A major reason for proposed mandated benefits is that federal and state governments want to shift many of the social costs for health care and other expenditures to employers, thus relieving some of the budgetary pressures.

    ANSWER: True, 495

66. A problem with workers' compensation systems is that an injured employee who collects cash benefits and medical care can also take legal action against the employer for work-related injuries.

    ANSWER: False, 496
    In exchange for workers' compensation, employees give up the rights of legal actions and awards.

67. The Worker Adjustment and Retraining Notification Act (WARN) of 1988 requires employers to give severance pay to laid-off and redundant workers.

    ANSWER: False, 498
    The WARN Act requires 60 day's notice if a mass layoff or facility closing is to occur, but the act does not require employers to give severance pay.

68. The mandatory retirement age has been increased to 70.

    ANSWER: False, 498
    A 1986 amendment to the ADEA prohibits mandatory employment at any age for most employees.

69. ERISA requires many companies to offer retirement plans to all employees if they are offered to any employee.

    ANSWER: True, 502

70. Employee who voluntarily resign or are terminated before being vested, accrue no pension rights except the funds that they have contributed.

    ANSWER: True, 502-503

71. In *Arizona Governing Committee v. Norris*, the Supreme Court prohibited pension plans from using gender-specific mortality tables when determining benefits.

    ANSWER: True, 504

72. A health maintenance organization (HMO) is a health care provider that contracts with an employer or employer group to provide health-care services to employees at a competitive rate.

    ANSWER: False, 506
    This is a description of a preferred provider organization (PPO).

73. A co-payment strategy requires employees to pay a portion of the cost of both insurance premiums and medical care.

    ANSWER: True, 508

74. COBRA allows employees who leave a job, either voluntarily or involuntarily, to continue participation in the employers' group health plan for a period of time.

    ANSWER: True, 509

75. The idea behind social and recreational programs is to promote employee happiness and team spirit.

    ANSWER: True, 511

76. The Family and Medical Leave Act of 1993 includes federal, state, and private employers.

    ANSWER: True, 513

77. A provision of the Family and Medical Leave Act of 1993 permits employers to require that employees take off a block of time rather than intermittent periods to ease employer scheduling problems.

    ANSWER: False, 513
    The act specifies that the leave may be intermittent rather than in one block.

78. Under the FMLA, employees can be required to use all paid-up vacation and personal leave before taking unpaid leave.

    ANSWER: True, 513

79. Employees who use an on-site child-care facility have a more positive attitude towards management and the employer.

    ANSWER: True, 514

80. New federal laws require employers to treat spousal equivalents and domestic partners on the same basis as spouses of married employees when providing benefits.

    ANSWER: False, 515
    While some states and cities have passed laws requiring domestic partner benefits, there are no such federal laws.

Essay

81. Discuss the role of benefits as a component of the total compensation package.

    ANSWER: 492-494
    Spending on benefits exceeds 40% of overall payroll costs. They help an organization compete in a tight labor market. Changing demographics has focused attention on health-care, retirement, and family-friendly benefits. Benefits attempt to protect employees and their families from financial risks and also provide some tax advantages.

82. What benefits are mandated by federal law? How are they funded?

    ANSWER: 494-495
    Mandated benefits include social security (funded by payroll taxes on employers and employees), workers' compensation and unemployment compensation (insurance purchased by employers), and family and medical leave, military reserve time off, and election and jury leaves (unpaid, but overhead costs paid by employer). In addition there are mandates for extended and portable health-care insurance.

83. What are the major provisions of the Employee Retirement Income Security Act? How has this legislation affected retirement benefits?

    ANSWER: 502
    ERISA does not mandate pension plans, but regulates plans to assure that employees who have put money into them or depend on a pension for retirement funds actually will receive the money when they retire. ERISA requires that retirement plans must be offered to all employees if they are offered to any, sets minimum funding requirements, and requires termination insurance. Defined-contributions plans are becoming more common.

84. Explain why health-care cost management has become important. Discuss several strategies available for controlling costs.

    ANSWER: 505-508
    An aging population, government mandates such as COBRA and HIPAA, and increasing medical costs have caused some organizations to drop health-care benefits, while others use managed care plans including PPOs and HMOs. Other strategies for controlling costs include co-payments and utilization reviews.

85. What family-oriented benefits are being offered by employers? Which of these are mandated by the federal government?

    ANSWER: 512-516
    The FMLA mandates unpaid leaves for eligible employees. Voluntary family-oriented benefits include adoption benefits, child care, elder care, and benefits for domestic partners and spousal equivalents.

Chapter 16

Health, Safety, and Security

Multiple Choice

1. _____ management practices in organizations strive to maintain the overall well-being of individuals.
   A. Safety
   B. Health
   C. Ergonomics
   D. Security

   ANSWER: B, 530

2. Safety is defined as
   A. the protection of employees while on work premises or work assignments.
   B. the protection of employer facilities from unauthorized access.
   C. a general state of physical, mental, and emotional well-being.
   D. a condition in which the physical well-being of people is protected.

   ANSWER: D, 530

3. The purpose of _____ is the protection of employer facilities and equipment from unauthorized access and protection of employees while on work premises or work assignments.
   A. security
   B. safety
   C. ergonomics
   D. enforcement

   ANSWER: A, 530

4. According to the text, _____ may also include providing emergency assistance programs to employees who encounter health problems while traveling on business internationally.
   A. health maintenance
   B. diplomacy
   C. security
   D. safety

   ANSWER: C, 531

5. The primary health, safety, and security responsibilities in an organization usually fall on
   A. safety teams.
   B. supervisors and managers.
   C. industrial engineers.
   D. HR specialists.

   ANSWER: B, 531

6. In a typical division of health, safety, and security responsibilities
   A. the HR unit monitors the health and safety of employees daily.
   B. the HR unit investigates accidents.
   C. the HR unit monitors the workplace for security problems.
   D. the HR unit develops the safety reporting system.

   ANSWER: D, 531

7. Who is responsible for workers' compensation costs?
   A. employers
   B. employees
   C. employees and employers jointly
   D. state and local government

   ANSWER: A, 532

8. What is the purpose of workers' compensation laws?
   A. to protect employees from dangerous and unhealthy working conditions.
   B. to promote worker safety through the enforcement of safety regulations.
   C. to provide payments for lost wages, medical bills, and for retraining if the worker cannot go back to the old job.
   D. to ensure that employers are held liable for injuries suffered at work.

   ANSWER: C, 532

9. Prior to the passage of workers' compensation laws, what was the attitude of most employers and society about workplace safety?
   A. Employers must try to minimize health and safety risks in the workplace.
   B. Safety was the employee's responsibility.
   C. Most accidents are caused by employees impaired by drugs or alcohol.
   D. Most workplaces are designed to promote safety so as to avoid lawsuits from injured employees.

   ANSWER: B, 532

10. What could be the impact on employers who make accommodations for injured employees through light-duty work?
    A. They could be liable for increased workers' compensation premiums due to increased risk.
    B. They would be violating ADA rules.
    C. They will be held liable for any accidents caused by the injured employee.
    D. They may be undercutting what really are essential job functions, as defined by the ADA.

    ANSWER: D, 534

11. The ADA requires that information from all medical examinations and inquiries
    A. be maintained separately from all other confidential files.
    B. be given to the employee. No copies may be made or kept by the employer.
    C. be made available to relevant supervisors who need to make reasonable accommodations for any identified disabilities.
    D. be filed with all other confidential information, with restricted access.

    ANSWER: A, 534

12. Which of the following is a restriction under the child-labor laws, as found in the Fair Labor Standards Act?
    A. The FLSA has set the minimum age for most employment at 14.
    B. Individuals from 14-16 years old are restricted to an eight-hour day.
    C. The minimum age is 18 for hazardous occupations.
    D. Children under 18 are restricted to an eight-hour day on weekends.

    ANSWER: C, 533

13. _____ was passed to "assure as far as possible every working man or woman in the Nation safe and healthful working conditions and to preserve our human resources."
    A. Worker's Compensation legislation
    B. The Occupational Safety and Health Act
    C. The Fair Labor Standards Act
    D. The Wagner Act

    ANSWER: B, 534

14. Every employer engaged in commerce who has _____ employees is covered by OSHA?
    A. over 15
    B. at least 25
    C. ten or more
    D. one or more

    ANSWER: D, 534

15. Which of the following are exempt from the Occupational Safety and Health Act?
    A. federal, state and local government employees
    B. employees of firms holding government contracts
    C. commercial organizations with fewer than 15 employees
    D. farmers with fewer than 20 employees

    ANSWER: A, 534

16. The general duty clause of the Occupational Safety and Health Act refers to
    A. strictly following all established standards.
    B. investigating any and all organizational accidents.
    C. areas in which no standards have been adopted.
    D. the philosophy and ideals of safe management.

    ANSWER: C, 536

220 Chapter 16

17. The Occupational Safety and Health Act states that employers have a *general duty*
    A. to obey all rules and regulations developed by the OSHA.
    B. to provide safe and healthy working conditions.
    C. to inform OSHA when there are no rules to apply in a specific situation.
    D. to develop safety and health standards unique to each place of employment.

    ANSWER: B, 536

18. Workers have the right to walk off a job and refuse to work if
    A. they are not receiving fair pay for the hazards presented.
    B. they have tried at least two alternative procedures which didn't work to solve the problem.
    C. management has tried to alleviate the problem, but has not succeeded.
    D. the employee's fear is objectively reasonable.

    ANSWER: D, 536

19. In a court case involving reproductive health, the Supreme Court held that Johnson Controls' policy of _____ violated the Civil Rights Act and the Pregnancy Discrimination Act.
    A. banning women of childbearing capacity from certain jobs to protect unborn children from the toxic effects of lead
    B. refusing to include abortion services in its medical insurance plan
    C. requiring pregnant women to take unpaid leave prior to giving birth
    D. not making reasonable accommodation for employees in the later stage of pregnancy

    ANSWER: A, 537

20. The federal Hazard Communication Standard requires uses of hazardous chemicals
    A. to limit the amount of time that an employee can work in areas where the chemicals are stored.
    B. to provide medical insurance for all employees working with the chemicals.
    C. evaluate, classify, and label these substances.
    D. to keep detailed records of any accident involving these substances.

    ANSWER: C, 537

21. OSHA representatives who conduct inspections are called
    A. government safety controllers.
    B. compliance officers.
    C. safety and health consultants.
    D. security officers.

    ANSWER: B, 538

22. What was the Supreme Court decision in *Marshall v. Barlow's, Inc.*?
    A. The no-knock provisions are a necessary part of OSHA investigations.
    B. The Fourth Amendment does not apply to government safety inspections.
    C. Inspectors must produce reasonable cause before getting a search warrant.
    D. Safety inspectors must produce a search warrant if an employer refuses to allow an inspector into the plant voluntarily.

    ANSWER: D, 538-539

Health, Safety, and Security   221

23. Whether or not a citation is issued for OSHA violations depends on
   A. the severity and extent of the problem and on the employer's knowledge of them.
   B. whether the violation is a breach of the *general duty* clause.
   C. the past record of the employer in correcting previous problems.
   D. whether a complaint had been filed by an employee.

   ANSWER: A, 539

24. The absence of guard railings to prevent employees from falling three stories into heavy machinery is an example of a(n) _____ violation.
   A. serious
   B. other than serious
   C. imminent danger
   D. *de minimis*

   ANSWER: C, 540

25. _____ violations could have an impact on employees' health or safety but probably would not cause death or serious injury.
   A. Serious
   B. Other-than-serious
   C. Dangerous
   D. *De minimis*

   ANSWER: B, 540

26. Lack of doors on toilet stalls is a common example of
   A. an other-than-serious violation.
   B. a situation that is not an OSHA violation.
   C. picky OSHA regulations.
   D. a *de minimis* violation.

   ANSWER: D, 540

27. An employer who has been warned of a safety violation, but does not correct the situation would be cited for
   A. a willful and repeated violation.
   B. a serious violation.
   C. a *de minimis* violation.
   D. an imminent danger violation.

   ANSWER: A, 540

28. If an employer has been warned of a safety violation, but does not correct the situation, and a death occurs,
   A. the employer is fined 25 percent of yearly gross income.
   B. workers' compensation insurance will not be required to pay, leaving the employer liable for civil litigation on the grounds of gross negligence.
   C. a jail term of six months can be imposed on the managers responsible.
   D. the business may be shut down for up to one year.

   ANSWER: C, 540

222   Chapter 16

29. Which employers are not required to keep detailed records for inspection by OSHA representatives?
    A.   employers with no government contracts or subcontracts
    B.   those with good safety records in previous years and with fewer than 10 employees
    C.   employers not engaged in interstate or foreign commerce
    D.   those with fewer than 25 employees in specified "safe" businesses

    ANSWER: B, 540

30. Which of the followings organizations are required to complete OSHA form 200?
    A.   firms with good safety records in previous years and with fewer than 10 employees
    B.   large organizations involved in interstate or foreign commerce
    C.   firms with a record of willful and repeated violations
    D.   firms having frequent hospitalizations, injuries, or illnesses and/or work-related deaths

    ANSWER: D, 540

31. Employers are required to calculate _____ by figuring the number of lost-time cases, the number of lost workdays, and the number of deaths.
    A.   accident severity rates
    B.   injury/illness rates
    C.   accident frequency rates
    D.   disability injuries

    ANSWER: A, 540

32. At the heart of safety management is(are)
    A.   safety policies and discipline.
    B.   safety committees consisting of employees from all departments.
    C.   an organizational commitment to a comprehensive safety effort.
    D.   routine inspections by OSHA compliance officers.

    ANSWER: C, 543

33. The _____ approach to safety management focuses on designing jobs, developing and implementing safety policies, and using safety committees.
    A.   engineering
    B.   organizational
    C.   systems
    D.   individual

    ANSWER: B, 544

34. Which of the following was not listed as part of the engineering approach to safety management?
    A.   designing work environment
    B.   reviewing equipment
    C.   ergonomics
    D.   designing jobs

    ANSWER: D, 544

35. With respect to safety committees, an employer may be in violation of the National Labor Relations Act if
    A. managers compose a majority on the committee.
    B. workers are excluded from participation.
    C. participation is compulsory.
    D. the committee lacks top management support.

    ANSWER: A, 544

36. The EPA defines _____ as a situation in which occupants experience acute health problems and discomfort that appear to be linked to time spent in a building.
    A. environmental chronic disease
    B. worker sensitivity effects
    C. sick building syndrome
    D. employee/work site interactions

    ANSWER: C, 546

37. Which of the following was given as a cause for health problems when working in certain buildings?
    A. environmental controls are easily manipulated by employees
    B. operators try to cut corners to save energy
    C. employees open windows which interferes with the ventilation system
    D. an over dependence on computer-related equipment

    ANSWER: B, 547

38. _____ is the proper design of the work environment to address the physical demands experienced by people.
    A. Occupational safety and health
    B. Environmental design
    C. Industrial physiology
    D. Ergonomics

    ANSWER: D, 547

39. An ergonomist studies _____ aspects of a job.
    A. physiological, psychological, and engineering design
    B. social and cultural
    C. environmental quality
    D. safety and security

    ANSWER: A, 547

40. _____ occur when workers repetitively use the same muscles to perform tasks, resulting in muscle and skeletal injuries.
    A. Arthritic disorders
    B. Joint failures
    C. Cumulative trauma disorders
    D. Multiple sclerosis

    ANSWER: C, 548

Chapter 16

41. The _____ industry has the highest level of cumulative trauma disorders.
    A. fast food
    B. meat-packing industry
    C. agricultural
    D. garment

    ANSWER: B, 548

42. Carpal tunnel syndrome is an injury common to people who
    A. spend most of the work day standing or leaning over a counter.
    B. work in places with constant loud noises.
    C. perform work that produces constant eye strain.
    D. put their hands through repetitive motions.

    ANSWER: D, 548

43. _____ approach safety from the perspective of a proper match of people to jobs and emphasize fatigue reduction and employee training.
    A. Industrial psychologists
    B. Safety consultants
    C. Industrial engineers
    D. HR specialists

    ANSWER: A, 548

44. Which of the following statements is true?
    A. People who are dissatisfied with their jobs have higher accident rates.
    B. "Accident proneness" is a personality disorder.
    C. People who work the "graveyard" shifts have higher accident rates.
    D. Research has found no relationship between accident rates and the amount of overtime worked.

    ANSWER: C, 550

45. For employers, the greatest problems associated with employees having life-threatening illnesses such as AIDS or cancer is
    A. the increased need for sensitivity at all levels of the organization.
    B. the eventual decline in productivity and attendance brought on by progressive deterioration.
    C. providing reasonable accommodation for the employees with life-threatening illnesses.
    D. maintaining health benefits.

    ANSWER: B, 551

46. Many companies feel that it is unnecessary to adopt specific policies that deal solely with AIDS for the following reason:
    A. They are waiting for government guidelines on treating AIDS as a disability.
    B. Most AIDS victims die before the issue develops into a problem.
    C. They already have adequate disability programs in existence.
    D. They do not want to draw attention to the problem and alarm employees.

    ANSWER: D, 552

47. Which of the following statements regarding workplace smoking is false?
    A. The courts have played an active role in addressing the smoking-at-work issue.
    B. Employers have a positive view of state and local anti-smoking laws.
    C. Employees who smoke tend to adjust to a smoking ban within a few weeks.
    D. Smoking cessation workshops do seem to reduce smoking by employees.

    ANSWER: A, 552

48. _____ is the use of illicit substances or the misuse of controlled substances, alcohol, or other drugs.
    A. Stress defense
    B. Drug addiction
    C. Substance abuse
    D. Dependency

    ANSWER: C, 552

49. Which of the following groups has the highest incidence of substance abuse at work?
    A. African-American single mothers
    B. white men aged 19 to 23
    C. white-collar males
    D. unmarried men and women 45 to 60

    ANSWER: B, 552

50. The most common employer response when a worker tests positive for drug use is
    A. immediate termination.
    B. disciplinary action such as suspension or probation.
    C. avoidance, doing nothing.
    D. referral to counseling and treatment.

    ANSWER: D, 552

51. What is a fitness-for-duty test?
    A. an attempt to detect impairment before putting a person behind dangerous equipment
    B. a medical examination to check for serious illness or disease
    C. an investigation into possible illegal drug and/or alcohol use
    D. a stress test

    ANSWER: A, 553

52. Under the Americans with Disabilities Act,
    A. the practicing illegal drug abuser is considered disabled.
    B. addiction to alcohol is not considered a disability.
    C. drug and alcohol addiction is generally regarded as a disease, similar to mental disorders.
    D. recovering substance abusers are not considered disabled.

    ANSWER: C, 553

Chapter 16

53. Which of the following is true about substance abuse and the workplace?
    A. Drug use is the cause of most employee theft.
    B. The organization can be held liable for injuries to others caused by an employee's drug use.
    C. Supervisors can usually identify substance abusers by their overt behavior.
    D. Drug use at work is highest among minority men.

    ANSWER: B, 553

54. The recommended action for supervisors when confronting substance abusers, which has been endorsed legally, is
    A. automatic referral to an employee assistance program (EAP).
    B. disciplinary action.
    C. a probationary period which includes random drug and alcohol testing.
    D. a firm choice between help and discipline.

    ANSWER: D, 553-554

55. _____ are designed to maintain or improve employee health before problems arise.
    A. Wellness programs
    B. Health maintenance programs
    C. Preventative programs
    D. Education/awareness programs

    ANSWER: A, 555

56. _____ provide(s) counseling and other help to employees having emotional, physical, or other personal problems.
    A. An ombudsman
    B. HR specialists
    C. Employee assistance programs
    D. A wellness program

    ANSWER: C, 555

57. Which of the following was not listed as a typical area addressed by EAPs?
    A. counseling for marital and family problems
    B. educational assistance
    C. termination/outplacement assistance
    D. financial counseling

    ANSWER: B, 556

58. _____ is(are) the second leading cause of workplace fatalities in the United States, second only to transportation-related deaths.
    A. Falls
    B. Fires and explosions
    C. Exposure to harmful substances
    D. Homicide

    ANSWER: D, 556

59. Which of the following industries experiences the highest rate of workplace homicide?
    A. taxi cabs
    B. post office
    C. jewelry stores
    D. public schools

    ANSWER: A, 557

60. Conducting a comprehensive analysis of the vulnerability of an organization's security is the purpose of
    A. an OSHA inspection.
    B. stress assessment.
    C. a security audit.
    D. vulnerability assessment.

    ANSWER: C, 559

True and False

61. The term "security" refers to protection of the physical well-being of people.

    ANSWER: False, 530
    This is a definition of "safety." Security refers to the protection of employer facilities and equipment, and to protection of employees.

62. Workers' compensation laws were passed as an amendment to the federal Occupational Safety and Health Act of 1970.

    ANSWER: False, 532
    Workers' compensation laws have been passed at the state level of government.

63. Prior to the passage of workers' compensation laws, employers and society assumed that safety was the employee's responsibility.

    ANSWER: True, 532

64. Employers are required to provide workers' compensation insurance for employees working at home via telecommuting.

    ANSWER: True, 532

65. The ADA encourages employers, in an attempt to reduce workers' compensation costs, to make accommodations for injured employees through light-duty work.

    ANSWER: False, 534
    Such action may undercut what really are essential job functions. By making accommodations for injured workers, the employer may be required to make accommodations for job applicants with disabilities.

Chapter 16

66. The "general duty" clause of the Occupational Safety and Health Act requires that in areas where there are no safety standards, the employer has a general duty to provide safe and healthy working conditions.

    ANSWER: True, 536

67. The Occupational Safety and Health Act specifically states that employees who report safety violations to OSHA cannot be punished or dismissed by their employer.

    ANSWER: True, 536

68. OSHA has issue regulations to eliminate or minimize occupational exposure to hepatitis B virus (HBV) and human immunodeficiency virus (HIV).

    ANSWER: True, 537

69. Under current OSHA regulations, an employer cannot refuse entry to an OSHA inspector. Instead of allowing an employer time to "tidy up", this *no-knock provision* permits inspection of normal operations.

    ANSWER: False, 539
    In *Marshall v. Barlow's Inc., 1978,* the Supreme Court ruled that safety inspectors must produce a search warrant if an employer refuses to allow an inspector into the plant voluntarily.

70. Other-than-serious violations could have an impact on employees' health and safety but probably would not cause death or serious harm.

    ANSWER: True, 540

71. Overall, it appears that OSHA regulations have not had any significant impact in reducing the number of work-related accidents and injuries.

    ANSWER: False, 541
    While studies have shown that OSHA has had a positive impact, others have shown that OSHA has had no impact.

72. Many employers pay little attention to OSHA because they have only a small chance of being inspected.

    ANSWER: True, 542

73. The Environmental Protection Agency (EPA) defines *sick building syndrome* as a situation in which occupants experience acute health problems and discomfort that appear to be linked to time spent in a building.

    ANSWER: True, 546

74. Ergonomically correct workstations focus on chair adjustment and support, station height, lighting glare, noise levels, and document placement.

    ANSWER: True, 547

75. Cumulative trauma disorders occur when a worker is required to stand for long periods of time, in the same place, while working.

ANSWER: False, 548
CTDs occur when workers repetitively use the same muscles to perform tasks, resulting in muscle and skeletal injuries.

76. Research has found no significant differences in accident rates of employees working different shifts. Day-shift workers had the same rate of accidents as employees who work late-night shifts.

ANSWER: False, 550
Employees working the "graveyard" shifts have higher accident rates than those on day or evening shifts.

77. It is estimated that only 25% of the larger employers in the United States have a policy on life-threatening illness such as AIDS.

ANSWER: True, 552

78. OSHA has issued regulations which bans all smoking in the workplace.

ANSWER: False, 552
There are no national laws regulating smoking in the workplace.

79. To reduce the risk of workplace violence, it is recommended that employers discharge employees for behaviors that often precede violent acts.

ANSWER: False, 558
Employers may face legal action for discharging employees for behaviors that often precede violent acts.

80. A disaster plan involves conducting a comprehensive analysis of the vulnerability of an organization's security.

ANSWER: False, 559
A security audit involves such an analysis. A disaster plan addresses how to deal with natural disasters such as floods, fires, and civil disobedience.

Essay

81. Define the terms "health" and "safety." Discuss the impact of workers' compensation laws, the ADA, and the FLSA on workplace safety.

ANSWER: 530-534
Health is a general state of physical, mental, and emotional well-being. Safety refers to protecting the physical well-being of people. Workers' compensation laws, passed by all 50 states, require employers to contribute to an insurance fund to compensate employees for work-related injuries. Under the ADA, action taken to accommodate an injured worker may create a precedent for hiring workers with disabilities. The ADA requires medical data to be kept separate from other confidential files. The FLSA sets the minimum age for hazardous occupations.

230 Chapter 16

82. What are the basic provisions of the Occupational Safety and Health Act of 1970? What is required of the organization to be in compliance? What is required of managers under this law? What are the responsibilities of individual employees?

ANSWER: 534-541
OSHA states that all private employers have a general duty to provide safe and healthy working conditions, whether there are specific standards or not. The act provides for inspections by compliance officers who can issue citations for violations categorized from *de minimis* to imminent danger. There are extensive record-keeping requirements. The employer is responsible for complying with all OSHA provisions. The individual employees have no such responsibility.

83. There are three different approaches to safety management - organizational, engineering, and individual. Discuss the focus of each of these approaches, giving examples of actions that can be taken to improve worker safety.

ANSWER: 543-551
The focus of the organizational approach is designing jobs, developing and implementing safety policies, using safety committees, and coordinating accident investigations. The engineering approach involves designing work environments, reviewing equipment, and applying ergonomic principles. The individual approaches attempts to identify and modify behaviors that can lead to accident. It involves safety training and incentive programs.

84. Would you recommend that an organization ban smoking in the workplace? Discuss your recommendation with respect to OSHA and the ADA.

ANSWER: 552
OSHA requires a healthy work environment, but there are no regulations regarding smoking. The ADA does not identify smoking as a disability. A multiple of state and local laws regulate smoking in the workplace. Many employers have established no-smoking policies and offer smoking cessation workshops.

85. Define the term "security" with respect to the workplace. What actions can an employer take to minimize the risk of workplace violence?

ANSWER: 556-560
Security involves the protection of employer facilities and equipment from unauthorized access and protection of employees while on work premises or work assignments. To minimize the risk of workplace violence, an employer can conduct a security audit/vulnerability analysis, control access to the physical facilities, screen job applicants, and have sufficient security personnel.

Chapter 17

Employee Rights and Discipline

Multiple Choice

1. It has been stated that: "rights do not exist in the abstract. They exist only when
   A. public policy accepts something as a right."
   B. someone is successful in demanding their practical applications."
   C. the judicial system rules that certain activities are rights."
   D. they are fully documented and accepted."

   ANSWER: B, 566

2. A _____ belongs to a person by law, nature, or tradition.
   A. responsibility
   B. duty
   C. lifestyle choice
   D. right

   ANSWER: D, 566

3. Rights are offset by
   A. responsibilities.
   B. traditions.
   C. laws.
   D. contracts.

   ANSWER: A, 566

4. Duties or obligations to be accountable for actions are
   A. contracts.
   B. laws.
   C. responsibilities.
   D. rights.

   ANSWER: C, 566

Chapter 17

5. If an employee has the right to a safe working environment, the employer has
   A. the right to expect the employee to assist in providing it.
   B. an obligation to provide a safe workplace.
   C. the right to demand compliance with all necessary rules.
   D. the responsibility to compensate the employee for any workplace injury.

   ANSWER: B, 566

6. The _____ nature of rights and responsibilities suggests that each party to an employment relationship should regard the other as having equal rights and should treat the other with respect.
   A. adversarial
   B. contractual
   C. legal
   D. reciprocal

   ANSWER: D, 566

7. Employees' _____ are the result of specific laws passed by federal, state, or local governments.
   A. statutory rights
   B. responsibilities
   C. contractual obligations
   D. contractual rights

   ANSWER: A, 566

8. An employee's _____ are based on a specific agreement with an employer.
   A. reciprocal rights
   B. legal rights
   C. contractual rights
   D. statutory rights

   ANSWER: C, 567

9. An agreement in which an employee who is being terminated agrees not to sue the employer in exchange for specific benefits is called a(n)
   A. employment contract.
   B. separation agreement.
   C. employment-at-will understanding.
   D. reciprocal agreement.

   ANSWER: B, 567

10. Provisions stating that if the individual leaves the organization, existing customers and clients cannot be solicited for business for a specific period of time, are contained in a(n)
    A. noncompete covenant.
    B. employment contract.
    C. separation agreement.
    D. nonpiracy agreement.

    ANSWER: D, 567

Employee Rights and Discipline 233

11. Which act made the theft of trade secrets a federal crime?
    A. The Economic Espionage Act of 1996
    B. The Sherman Antitrust Act of 1890
    C. The National Labor Relations Act of 1935
    D. The McCain-Feingold Act of 1998

    ANSWER: A, 569

12. Rights and responsibilities of the employee to the employer may be spelled out in which of the following?
    A. statutory laws
    B. reciprocal agreements
    C. a job description
    D. an employment-at-will understanding

    ANSWER: C, 568

13. A number of court decisions have held that if an employer hires someone for an indefinite period of time
    A. the employer can terminate the employee at will.
    B. the employer has created an implied contract.
    C. the employee has an obligation to remain working for the employer.
    D. a psychological contract exists.

    ANSWER: B, 568-569

14. Employment-at-will is a common-law doctrine stating that
    A. an employee can resign from a job, with notice or without notice, at any time.
    B. employers can fire whomever they please, for any reason or for no reason.
    C. an employee has a guaranteed right to a job until retirement.
    D. employers have the right to hire, fire, demote, or promote whomever they choose, unless there is a law or contract to the contrary.

    ANSWER: D, 570

15. Which of the following was not given as a defense of employment-at-will (EAW)?
    A. Challenging EAW violates the employers' right to good faith and fair dealing.
    B. The right of private ownership of a business guarantees EAW.
    C. Interfering with EAW reduces productivity in the firm and in the economy.
    D. EAW defends employees' right to change jobs, as well as employers' right to hire and fire.

    ANSWER: A, 570

16. Which of the following is an argument defending employment-at-will (EAW)?
    A. Without a written agreement, there was no contract for life-time employment.
    B. The right to make a profit is part of our economic system.
    C. Interfering with EAW reduces productivity in the firm and in the economy.
    D. The business is located in a right-to-work state.

    ANSWER: C, 570

17. Which of the following has been recognized by the courts as a rationale for concluding wrongful discharge in an employment-at-will suit?
    A. The employee is ineligible for unemployment insurance.
    B. The reason the employee was fired violates public policy.
    C. Downsizing is for other than economic objectives.
    D. The probationary employee status is unfair.

    ANSWER: B, 570

18. When challenging employment-at-will, the _____ approach is based on the premise that an employee will not be fired as long as he or she does the job.
    A. psychological contract
    B. union contract
    C. good faith and fair dealing
    D. implied employment contract

    ANSWER: D, 572

19. How have the courts treated unionized workers and employment-at-will actions?
    A. Unionized workers cannot pursue EAW actions as at-will employees, because they are covered by the grievance-arbitration process.
    B. Unionized workers can also pursue EAW actions.
    C. Unionized workers cannot pursue EAW actions in right-to-work states.
    D. Unionized workers can only be discharged for just cause as spelled out in the union contract.

    ANSWER: A, 572

20. In the landmark EAW case, *Fortune v. National Cash Register Company,* Fortune was fired shortly after winning a large order which would have earned him a big commission. The courts ruled that
    A. permitting NCR to fire in these circumstances was against public policy.
    B. the EAW doctrine gave NCR the right to downsize its workforce at will.
    C. by firing him, NCR violated the covenant of good faith and fair dealing.
    D. NCR had a right to fire Fortune in the absence of an employment contract.

    ANSWER: C, 572

21. _____ is defined as "sufficient justification for taking employment-related actions."
    A. Constructive discharge
    B. Just cause
    C. Due process
    D. Procedural justice

    ANSWER: B, 572

22. Dismissal for _____ usually is spelled out in union contracts.
    A. any reason
    B. rule breach
    C. behavioral consequences
    D. just cause

    ANSWER: D, 572

Employee Rights and Discipline 235

23. _____ is most often found when an employer deliberately makes conditions intolerable in an attempt to get an employee to quit.
    A. Constructive discharge
    B. Just-cause dismissal
    C. Harassment
    D. At-will discharge

    ANSWER: A, 572

24. Which of the following would be a criterion for determination of just cause for disciplinary action?
    A. Did the behavior occur on-the-job?
    B. What was the performance and discipline record of this employee?
    C. Was the employee warned of the consequences of the conduct?
    D. What is the employee's race, sex, or national origin?

    ANSWER: C, 573

25. In employment settings, _____ is the opportunity for individuals to explain and defend their actions against charges of misconduct or other reasons.
    A. progressive discipline
    B. due process
    C. legal constraints
    D. "Georgian" rights

    ANSWER: B, 574

26. People decide how favorable their outcomes are by comparing them with those of others, given their relative situations. This decision involves the concept of
    A. procedural justice.
    B. just treatment.
    C. equitable treatment.
    D. distributive justice.

    ANSWER: D, 574

27. Procedural justice deals with which of the following questions?
    A. Was the procedure used to make the decision fair?
    B. Were the outcome equitably distributed?
    C. Is the way the outcomes were distributed fair?
    D. Would a reasonable person agree with the decision?

    ANSWER: A, 574

28. For unionized employees, due process usually refers to
    A. protection from arbitrary actions by management.
    B. a right to participate in union activities.
    C. the rights to use the grievance procedure specified in the union contract.
    D. the right to sue both the union and management for wrongful discharge.

    ANSWER: C, 574

Chapter 17

29. Which of the following is not a common alternative dispute resolution method?
    A. arbitration
    B. HR review board
    C. Peer review panel
    D. ombudsman

    ANSWER: B, 575

30. _____ uses a neutral third party who renders a decision.
    A. Mediation
    B. Peer review
    C. The ombudsman
    D. Arbitration

    ANSWER: D, 575

31. A person outside the normal chain of command who acts as a problem solver for management and employees is known as a(n)
    A. ombudsman.
    B. arbitrator.
    C. mediator.
    D. peer review panelist.

    ANSWER: A, 576

32. The Privacy Act of 1974, which includes provisions affecting HR record-keeping systems,
    A. protects employers who keep details of employees' off-the-job behavior.
    B. prevents employers from investigating the off-the-job behavior of employees.
    C. applies only to federal agencies and organizations supplying services to the federal government.
    D. requires employees to keep all personnel records confidential.

    ANSWER: C, 576

33. Which of the following is recommended by most lawyers about employee records?
    A. keep all medical, disciplinary, and performance reports together in a separate confidential file.
    B. release only the most basic employment history, such as job title, duties of employment, and ending salary
    C. permit an employee to review all records in his or her employment file
    D. to avoid law suits, keep only essential HR information on each employee

    ANSWER: B, 578

34. Individuals who report real or perceived wrongs committed by their employers are called
    A snitches.
    B. public watchdogs.
    C. Naderites.
    D. whistle-blowers.

    ANSWER: D, 578

35. What has been the impact of the Electronic Communications Privacy Act of 1986 regarding employer monitoring of e-mail and voice mail?
    A. Entities that provide electronic communications services may have access to stored electronic communications.
    B. Employers cannot use electronic monitoring as part of the ordinary course of business.
    C. Only government agencies can monitor electronic communications.
    D. The act does not apply to employers monitoring employee's electronic mail.

    ANSWER: A, 580

36. Constitutional rights in the areas of due process, search and seizure, and privacy protect
    A. all employees.
    B. only those individuals employed in the private sector.
    C. an individual only against the activities of the government.
    D. employees from self-incrimination, such as providing urine samples.

    ANSWER: C, 583

37. Which of the following statements is true about polygraph testing?
    A. A certified professional must read and interpret polygraph test results before they can be admitted in court.
    B. The Polygraph Protection Act prohibits the use of polygraphs for most preemployment screening.
    C. The American Psychological Association has certified the validity of polygraph tests.
    D. Polygraph tests accurately measure changes in the heart rate when a person lies.

    ANSWER: B, 583-584

38. The Polygraph Protection Act
    A. prohibits government contractors from using polygraphs for drug testing.
    B. provides guidelines for the use and interpretation of polygraph tests.
    C. permits government agencies to use polygraphs but only for new employees.
    D. prohibits the use of polygraphs for judging a person's honesty while employed.

    ANSWER: D, 584

39. Which of the following statements is false about paper-and-pencil honesty tests?
    A. Because of their nature, they are unlikely to be prohibited under the Fifth Amendment (which protects persons from compulsory self-incrimination) in public-sector employment.
    B. The tests have generally been shown to be valid.
    C. Honesty tests do not violate any legal rights of employees if employers adhere to state laws.
    D. Because they are not restricted by the Polygraph Protection Act, they have become popular.

    ANSWER: A, 584

238 Chapter 17

40. Which of the following actions can an employer take in response to an employee's off-the-job behavior?
    A. Reassign a homosexual worker when other employees refuse to work with him.
    B. Forbid employees from dating one another.
    C. Take disciplinary action when there are clear job-related consequences.
    D. Prohibit the private use of legal products (like tobacco and alcohol).

    ANSWER: C, 584

41. The Drug-Free Workplace Act of 1988 requires
    A. tobacco and alcohol to be regulated as controlled substances.
    B. government contractors to take steps to eliminate employee drug usage.
    C. that employers cease testing for the off-the-job drug use of its workers.
    D. that government contractors establish drug-awareness programs.

    ANSWER: B, 584

42. For U.S. government contractors, what is the major consequence of not providing employees with a drug free environment?
    A. The contractor becomes liable for criminal law suits.
    B. The contractor is liable for civil law suits by employees concerned about personal security.
    C. State governments may require additional workers' compensation insurance.
    D. The company may lose its government contracts.

    ANSWER: D, 584

43. Employee attitudes towards drug testing can be described as follows:
    A. Drug testing appears to be most acceptable when employees see the procedures being used as fair.
    B. There is more tolerance for drug use and drug users now than before.
    C. Drug testing is still regarded as an unacceptable invasion of privacy, and as such is not acceptable to most employees.
    D. To be accepted, all employees should be routinely tested.

    ANSWER: A, 585

44. Drug testing policies used by employers include each of the following, except:
    A. random testing of everyone at periodic intervals.
    B. testing only when there is probable cause.
    C. testing before new, complicated equipment is installed.
    D. testing after accidents.

    ANSWER: C, 585

45. Where there is a choice among actions, _____ act as general guidelines that regulate organizational actions.
    A. procedures
    B. policies
    C. practices
    D. HR recommendations

    ANSWER: B, 586

46. _____ are general in nature, while _____ are specific to the situation.
    A. Procedures and rules; policies
    B. Procedures; rules and regulations
    C. Rules; policies and procedures
    D. Policies; procedures and rules

    ANSWER: D, 586

47. _____ are customary methods of handling activities.
    A. Procedures
    B. Practices
    C. Rules
    D. Policies

    ANSWER: A, 586

48. "Specific guidelines that regulate and restrict the behavior of individuals" is a definition of
    A. policies.
    B. procedures.
    C. rules.
    D. practices.

    ANSWER: C, 586

49. A(n) _____ is a formal method of obtaining employee input and upward communication.
    A. employee handbook
    B. suggestion system
    C. TQM action
    D. teleconference

    ANSWER: B, 590

50. Discipline is _____ that enforces organizational rules.
    A. an outcome
    B. negative reinforcement
    C. punishment
    D. a form of training

    ANSWER: D, 591

51. The disciplinary system can be viewed as an application of _____ for marginal or unproductive employees.
    A. behavior modification
    B. punishment
    C. negative rewards
    D. a public rebuke

    ANSWER: A, 591

240   Chapter 17

52. The best discipline is clearly
    A.   administered in public.
    B.   administered off-the-job.
    C.   self discipline.
    D.   positive reinforcement.

    ANSWER: C, 591

53. The _____ approach builds on the philosophy that violations are actions that usually can be constructively corrected without penalty.
    A.   behavior modification
    B.   positive discipline
    C.   progressive discipline
    D.   problem-solving

    ANSWER: B, 592

54. What should be the goal of counseling as a part of the discipline process?
    A.   using penalties to discourage undesirable behavior.
    B.   reinforcing organizational procedures and rules
    C.   avoiding law suits
    D.   heighten employee awareness of organizational policies and rules.

    ANSWER: D, 592

55. _____ incorporates a sequence of steps into the shaping of employee behaviors.
    A.   Progressive discipline
    B.   Step-wise punishment
    C.   Behavior modification
    D.   Employee counseling

    ANSWER: A, 593

56. When actions to modify behavior become more severe as the employee continues to show improper behavior, it is called
    A.   behavior conditioning.
    B.   operant conditioning.
    C.   progressive discipline.
    D.   counseling and discipline.

    ANSWER: C, 593

57. Progressive discipline procedures, from verbal caution through dismissal if necessary, are best applied for which of the following offenses?
    A.   intoxication at work.
    B.   absenteeism and tardiness.
    C.   possession of weapons.
    D.   falsifying employment application.

    ANSWER: B, 593

Employee Rights and Discipline 241

58. For discipline to be effective it must be
    A. publicly administered to "set an example."
    B. administered at a later date after tempers have cooled.
    C. selectively applied.
    D. aimed at the behavior, not at the employee personally.

    ANSWER: D, 594

59. Which of the following statements is *false*?
    A. Discipline can only harm performance.
    B. Consistent discipline informs people about what they can and cannot do.
    C. Effective discipline is handled impersonally.
    D. Effective discipline requires accurate, written record keeping.

    ANSWER: A, 595

60. The final stage in the discipline process is
    A. arbitration.
    B. counseling.
    C. termination.
    D. mediation.

    ANSWER: C, 596

True and False

61. Legal rights correspond to moral rights in that they belong to a person by nature or tradition.

    ANSWER: False, 566
    Legal rights may or may not correspond to moral rights. Legal rights belong to a person by law, moral rights by nature or tradition.

62. Rights and responsibilities are reciprocal in nature.

    ANSWER: True, 566

63. Courts are ruling that content of an employee handbook constitute a contract between an employer and its employee.

    ANSWER: True, 569

64. The employment-at-will doctrine provides workers with protection from arbitrary and capricious discharge through grievance procedures.

    ANSWER: False, 570
    EAW is a common-law doctrine stating that employers have the right to hire, fire, promote, or demote whomever they choose, unless there is a law or contract to the contrary.

Chapter 17

65. In general, unionized workers cannot pursue employment-at-will actions as at-will employees, because they are covered by an alternative remedy: the grievance-arbitration process.

    ANSWER: True, 572

66. When an employee is dismissed for a well-documented breach of the organization's rules, it is a "just cause" termination.

    ANSWER: True, 572

67. If an employer deliberately makes conditions intolerable in an attempt to force an employee to resign, it is called a "wrongful termination."

    ANSWER: False, 572
    Constructive discharge occurs when an employer makes conditions so intolerable as to force a reasonable employee to resign.

68. The Privacy Act of 1974 applies only to federal agencies and organizations supplying services to the federal government.

    ANSWER: True, 576

69. Whistle-blowers are more likely to lose their jobs in public employment than in private employment, because most civil rights laws specifically exclude federal, state, and local governments from coverage.

    ANSWER: False, 579
    Most civil service systems have rules protecting whistle-blowers. There is no comprehensive whistle-blowing law that protects private-sector employees.

70. The Fifth Amendment prohibits employers from monitoring employees' voice mail, e-mail, and computer files.

    ANSWER: False, 580
    The Fifth Amendment applies to actions of government. However, the Electronic Communications Privacy Act of 1986 provides some limited protection, except the employer can monitor systems and equipment that it provides to its employees.

71. The Polygraph Protection Act prohibits the use of polygraphs for most preemployment screening and for judging a person's honesty while employed.

    ANSWER: True, 583-584

72. Federal law prohibits employers from firing workers for engaging in legal activities when away from the job.

    ANSWER: False, 584
    While many workers believe that their employers have no right to question employees' private lives, there is no federal legal protection.

Employee Rights and Discipline

73. Drug testing by employers violates an employee's constitutional right to protection from unreasonable search and seizure.

    ANSWER: False, 584
    The Supreme Court has ruled that certain drug-testing plans do not violate the Constitution. The search and seizure provision of the Constitution applies to actions of government.

74. The Drug-Free Workplace Act of 1988 permits federal officials to conduct random drug testing of federal government employees.

    ANSWER: False, 584
    The Act requires government contractors to take steps to eliminate employee drug use. This may involve drug testing by private-sector employers.

75. Employers who conduct preemployment drug tests have found that substance abusers do not even apply for employment.

    ANSWER: True, 585

76. One suggested method of avoiding costly law suits claiming that an implied contract was broken is to abandon all employee handbooks as a way to communicate HR policies to employees.

    ANSWER: False, 589
    Employee handbooks are a recommended reference source for company policies and rules. Not having a handbook can lead to costly litigation. The language in the handbook should be reviewed by legal counsel.

77. It is recommended that employers use disclaimers in all employee handbooks.

    ANSWER: True, 589

78. Discipline is a form of training that enforces organizational rules.

    ANSWER: True, 591

79. Effective discipline should be aimed at the behavior, not at the employee personally.

    ANSWER: True, 594

80. In most cases, discipline has a negative effect on performance.

    ANSWER: False, 594
    The reason for discipline is to improve performance. Lack of discipline can cause problems for the work group.

Chapter 17

Essay

81. What is an employment contract? Discuss the provisions typically included in a formal employment contract.

    ANSWER: 567-568
    An employment contract is an agreement that formally spells out the details of employment. Typical provisions include terms and conditions of employment, general job duties and expectations, compensation and benefits, confidentiality and secrecy, nonpiracy and noncompete agreements, nonsolicitation of current employees upon departure, and termination/resignation.

82. Explain the doctrine of employment-at-will. What is the relationship between this doctrine and the employment agreement?

    ANSWER: 570-572
    EAW is a common law doctrine stating that employers have the right to hire, fire, demote, or promote whomever they choose, unless there is a law or contract to the contrary. EAW defends employees' right to change jobs, as well as the employers' right to hire and fire. Wrongful discharge occurs when an employer terminates an individual for reasons that are illegal or improper

83. Explain the growth in alternative means for resolving disputes. Describe three methods of alternative dispute resolution.

    ANSWER: 575-576
    A major reason for the growth of alternative dispute resolution is dissatisfaction with the expense and delays common in the court system. Methods include arbitration, peer review panels, and ombudsmen.

84. Under what circumstances can an employer require drug testing? What tests are available? What are the legal consequences of drug testing?

    ANSWER: 584-586
    It is estimated that 70% of all uses of illegal drugs are employed. Private-sector employers can administer random drug tests at periodic intervals, test when there is probable cause, and/or test following an accident. In addition, job candidates can be tested as a condition of employment. The three types of drug tests are: hair radioimmunoassay, urinalysis, and fitness-for-duty. These tests are generally accurate. The Drug-Free Workplace Act of 1988 requires government contractors to take steps to eliminate employee drug use. Drug testing does not violate the Constitution. The Fifth Amendment does not apply to non-government testing.

85. What is the purpose of employee discipline? Outline a typical disciplinary procedure. When discharge is appropriate, what actions can be taken to avoid a legal judgment?

    ANSWER: 591-596
    The purpose of discipline, a form of training that enforces organizational rules, is to improve individual, group, and organizational performance. A typical procedure progresses from verbal caution, written reprimand, suspension, to dismissal. Reasons for discharge should be documented and clearly stated. A witness should attend the termination meeting.

Chapter 18

Labor/Management Relations

Multiple Choice

1. A union is a formal association of workers that promotes the interests of its members through
    A. threats and strikes.
    B. collective action.
    C. negotiation.
    D. collective bargaining.

    ANSWER: B, 604

2. What is the primary reason why employees join unions?
    A. They want higher wages and believe that the union can pressure their employers to raise wages.
    B. They feel their benefits package is inadequate and want to bargain for an improved package.
    C. They fear losing their jobs to employees in foreign companies.
    D. They are dissatisfied with how they are treated by their employers and feel the union can improve the situation.

    ANSWER: D, 604

3. Which of the following is the HR unit's responsibility with unions in the typical division of responsibilities between the HR unit and operating managers.
    A. Monitor the climate for unionization and union relations.
    B. Avoid unfair labor practices during organizing efforts
    C. Administer the labor agreement on a daily basis
    D. Resolve grievances and problems between management and employees

    ANSWER: A, 606

4. The labor relations responsibilities of managers would include:
    A. Dealing with union organizing attempts at the company level
    B. Helping negotiate the labor agreements
    C. Administering the labor agreement on a daily basis
    D. Monitoring the climate for unionization and union relationships

    ANSWER: C, 606

Chapter 18

5. Unionism in the United States is different from other countries in the sense that
    A. the U.S. unions are highly regulated by the national government.
    B. the union movement in Italy, England, and Japan has been at the forefront of nationwide political trends.
    C. the cost of union membership is higher in most European countries.
    D. workers in the United States have the right not to join a union.

    ANSWER: B, 606

6. Unions in the United States typically have focused on
    A. achieving worker solidarity.
    B. increasing industrial democracy.
    C. maintaining due process for all workers.
    D. improving "bread-and-butter" issues for members.

    ANSWER: D, 606

7. Economists speculate that deregulation, foreign competition, and a larger number of people looking for jobs have
    A. sparked union decline.
    B. been caused by union militancy.
    C. prompted increased government regulations of the union/management relationship.
    D. been the catalyst for increases in union membership.

    ANSWER: A, 608

8. In 1806, when the shoemaker's union struck for higher wages, a Philadelphia court found
    A. union leaders guilty of civil disobedience.
    B. union members guilty of treason.
    C. union members guilty of engaging in a criminal conspiracy to raise wages.
    D. no crimes had been committed.

    ANSWER: C, 610

9. In 1886, the American Federation of Labor was formed to organize
    A. workers from any industry.
    B. skilled craft workers.
    C. workers from manufacturing industries.
    D. semiskilled and unskilled workers.

    ANSWER: B, 610

10. The Congress of Industrial Unions was founded in 1938 to focus on
    A. skilled craft workers.
    B. establishing one large union embracing all workers.
    C. organizing workers in the public sector.
    D. semiskilled and unskilled workers.

    ANSWER: D, 610-611

Labor/Management Relations

11. In 1926, the Railway Labor Act was passed to reduce transportation strikes, by
    A. giving railroad employees the right to organize and bargain collectively through representatives of their own choosing.
    B. preventing management from using the courts to interfere with union activities.
    C. limiting workers in "essential industries" such as transportation from going on strike.
    D. establishing the National Labor Relations Board to mediate labor disputes.

    ANSWER: A, 611

12. Passed in 1932, the _____ granted workers some rights to organize and freed union activity from court interference.
    A. Clayton Act
    B. Wagner Act
    C. Norris-LaGuardia Act
    D. Labor- Management Relations Act

    ANSWER: C, 611

13. Which act has been called the *Magna Carta* of labor in that it is pro-union?
    A. Landrum-Griffin
    B. Wagner
    C. Railway Labor
    D. Taft-Hartley

    ANSWER: B, 611

14. Which agency, set up as an impartial umpire of the organizing process, enforces all of the provisions of the labor relations acts?
    A. Federal Workers Protection Board
    B. U.S. Department of Labor
    C. Federal Labor-Management Conciliation Authority
    D. National Labor Relations Board

    ANSWER: D, 612

15. Which act prohibited employers from undertaking certain unfair labor practices?
    A. The Wagner Act
    B. The Railway Labor Act
    C. The Landrum-Griffin Act
    D. The Taft-Hartley Act

    ANSWER: A, 612

16. Which act, passed in 1947, answered the concerns of many that unions had become too strong, and attempted to balance the collective bargaining equation?
    A. The Norris-LaGuardia Act
    B. The Landrum-Griffin Act
    C. The Taft-Hartley Act
    D. The Wagner Act

    ANSWER: C, 612

17. A firm that requires individuals to join a union before they can be hired is called
    A. a limited-employment shop.
    B. a closed shop.
    C. an agency shop.
    D. a union shop.

    ANSWER: B, 613

18. A union shop
    A. requires employees who refuse to join a union to pay equivalent amounts equal to union dues and fees for the union's representative services.
    B. requires individuals to join a union before they can be hired.
    C. prohibits the employer from contracting out work to non-union firms.
    D. requires that an employee join a union, usually 30 to 60 days after being hired.

    ANSWER: D, 613

19. Right-to-work laws are state laws that prohibit
    A. both the closed chop and the union shop.
    B. all agency shops.
    C. closed shops.
    D. unions from organizing in a particular state.

    ANSWER: A, 613

20. The Landrum-Griffin Act was aimed at
    A. giving workers the right to engage in union activities.
    B. defining unfair labor practices of both employers and union officials.
    C. protecting the rights of individual union members from union corruption.
    D. defining the behaviors expected during collective bargaining.

    ANSWER: C, 613

21. As a result of the Civil Service Reform Act of 1978,
    A. federal contractors are required to negotiate in good faith.
    B. wages and benefits are not subject to bargaining for employees of the federal government.
    C. federal contractors cannot hire replacement workers during a strike.
    D. union pension funds are financially sound.

    ANSWER: B, 613

22. A(n) _____ is one whose members do one type of work, often using specialized skills and training.
    A. membership guild
    B. apprenticeship guild
    C. industrial union
    D. craft union

    ANSWER: D, 614

23. Which type of union has many persons working in the same industry or company, regardless of job held.
    A. industrial union
    B. craft union
    C. company union
    D. federated union

    ANSWER: A, 614

24. A _____ is a group of autonomous national and international unions.
    A. conciliation
    B. union congress
    C. federation
    D. union organization

    ANSWER: C, 614

25. Who operates the local union headquarters, helps negotiate contracts with management, and becomes involved in attempts to unionize employees in other organizations?
    A. the union steward
    B. the business agent
    C. the national union
    D. the chief negotiator

    ANSWER: B, 615

26. An employee of the firm who is elected to serve as the first-line representative of unionized workers is the
    A. union organizer.
    B. member rep.
    C. business agent.
    D. union steward.

    ANSWER: D, 615

27. The process of unionization may begin in one of two ways, including
    A. a request from individual workers expressing a desire to unionize.
    B. a refusal by management to communicate with the union.
    C. a change in state law regarding open shops.
    D. an inquiry from the National Labor Relations Board.

    ANSWER: A, 615

28. The practice in which unions give written publicity to employees to convince the employees to sign authorization cards is known as
    A. external influence.
    B. authorizing.
    C. handbilling.
    D. union relations.

    ANSWER: C, 616

29. _____ is the practice in which unions use paid organizers to apply for jobs at a targeted employer for the purpose of trying to organize other workers.
   A. Espying
   B. Salting
   C. Penetrating
   D. Intruding

   ANSWER: B, 616

30. If _____ of the employees in the targeted group sign authorization cards, the union can request that an election be held.
   A. more than 20 percent
   B. two-thirds
   C. a majority
   D. at least 30 percent

   ANSWER: D, 616

31. A _____ is composed of all employees eligible to select a single union to represent and bargain collectively for them.
   A. bargaining unit
   B. contract unit
   C. targeted unit
   D. negotiating unit

   ANSWER: A, 617

32. A number of legal tactics may be used by management representatives to try to defeat a unionization effort. These include:
   A. threatening to close down or move the company if a union is voted in.
   B. asking employees how they plan to vote or if they have signed authorization cards.
   C. showing employees articles about unions and relating negative experiences others have had elsewhere.
   D. urging employees to persuade others to vote against the union.

   ANSWER: C, 617

33. Which of the following activities by management would be considered an unfair labor practice during the unionization process?
   A. Forbid distribution of union literature during work hours in work areas.
   B. Promise employees pay increases if they vote against the union.
   C. Tell employees the disadvantages of having a union.
   D. Enforce disciplinary policies and rules in a consistent and fair manner.

   ANSWER: B, 617

34. To win the election, the union must receive
   A. a majority of the votes of those who signed authorization cards.
   B. two thirds of the votes cast.
   C. the votes of the majority of the employees in the bargaining unit.
   D. the votes of the majority of those voting.

   ANSWER: D, 618

35. Once certified, the union will
    A. attempt to negotiate a contract with the employer.
    B. assess union dues.
    C. collect the costs associated with the unionization process from the employer.
    D. demand improved wages and benefits for the members of the bargaining unit.

    ANSWER: A, 618

36. _____ is the process whereby a union is removed as the representative of a group of employees.
    A. Deunionization
    B. Union busting
    C. Decertification
    D. Derepresentation

    ANSWER: C, 618

37. The process whereby representatives of management and workers negotiate over wages, hours, and other terms and conditions of employment is called
    A. arbitration.
    B. collective bargaining.
    C. power bargaining.
    D. labor/management negotiations.

    ANSWER: B, 618

38. Which of the following best describes the collusion strategy?
    A. It produces conflict between the representatives of the employer and the union.
    B. It causes conflict among the union members.
    C. It generally leads to be best possible contract between the employer and the workers.
    D. It is illegal.

    ANSWER: D, 619

39. In order to reserve to the employer the right to manage, direct, and control its business, virtually all labor contracts include a _____ provision.
    A. management rights
    B. no challenge
    C. shareholders' prerogative
    D. flexibility

    ANSWER: A, 619

40. _____ refers to provisions to aid the union in obtaining and retaining members.
    A. Union affiliation clauses
    B. Union rights
    C. Union security provisions
    D. Union-management collusion

    ANSWER: C, 620

252   Chapter 18

41. Which of the following has been identified as a mandatory subject for bargaining?
    A. performance bonds
    B. wages
    C. no-strike or lockout clause
    D. benefits for retired employees

    ANSWER: B, 621

42. If both parties agree, bargaining over _____ issues is allowed.
    A. optional
    B. joint
    C. acceptable
    D. permissive

    ANSWER: D, 621

43. Which of the following bargaining issues would require either party to take illegal action?
    A. giving preference in hiring to individuals who have been union members
    B. requiring employees to take annual physical exams
    C. management and unions negotiating before setting product prices
    D. requiring management to deduct union dues from employee payroll checks

    ANSWER: A, 621

44. If the organization argues that it cannot afford to pay what the union is asking, the employer must
    A. declare bankruptcy.
    B. provide full financial disclosure information.
    C. provide necessary financial data if requested.
    D. still negotiate in "good faith" until an agreement is reached.

    ANSWER: C, 621

45. In _____, the parties agree to send representatives who can bargain and make decisions, rather than people who do not have the authority to commit either group to a decision.
    A. labor/management negotiations
    B. good-faith negotiations
    C. honest bargaining
    D. collective bargaining

    ANSWER: B, 623

46. The process by which union members vote to accept the terms of a negotiated labor agreement is called
    A. authorization.
    B. certification.
    C. localization.
    D. ratification

    ANSWER: D, 623

47. The process by which a third party attempts to keep the union and management negotiators talking so that they can reach a voluntary settlement, is known as
    A. conciliation.
    B. arbitration.
    C. mediation.
    D. resolution.

    ANSWER: A, 623

48. _____ is the process by which a third party assists negotiators in their discussions and also suggests settlement proposals.
    A. arbitration.
    B. conciliation.
    C. mediation
    D. resolution.

    ANSWER: C, 623

49. In _____, negotiating parties submit their disputes to a third party to make a decision.
    A. conciliation.
    B. arbitration.
    C. mediation
    D. resolution.

    ANSWER: B, 623

50. Union members refuse to work in order to put pressure on an employer during a
    A. close-down.
    B. lockout.
    C. boycott.
    D. strike.

    ANSWER: D, 623

51. In a _____, management shuts down company operations to prevent union members from working.
    A. lockout
    B. strike
    C. close-down
    D. boycott

    ANSWER: A, 623

52. What type of strikes occur when the parties fail to reach agreement during collective bargaining?
    A. wildcat
    B. jurisdictional
    C. economic
    D. sympathy

    ANSWER: C, 624

53. _____ strikes occur during the life of the collective bargaining agreement without approval of union leadership and violate a no-strike clause in a labor contract.
    A. Unfair labor practice
    B. Wildcat
    C. Economic
    D. Jurisdictional

    ANSWER: B, 624

54. Strikers can be discharged or disciplined for participating in a(n)
    A. unfair labor practices strike.
    B. economic strike.
    C. jurisdictional strike.
    D. wildcat strike.

    ANSWER: D, 624

55. In a(n) _____, an employer is free to replace the striking workers; but in a(n) _____, workers who want their jobs back at the end of the strike must be reinstated.
    A. economic strike; unfair labor practices strike
    B. unfair labor practices strike; jurisdictional strike
    C. jurisdictional strike; wildcat strike
    D. economic strike; sympathy strike

    ANSWER: A, 624

56. The TEAM act, if passed by Congress, would amend the Wagner Act to
    A. permit employee-owned businesses to form worker-management teams to mutually decide on such matters as pay, benefits, and hours of work.
    B. exempt employee-owned businesses from the Wagner Act provisions.
    C. allow nonunion employees in team-based situations to work with management concerning working conditions and workplace situations.
    D. prohibit management from interfering with work-based teams.

    ANSWER: C, 626

57. What is the difference between a complaint and a grievance?
    A. They are different names for the same thing.
    B. A grievance is a complaint that has been put in writing and made formal.
    C. Grievances are more informal, and do not follow a set procedure.
    D. Complaint relate to money issues; grievances to supervisory behavior.

    ANSWER: B, 627

58. _____ are formal communications channels designed to settle a grievance as soon as possible after the problem arises.
    A. Contract procedures
    B. Legal processes
    C. Arbitration courts
    D. Grievance procedures

    ANSWER: D, 628

59. An employee's _____ means that a unionized employee generally has a right to union representation if he or she is being questioned by management and if discipline may result.
    A. *Weingarten* rights
    B. *Taft-Hartley* rights
    C. constitutional rights
    D. *Landrum-Griffin* rights

    ANSWER: A, 628

60. _____ is a means by which disputes arising from different interpretations of a labor contract are settled by a third party.
    A. Mediation
    B. Court-ordered negotiation
    C. Grievance arbitration
    D. The Department of Labor negotiating team

    ANSWER: C, 629

True and False

61. Class consciousness and conflict between the working class and the management class is a primary cause of unionization attempts in the United States.

    ANSWER: False, 606

    U.S. unions have primarily focused on "bread and butter" issues such as wages, job security, and benefits. The European unions, however, are more concerned with class consciousness and conflict.

62. The American Federation of Labor (AFL) was formed as a federation of independent unions that represented semiskilled and unskilled workers.

    ANSWER: False, 610
    The aim of the AFL was to organize skilled craft workers.

63. The Wagner Act declared, in effect, that the official policy of the U.S. government was to encourage collective bargaining.

    ANSWER: True, 611

64. The National Labor Relations Board (NLRB) is an independent board, not influenced by politics in any way.

    ANSWER: False, 612
    The NLRB has altered its emphasis depending on what political party is in power to appoint members.

65. The Wagner Act allows the president of the United States to declare that a strike presents a national emergency. The president can delay such a strike up to 80 days, called a *cooling-off period*.

    ANSWER: False, 613
    This is a provision of the Taft-Hartley Act.

66. The Taft-Hartley Act allowed states to pass laws that granted a person the right to work without having to join a union.

    ANSWER: True, 613

67. The Landrum-Griffin Act was passed to protect the rights of individual union members from corruption in the union, and to ensure the democratic rights of union members.

    ANSWER: True, 613

68. The process of unionization may begin with a union targeting an industry or a company.

    ANSWER: True, 615

69. Once the unionizing efforts begin, management activities must conform to the requirements established by the NLRB. Union leaders, however, are not similarly restricted.

    ANSWER: False, 615-616
    All activities of management and unions must conform to NLRB requirements.

70. The practice of "salting" involves unions' hiring and paying people to apply for jobs at certain companies. When the people are hired, they begin union organizing efforts.

    ANSWER: True, 616

71. The Supreme Court has ruled that "salting" is an unfair labor practice of the unions.

    ANSWER: False, 616
    The Supreme Count has ruled that refusing to hire otherwise qualified applicants, even if they are also paid by the union, violates the Wagner Act.

72. During the unionization process, managers cannot urge employees to persuade others to vote against the union.

    ANSWER: True, 617

73. Unfair labor practices of management include forbidding the distribution of union literature during work hours in work areas.

    ANSWER: False, 617
    Managers may forbid distribution of union literature during work hours in work areas.

74. A majority of employees in the bargaining unit must vote for the union.

    ANSWER: False, 618
    A majority of those voting is required.

75. One union security provision involves requiring union membership of all employees, subject to right-to-work laws.

    ANSWER: True, 620

76. The Wagner Act clearly expects management and the union to bargain over wages, hours, and other terms and conditions of employment.

    ANSWER: True, 621

77. Such issues as giving preference to individuals who have been union members when hiring employees, are permissible issues that may be bargained over if both parties agree.

    ANSWER: False, 621
    This is an illegal issue.

78. The process of conciliation is a means of deciding a dispute in which negotiating parties submit the dispute to a third party to make a decision.

    ANSWER: False, 623
    Conciliation is the process by which a third party attempts to keep union and management negotiators talking so that they may reach a voluntary settlement.

79. During an unfair labor practices strike, workers who want their jobs back at the end of the strike must be reinstated.

    ANSWER: True, 624

80. Grievance arbitration is a formal channel of communications used to resolve grievances.

    ANSWER: False, 629
    A grievance procedure is a formal channel of communication.

Essay

81. What is the current "state of labor unions" in the United States?

    ANSWER: 606-610
    Unions membership has fallen from over 30% of the workforce in 1945 to less than 14% today. Unlike most other countries, U.S. unions are primarily concerned with "bread and butter" issues of wages, benefits, and job security, many of which have been passed into law. Deregulation, foreign competition, geographic changes have also caused union decline. The only increase in union membership appears to be among federal government employees.

Chapter 18

82. What is the "National Labor Code?" What has been its impact on labor/management relations?

    ANSWER: 611-614
    Three acts comprise the National Labor Code: The Wagner Act (1935), the Taft-Hartley Act (1947), and the Landrum-Griffin Act (1959). Together they give workers the right to organize, define unfair labor practices of management and unions, and protect the rights of union members from corrupt union officials. They also give workers the right not to participate in union activities.

83. An employee at your factory has shown you a union leaflet she was given in the parking lot this morning. Discuss the possible significance of the leaflet and what you might expect to happen as a result of this leaflet.

    ANSWER: 615-619
    This leaflet, or "handbill", is probably a request to sign authorization cards. If 30% of the factory employees sign a card, a representation election must be held. A simple majority of workers voting in the election will determine if the union is certified as the legal representative of the employees. The employer is then required to collectively bargain with the union.

84. What is the role of collective bargaining in union/management relations? Describe a typical collective bargaining process.

    ANSWER: 618-624
    Collective bargaining is the process whereby representatives of management and workers negotiate over wages, hours, and other terms and conditions of employment. Management is required to collectively bargain once a union has been certified. The process begins with demands from the union and proposals from management. Negotiation continues in good faith. If an agreement is reached it is ratified by the employees. Alternatively, if a bargaining impasse occurs, disputes can be taken to conciliation, mediation, or arbitration. If a deadlock cannot be resolved, a strike or lockout may result.

85. Why is grievance management essential in both union and nonunion organizations? Describe the steps in a typical grievance procedure.

    ANSWER: 627-629
    A grievance is a complaint that has been put in writing and made formal. It is crucial for nonunion employers to have an effective grievance procedure. Failure to have one may result in employee dissatisfaction and union representation. For union organizations, the grievance procedure is spelled out in the contract. A typical procedure begins with the employee discussing the grievance with the union steward and the supervisor ... the steward discusses it with the supervisors manager ... union grievance committee with the plant manager or HR department ... national union with company's general manager ... impartial umpire or arbitrator.